OBJECT TO BE DESTROYED

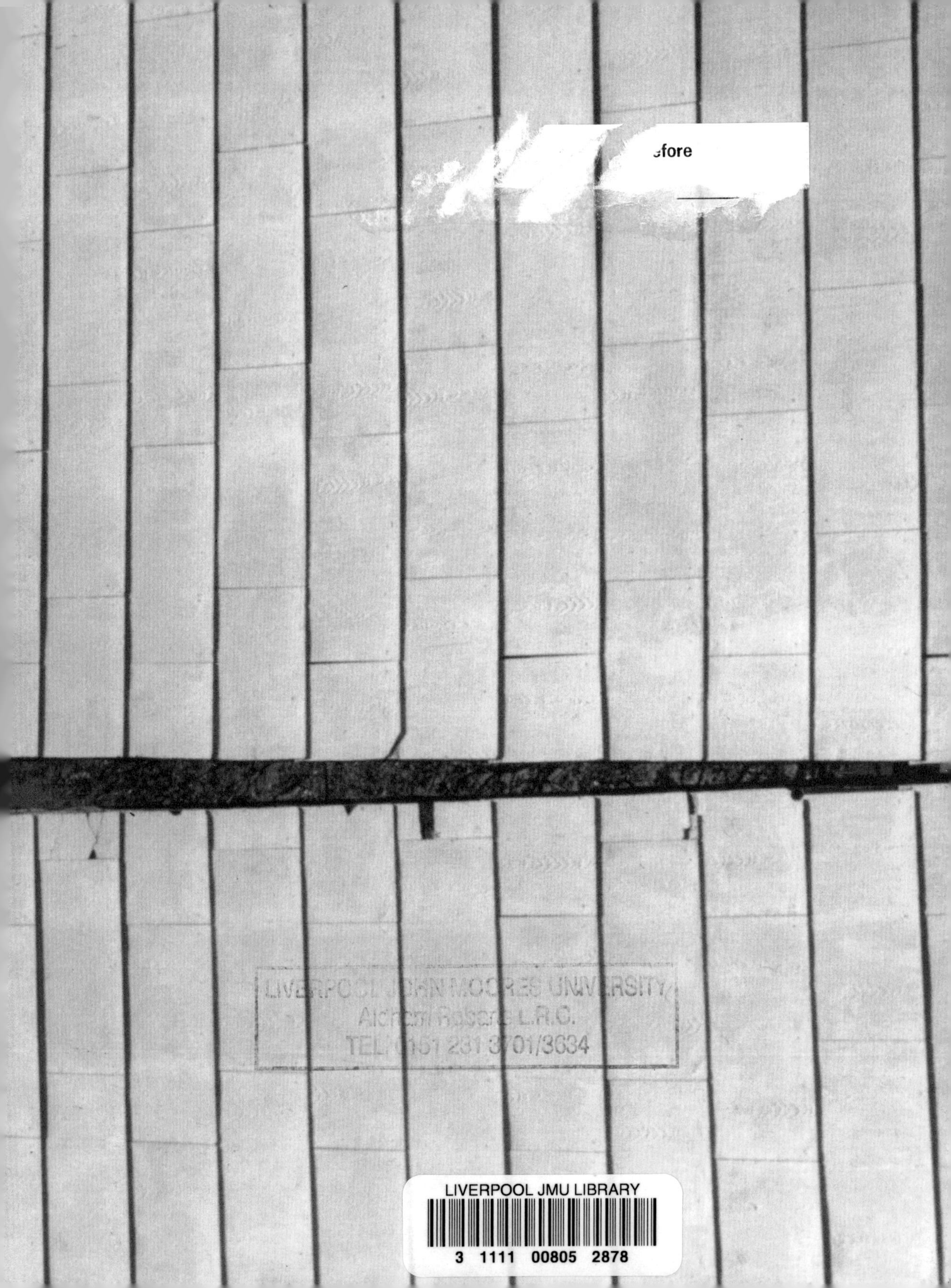

LIVERPOOL JOHN MOORES UNIVERSITY
Aldham Robarts L.R.C.
TEL. 0151 231 3701/3634
LIVERPOOL JMU LIBRARY
3 1111 00805 2878

OBJECT TO BE DESTROYED

THE WORK OF GORDON MATTA-CLARK

PAMELA M. LEE

THE MIT PRESS · CAMBRIDGE, MASSACHUSETTS · LONDON, ENGLAND

© 2000 Massachusetts Institute of Technology
All works by Gordon Matta-Clark (and pictures of the artist) are reproduced courtesy of The Estate of Gordon Matta-Clark, Weston, CT, unless otherwise noted.
All rights reserved. No part of this book may be reproduced in any form, by any electronic or mechanical means (including photocopying, recording, or information storage and retrieval) without permission in writing from the publisher.

This book was set in Adobe Garamond by Graphic Composition, Inc. and was printed and bound in the United States of America.

Library of Congress Cataloging-in-Publication Data
Lee, Pamela M.
Object to be destroyed : the work of Gordon Matta-Clark / Pamela M. Lee
p. cm.
Includes bibliographical references and index.
ISBN 0-262-12220-0 (hc : alk. paper)
1. Matta-Clark, Gordon, 1943–1978—Criticism and interpretation. 2. Deconstructivism (Architecture)—Influence. I. Matta-Clark, Gordon, 1943–1978. II. Title.
N6537.M3947L44 1999
709′.2—dc21 99-17978
CIP

FOR MY FAMILY

CONTENTS

ACKNOWLEDGMENTS

There are very few certainties in historical research, but if there was one thing certain about Gordon Matta-Clark, it was his sociability. It is appropriate, then, to acknowledge the social horizon behind the present work. If I have made claims for a "workless" community in my writing, the following individuals give the lie to my own theoretical leanings.

This book could not have been written without the extraordinary support of Jane Crawford, Matta-Clark's widow, who opened her home and the Matta-Clark archives to me during the course of writing my doctoral thesis and then revising the manuscript as a book. All historians should be so lucky to work with such a generous, warm, and open-minded individual; she has facilitated this project in every way imaginable while allowing the peculiarities of my own interpretation to emerge. My deepest gratitude and respect for her knowledge, patience, and time. Sincere thanks as well to Bob and Jessamyn Fiore. I also wish to acknowledge the late Anne Alpert, Caroline Goodden Ames, Daniel Buren, Florent Bex, Jene Highstein, Nancy Holt, Dan Graham, and Louise Lawler for their invaluable insights. And my respect to those individuals whose writing, research, and interviews regarding Matta-Clark came before, particularly Joan Simon, Judith Russi Kirshner, and Donald Wall.

At Harvard University, where this book originated as my doctoral thesis, I am inspired by and deeply indebted to my adviser, Yve-Alain Bois, whose teaching provided a number of models out of which some of the following ideas first developed, and whose support and advice has always been crucial. Joseph Koerner's teaching and writing have also exerted an enormous influence on my thinking, and I am obliged to him as my second reader. Many thanks to Ewa Lajer-Burcharth, Neil Levine, and Benjamin Buchloh for sharing their knowledge on particular aspects of what follows. And because the thesis was completed with the support of a Wyeth Fellowship from the Center for Advanced Study in the Visual Arts, Washington, D.C., I am grateful to Hank Millon for the opportunity to learn from an amazing community of scholars. I want to acknowledge a number of friends and colleagues I made at CASVA for their support and comments on the work, including Jenny Anger, Hubert Damisch, Michael Ann Holly, Sandy Isenstadt, Jeffrey Schnapp, and Gennifer Weisenfeld.

The manuscript was revised at Stanford University, and I thank all my colleagues in the Department of Art and Art History; but I must single out Scott Bukatman and Alexander Nemerov. Most important, I thank Leah Dickerman, the finest comrade in modernism and everyday life. Finally, a medal should be awarded to Gwen Allen, an ever-patient research assistant, who put up with more than her fair share of garbage and Englewood, New Jersey.

Outside of Stanford, I am pleased to acknowledge the friendship of four remarkable women: Maria Gough, Karin Higa, Juliet Koss, and Christine Mehring. No less remarkable are: Russell Ferguson, David Joselit, Jennifer Lee, Tom Lentz, Richard Meyer, Eric Miles, Helen Molesworth, Steven Nelson, Ellen Tepfer, Frazer Ward, and Sarah Whiting (and Darnell Witte-Whiting by proxy.) Thanks also to those who granted my thinking on Matta-Clark a receptive audience before the publication of this book, in both written and spoken form, including Sabine Breitwieser, Jean-Pierre Criqui, Joe Day, Hal Foster, Silvia Kolbowski, Sylvia Lavin, and Anthony Vidler. And to Roger Conover, editor at The MIT Press, thank you for your commitment to this project.

For all its rhetoric of liminality, this book finds its center with my family. This work is dedicated to my parents, Fred and Margaret Lee, and to my sisters Felicia, Serena, and Sondra.

INTRODUCTION: GORDON MATTA-CLARK AND THE QUESTION OF "WORK"

It is the spring of 1974. On a small plot of land in Englewood, New Jersey, stands a two-story frame house, an unremarkable building abandoned to weeds and time (figure I.1). One of dozens of homes lining this stretch of suburbia, it is strangely familiar, so commonplace as to invite both recognition and dismissal. It is a monumental blankness. A tired and lumbering thing faced in clapboard siding and crowned by a pitched roof, it bears the years dejectedly, the ruin of a middle-class existence.

Yet from March to June of this year, the house will undergo a striking metamorphosis. An artist named Gordon Matta-Clark will approach the building as no other. Using a chainsaw as his principle tool, he will cleave the building in half with two parallel cuts, chisel off its eaves, gouge out the material from its center, score walls, floors, ceilings. Then he will tip the house back on its cinderblock foundations, so that its bluntly rectalinear gestalt will be fractured by a deep and widening cleft, sliced neatly in two like a deck of cards. Any and all possessions left behind—any trace of its previous tenants—will be quickly, expeditiously removed, consigned to the basement like detritus.

Transformed into a startling sculptural environment, the house admits a new audience. A busload of the artist's friends, many of them the important artists of the day, will pay the work a visit from Manhattan. They will remark on its tenebrous interior as they track its brilliant accidents of light—how, clocking the day like a giant sun dial, the house registers the temporal drift of its site through the fall of shadows within. Some will read the work as metaphor: the readymade symbolism of a house divided. Others will attend to its chiasmatic play of surface and void. Above all, the precarious balance the work strikes between exterior and interior, urban and suburban, public and private, violence and en-

I.1 Gordon Matta-Clark, *Splitting,* 1974, 322 Humphrey Street, Englewood, New Jersey.

lightenment causes many to check themselves, to still their movements as they negotiate their way through the space. From room to room and floor to floor, they will pad about gingerly, as if the cut threatened to swallow them whole.

Not that they need worry, though, for the house has been scheduled to be demolished all along. Its imminent destruction is what granted the artist the use of it in the first place. For with the imperatives of real estate beckoning, speculation taking its course, the lot will be cleared for its property value. Before this happens, though, photographs will be taken of the work and a grainy, noiseless film will bear witness to its making. Some articles will make their way into the contemporary art press. An artist's book will likewise appear. But save for some fragments of architecture the artist preserved—and save for the documentation itself—the work in question, Splitting, *has all but ceased to exist.*

▪ ▪ ▪

This is a book about works like *Splitting,* the question of their temporality, and the conjugation of artistic, social, and architectural phenomena they set in relief. It is a book about Gordon Matta-Clark (1943–1978), an American artist active in the seventies who is best known for his "building cuts": sculptural transformations of abandoned buildings produced by cutting and dismantling a given architectural site. A catalytic figure in the history of New York's SoHo, Matta-Clark is remembered by his peers for his boundless sense of community, his legendary sociability, and his dynamic artistic persona. Working in both the United States and Europe, he brought an acutely social dimension to his art making, played out through the terms of architectural space.

Yet while Matta-Clark was highly respected during his short life—and though his work is honored in artistic and architectural circles today—he remains largely obscure within the history of art. Although two major retrospectives of his work have been staged since the mid-eighties, much of the writing on the artist has tended toward the essayistic or commemorative, understandable given his tragic death at the age of thirty-five. The failure to account for his art in a sustained manner may also seem the result of its ephemeral character, the fact that the building cuts no longer exist. Yet *Object to Be Destroyed* offers another reading. It suggests that Matta-Clark's work has not been considered historically as much for its historiographic dimensions as for its physical inaccessibility to a contemporary audience.

This book hopes to redress this problem of art historical omission. It discusses Matta-Clark's art in relation to the artistic practices of the sixties and seventies, principally site-specific strategies, process art, minimalism, and conceptual art. It seeks to consider the range of his artistic output—his building cuts, architectural fragments, photographs, cooking experiments, performances, and moldering objects—through contemporaneous debates on property, architecture, urbanism, and the institutional climate of art exhibition in the seventies. It identifies Matta-Clark's social horizon in the early years of SoHo artist culture and its construction as central to his own activities as an artist. Ultimately, it presents this work as countering a certain model of history, one bound inexorably to Hegelian models of progress and the lockstep march of its teleology.

What emerges from this brief gloss is a generalized consideration of treatment, namely, how does one approach an artist whose principle mode of production is bound up with the work's destruction? To what end were such deliberately ruinous objects put? And what historically specific considerations of architecture and urbanism follow from this body of work, at once parasitic and trenchant characteristics of the architect's profession? These questions are fundamental to what follows, but they eclipse a problem that recurs in the course of discussing and researching Matta-Clark's practice. For in grappling to articulate the formal and historical character of the building cuts—and ascribing the word "work" to his art in the process—one sounds a catachresis of theoretical and historical implications. Bluntly put, to speak of Matta-Clark's work as "work" enacts a critical paradox. His art begs the question of the status of the work of art, its ontological security. Certainly, the building cuts question this notion as it is traditionally imagined within Western aesthetics: as something perceived as total, finished, and whole; as a self-contained and rational thing; as something borne of the logic of *techne*.[1] But the notion of work here is doubly inflected, appealing also to the sense in which something is built or produced as an object of labor. That Matta-Clark referred to his principle activity as "unbuilding" points to the ways in which he was confronting the logic of artistic as well as architectural production. In contrast to an artistic "work" he offered instead a kind of artistic *play*—an idea of art as practice or use.[2]

If we also understand that a work of art is never really a "finished" thing—because its reception admits to an indissociable melding of past and present horizons, conditioned further by changing institutional temperaments—we can see how Matta-Clark's art forcefully registers its workless character. At one level, the building cuts stubbornly withhold hermeneutic closure insofar as they exist now only as residuum: fragments, photographs, films, documents. But Matta-Clark's works underscored this condition even when extant. Demanding the viewers' kinaesthetic passage throughout each site, the building cuts refused interpretive consolidation by its audience, radically destabilizing the terms of aesthetic experience through their dramatic shifts in scale and vertiginous mode of address. Ultimately, though, it was the work's condition of possibility that denied the givenness of the art object. Predicated on the very destruction of site, Matta-Clark's projects could no longer make claims for permanence (much less transcendance) because they were contingent upon the shifting temporalities of the built environment.

With the notion of the "work" in mind, consider again the example that opened our discussion, *Splitting*. If by some historicist feint we were to position ourselves as critics in the early seventies, how might we account for this startling object, a work whose visual audacity was matched only by the gesture of its self-effacement?

MATTA-CLARK'S ECONOMY

There was, in fact, a narrative from the period that served to rationalize such practices. Set as squarely within the era of conceptual art as we are, it bore a range of mysterious appelations: the disappearance or "dematerialization" of the art object, "Idea Art," "Post-Object Art," "Anti-Object Art," "Post-Aesthetic Art."[3] Priveleging the conception of the art object over the physical embodiment of the work as such, this narrative would appear to "emphasize the elimination of the art object," as one popular critic stated blankly.[4] Whereas traditional sculpture was weighty and massive, demanding of space and inviolable in its corporeal presence, its current state was trace-like, evanescent. Painting was to fare no better. By many historical accounts, it was already dead, analogously supplanted by word, text, philosophical proposition. As if fallen to an iconoclastic sweep, the "negative" character of the work of art was valorized as the end goal of the work itself.

Of course, this was only a fraction of the story, and hardly the most interesting part.[5] The journalistic commonplaces surrounding these gestures aroused the suspicion of both artists and critics, who challenged the notion of dematerialization on a number of different counts.[6] Similarly, while Matta-Clark identified strongly with conceptual artists—exhibiting with them, championing them, and socializing with them—his practice, I would argue, frustrates the conventions of "work" without reifying absence as popular conceptualist accounts were wont to do. I will describe his activities through the notion of a "sacrificial economy," a phrase that evokes both the social or ritualistic dimensions of sacrifice as well as the destruction around which such rituals are organized. Because this notion takes its cue from Georges Bataille's reading of the "general economy,"[7] a brief on this earlier formulation is in order.

In sum, the general economy is opposed to "restricted economies," systems which are functionalist and accumulative in nature and organized around the logic of progress and growth. The general economy, by contrast, locates destruction and a "luxurious squandering of energy" as one of society's first principles.[8] It demands that a system lose its excessive energy that cannot be harnessed for growth—"energy lost without profit" in the service of its own development.[9] Just how that system loses its energy may have either glorious or catastrophic consequences, depending on whether or not this condition is recognized as the basis of all social organization. "The ground we live on is little other than a field of multiple destructions," Bataille warns, "our ignorance only has this incontestable effect: it causes us to undergo what we could bring about in our own way, if we understood."[10]

The relevance of this formulation for the notion of the sacrificial economy is clear. But an important caveat follows from this treatment. To describe Matta-Clark's art as "sacrificial" is by no means to suggest that it was a celebratory embrace of the destruction of buildings, for nothing could be farther from his project. Operations that shared more with the wielding of a surgeon's knife than the indiscriminate crush of a wrecking ball, these were not decadent gestures, complicit with the demolition of architectural and social space. On the contrary, it is the broad claim of this book that Matta-Clark's practice takes account of its own activity—"brings it about in his own way," to follow Bataille—as intervening in the collective imperative to waste. His work provides a dialectical compliment to this expenditure, its "non-productive" use as artistic and social play.

Indeed, for all its seeming destructiveness, Matta-Clark's practice is decidedly *materialist* in its concerns. Materialist of a peculiar order, however, as it imagines that the condition of its own "worklessness" negotiates historical phenomena marginal to the 1970s. Matta-Clark's fascination with things embracing their own outmodedness—buildings and dumpsters, suburbs and sewers, trash heaps, catacombs, cities, property—occasions an improper history of that decade, a history constituted through its fallout. If the sixties are routinely described as the era in which social activism emerged within public consciousness, we can generalize safely by saying that artists grappled with the remains of such a project in the seventies. Matta-Clark's work, therefore, is a politics of things approaching their social exhaustion and the potential of their reclamation. It is a politics of the art object in relation to property; of the "right to the city" alienated by capital and the state;[11] of the retrieval of lost spaces; of communities reimagined in the wake of their disappearance; a politics of garbage and things thrown away.

This book is thus a history of the seventies—of a type—but it also reads Matta-Clark's work as a consideration of history itself. To say that Matta-Clark's work is "sacrificial," with all its resonances of loss as well as social ritual, is to challenge the terms by which history is traditionally read as "accumulative": as a *building* toward an ideal work in the service of progress; or as a vision of futurity at once founded upon and edified by the stockpiling of historical events. When Matta-Clark once observed that "only our garbage heaps are soaring as they fill up with history,"[12] he implicitly criticized any such ideologies of progress. As much as his art is founded on the waste matter of architecture, it is always in the process of undoing itself, *unbuilding* as the artist described it. The "Object to Be Destroyed," then, should not be understood as the destruction of buildings as such. Rather, Matta-Clark takes up the object's refuse as his own artistic intervention: at times playful, humorous, communal, and generous in spirit; at other moments, haunted by the loss of its temporal horizon.

WRITING ON MATTA-CLARK

I have no illusions about my struggles with writing around the work.
—Gordon Matta-Clark[13]

How many maps, in the descriptive or geographical sense, might be needed to deal exhaustively with a given space, to code and decode all its meanings and contents? It is doubtful whether a finite number can ever be given in answer to this sort of question. What we are most likely confronted with here is a sort of instant infinity
—Henri Lefebvre[14]

What map, then, could "deal exhaustively" with Gordon Matta-Clark? What legend could decode the historical import of an artist whose treatment of "worklessness" I argue for generally in this book? To write about an artist whose principal body of work no longer exists presents a peculiar set of methodological dilemmas for the art historian. By extension, the desire to produce a monograph around such an artist seems vaguely counterintuitive.

Not that the history of art is lacking in such practices. When we painstakingly reconstruct archaeological sites, say, or conjure the displaced fragment of a predella, we concede at once to both the speculative and the historicist presumptions of our discipline. In the spirit of such concessions, this book is monographic in its approach but only to a point. For one, it is neither exhaustive in discussing the entirety of Matta-Clark's output nor biographical in producing a seamless narrative of his life. At its base, it recognizes that Matta-Clark's art foregrounds the problem of its own mediation, and so presumes that many other "maps" on the artist will follow.

A brief note on terminology assumed throughout the text is important here, concerning the way "space" is related to Matta-Clark's art. Over the last few decades, the notion of "space" has assumed the status of theoretical fetish in the academy, losing something of its historical use value in the process. I have endeavored to avoid this trap by subscribing to an acutely dialectical reading of space, owing much to Henri Lefebvre's observations in *The Production of Space* (1974) and the earlier *Right to the City* (1968). Refusing notions of space as a plane upon which social relations are deposited and unilaterally produced—as an isotropic extension for modes of production as such—Lefebvre attends to the anticipatory and formative role of the actors on that space as a kind of use value or praxis. I wish to retain the heterogeneous sense of space that Lefebvre articulates, precisely by rejecting an account of Matta-Clark's work as passively mirroring its environmental surround.

The book attends to Matta-Clark's sacrificial or workless economies in a roughly chronological manner. Chapter 1, titled "The First Place," locates the beginnings of Matta-Clark's art and addresses the question of contextual influence. While context cannot be ignored in the historical treatment of art, this chapter takes to task the way it is uncritically assumed as accessible and transparent. Paradoxically, however, Matta-Clark's context or "first place" is harnessed in the service of revealing the limitations of contextual analyses: of both his "development" as an artist and a certain reading of site-specific art itself. First I speculate on Matta-Clark's relation to his father, the surrealist painter Roberto Matta, to consider how the site of the home serves as a principal metaphor of influence. Matta-Clark's work on the home undoes this logic, challenging the conventions of privacy and security attached to the domestic sphere, particularly within a suburban context. The second part of the chapter considers his time at Cornell University and his studies in architecture in the sixties. Finally, I consider his meeting at Cornell with Robert Smithson, which enormously influenced the younger artist. I draw upon Smithson's theories of entropy to ironize certain assumptions surrounding the inextricability of context, influence, and site-specific work.

What does it mean to have property? To what uses may property reasonably be put? And what are the theoretical convergences between notions of property, the constitution of the work of art, and the artistic subject? Chapter 2 considers Matta-Clark's early work in New York in relation to artists and the "right to the city." I discuss his involvement in the young community of SoHo—namely, his projects at 112 Greene Street and the restaurant Food—as well as his first building cuts in New York City. But the chapter also occasions a larger reading on the politics of property rights in New York at the time and the extent to which artists struggled with them. Matta-Clark's association with the loose collective known as Anarchitecture and his body of work known as the "Fake Estates" provide an insistent critique of the ways the space of New York city was rationalized in the seventies. To this end, I argue for a reading of property and personhood in Matta-Clark's work through the terms of expenditure or waste.

Chapter 3 argues against the trope of violence uncritically assumed in relation to Matta-Clark's art, suggesting that Matta-Clark's "violence" is directed against the terms of spatial experience. Close readings of two of his most important sites (*Days*

End and *Circus: The Caribbean Orange*) provide case studies. They are treated through two seemingly contradictory bodies of thought frequently appropriated in the criticism of the late sixties and seventies—the discourses of phenomenology, on the one hand, and the lessons of the sublime on the other; and they are related further to the examples of minimalist sculpture and land art, which preceded Matta-Clark's work historically. I suggest that the artist's alleged violence offers a critique of minimalism's phenomenological model through the uses of scale and the "cut" in his art, discussed as sublime. The building cuts externalize minimalism's concerns to the subject's shifting status within the built environment, opening onto the "violence" of architectural site and abstract space.

If Matta-Clark's work implicitly rejects a model of subjectivity as secure, how can it possibly engender a political impulse, contingent as that would seem to the faith placed in an autonomous historical actor? With chapter 4, Matta-Clark's projects in Paris, specifically *Conical Intersect,* are evaluated with regard to questions of community—namely, the struggle for community—drawing upon Walter Benjamin's reading of the "outmoded." While community was central to the entirety of Matta-Clark's work, I argue that his Parisian work partakes of the logic of a "workless" community—a community that recognizes the radical alterity of its members, by witnessing the passing of its own communal horizon. Set against the controversy surrounding the reconstruction of the Les Halles district in the sixties and seventies, as well as the building of the Centre Georges Pompidou, I read Matta-Clark's Parisian based work as providing a political critique through foregrounding the loss of community, much as Benjamin (whom the artist admired) detects the "revolutionary energy" of things about to fall into obsolescence in his meditation on Paris.

In conclusion, I think about the theoretical implications in treating Matta-Clark's legacy for art and architecture as well as the "souvenirs" of his projects. I also consider the status of the documentary photographs through which Matta-Clark's art is mediated today. The particular case of the attempt to save his Antwerp based project, *Office Baroque,* is finally outlined in order to think about the historiographic implications of preserving his work. And arising ultimately from this is a larger reading on the paradox embedded in the notion of contemporary art history—what it means to produce a history of the contemporary, of the time, that is nevertheless historical, past. The odd temporality of Matta-Clark's work, I argue, tells us much about the methodological presumptions of the historian herself.

Throughout, I hope to demonstrate that Matta-Clark's "work" refuses the traditional logic of work, however much my account is reasoned, rationalized, and systematic—the very means through which work is itself produced. The ironies implicit in such pursuits are unavoidable. But what these ironies suggest about Matta-Clark's art are ultimately productive, attesting to its critical sensibility, the paradoxes it lays bare about social space and the built environment. For Matta-Clark's art fully embraces the contradictions of both its production and reception, untethered as it is to fixed notions about the space of art in contemporary life.

OBJECT TO BE DESTROYED

1 THE FIRST PLACE

The history of art is a litany of places. Like a well-thumbed Baedeker, each monument dutifully inscribed, its narratives turn endlessly around the scene of the artist, as if the revelation of site could secure the meaning of the art produced. The names of these places recall schools and styles, networks and individuals, singular objects, histories long and complex. To trace the artist's itinerary would seem to yield understanding into his formation. And to map the artist's first place would be to circumscribe its origin.

But what of an artist whose relationship to site is discontinuous, aporetic? What of the first place of Gordon Matta-Clark? Labyrinthine, vertiginous, and disorienting in their scale and projection, Matta-Clark's building cuts interrogated the relationship between art and place at their very foundation. Constructed from outmoded buildings and produced from 1971 until his death in 1978, these Piranesiac irruptions into architectural mass unsettled the very act of spectatorship in the viewer's passage through space. But as if to externalize these concerns, to broaden the scope of their implicit critique, they also addressed the phenomenon of places in dizzying flux. In neighborhoods ranging from the slums of Manhattan to the boulevards of Paris, they dramatized the temporality of each site, the timeliness of architecture, through marking the disintegration of social space.

To seek the first place of such an artist would seem a questionable enterprise, yet this chapter attends to the most conventional routes of the art historian in thinking about Matta-Clark's consideration of site. His art will be seen here to challenge a seamless equation between place and causality, whether at the level of art historical biography or the reception of the site works themselves. Two places and two figures will be focused on along the way. I begin with the artist's home and his father, the surrealist painter Roberto Matta, to see how Matta-Clark ironizes the space of the house, traditionally regarded as a cipher of privacy, security, and absolute space. Second, Matta-Clark's place of education, Cornell University, and the mentor he encountered there, the artist Robert Smithson, will be read through an "entropic" inversion of the monument. At issue in both sections is that the notion of context—what might seem the first principle of site-specific art—cannot be assumed as transparent, nor can the mechanics of influence commonly attached to site.

HOMELINESS AND ABSENTEEISM: MATTA'S PLACE FOR MATTA-CLARK

A photograph taken in 1943 (figure 1.1), the year of Matta-Clark's birth, appears to provide pressing evidence as to the first place of the artist. Taken in New York City, it is among his earliest portraits, snapped by no less of an authority figure than his father Matta (Roberto Matta Echaurren). One turns to it, then, with some expectancy, as if it might shed light on the artist's domestic situation.

The small black and white photograph pictures the infant Gordon next to Giacometti's famous sculpture, *Invisible Object,* in the Patchin Place apartment shared by Matta and his wife Anne Clark. A strange, disquieting image of childhood, it bears virtually no resemblance to the baby picture genre, sacrificing the casual intimacy such images are wont to convey for the formal *gravitas* of an art photograph, a tenebrous composition relieved by the flashed surfaces of both the child's and the object's faces. In this detail is the absurdity of the image contained. The juxtaposing of the infant with a starkly fashioned, surreal object serves less to humanize the child than to objectify him, to render a soft and mewling thing into something stony and sculptural.

Whatever its aesthetic merits, the photograph bears witness to a decidedly unorthodox home, sharing nothing with the stock conventions of domesticity. A place in which Giacometti sculptures function like so much furniture, it was peopled by even more extraordinary personages—Andre Breton, Marcel Duchamp, Katherine Dreier, the surrealist circle recently emigrated to New York. Thus, the Matta household of the early forties is referred to tirelessly in the son's biographies as if to rationalize the child's inclination toward art and explain the qualities in his work described as surrealistic.[1] By turns, Gordon's birth figures into histories of surrealism as well. Born on June 22, 1943, the appearance of Gordon and his twin John Sebastian (Batan) "became legendary in the annals of Surrealism," since "the surrealists were all sufficiently conversant with ethnology to be aware of the specific beliefs that attach

to the birth of twins."[2] Certainly, the surrealist presence in the Matta household was unimpeachable, carrying nominal as well as social implications. The British painter Gordon Onslow-Ford, another recent surrealist exile, was the infant's namesake.

Yet if Matta's home socially condensed this art historical scene, fundamentally it was a place of exile, formed as a desperate community through the crisis of the Second World War. And any influence it may have had on the child was radically tempered by a crucial, personal note: the father's role in his sons' upbringing was shortlived. A few months after the twins' birth, Matta left Anne Clark, forcing her to raise the children alone. While she continued to socialize with her husband's circle after his departure, she describes the twins' access to the surrealists as limited.[3] By the time Matta moved back to Europe in 1948 after being expelled from the surrealist circle, the twins' access to their father grew even more remote: "I never saw him for more than an hour in my life,"[4] Matta reports on his relation to Gordon. The statement is patently false: Gordon spent a considerable amount of time with his father and his new family, and they corresponded frequently. Nonetheless, Matta's remark sheds light on his attitude toward raising the twins, whose childhood was peripatetic at best. Moving to South America and various parts of France within the first six years of their life, their situation was alleviated by Anne's marriage to the writer Hollis Alpert in 1950.

Matta-Clark wrestled for the rest of his short life with a simultaneous denial of his father's influence and a desire for his recognition. Every testimony devoted to the younger artist's rejection of the father is complemented by a discussion of Matta-Clark's need for his acceptance. "Although he never spoke about his father," his former partner Caroline Goodden (now Goodden Ames) recalls, "I realized that he had spent his whole life competing with him."[5] Other gestures attest to Matta-Clark's partial renunciation of the father. In 1970, not long out of college, the artist changed his surname by incorporating his mother's maiden name "Clark" within it.

The relationship between father and son would seem to recommend itself to the psychoanalytic model of influence famously described by Harold Bloom.[6] In the

1.1 Roberto Matta Echaurren, Gordon Matta as an infant with Giacometti sculpture, Patchin Place, NY, 1943.

dynamic just described, father and son are literally master and epigone: influence is treated as both paternal and artistic, with the younger artist's attempt to supersede his elder understood as an Oedipal reckoning. But the terms of this relationship are not so transparent, nor are the terms of this influence. Clearly Matta's legacy is not one of practical lessons about the making of art, but neither is it an absolute dismissal of the father's ways—a rejection of the father's name *in toto.* At stake, rather, is the condition of the father's absenteeism, a notion that speaks less to the permanent condition of his absence—or even his presence—than it does to the endless possibility of his return and leave taking.

Consider, then, the father's treatment of place, particularly the homestead, against the grain of Matta-Clark's own investigations. Born in Santiago, Chile, in 1912, Matta arrived in 1935 in Paris, where he served as a draftsman in the studio of Le Corbusier. For two years he labored on the architect's plan for the *Ville Radieuse,* a revised notion of the ideal city inspired by Taylorist models of efficiency and scientific management. In Le Corbusier's enormous treatise on the subject, the architectural plan is afforded enormous weight. "Plans are *not* politics," he inveighs. "Plans are the rational and poetic monument set up in the midst of contingencies . . . Contingencies should only be judged as they relate to the entity 'man'—and in connection with man."[7] Le Corbusier makes clear that the rationalizing of place *as plan* supersedes the range of contingencies, even as it is "set up in the midst of them." And, invariably, what guides the plan for Le Corbusier is the "entity of 'man,'" if a very particular kind of man, finding its apotheosis in the two-volume work *Le Modulor* (1948 and 1955).

Yet no matter how Le Corbusier's name resonated within architectural circles, Matta's association with the master inspired only derision from the surrealists, whom he was shortly to meet. Through an invitation from family friends, Matta was introduced to Salvador Dalí, who secured for him an audience with Breton. Matta describes the surrealists' characteristically sneering dismissal of the high modernist architect: "What, are you with Le Corbusier? How terrible!"[8] No doubt this recollection is surrealist puffery, revealing much about Matta's own blunt caricaturization of Le Corbusier's work, but his almost immediate conversion to the surrealist program was evident enough. Rejecting Le Corbusier's ratiocinated anthropomorphism, Matta observed that it failed to contain "the kind of man who lived there," unless that man was nothing short of a utopian subject, "a creature that lived in perfect harmony with the society and his work."[9]

Matta's refutation of an architecture perceived to be as streamlined and rationalized as its inhabitants found its primary exposition in his 1938 article in the surrealist journal *Minotaure.* Titled "Mathematique Sensible—Architecture du Temps," it called for an architecture that rejected the viability of linear and regularized designs.[10] "Mathématique Sensible" both mimicked and criticized Le Corbusier's notion of *mathématique raisonable,* the architect's conceit that "the transcendent forces of geometry must prevail" in design.[11] The essay was accompanied by Matta's illustration of a room in which non-regularized walls and sharply tilted planes housed "pneumatic" furniture and staircases that "mastered the abyss" (figure 1.2). Opening up onto vistas of deeply ambiguous space, it was inhabited by the kind of languid, amorphous figures that normally populated his canvases.

The text itself blusters with the force of a manifesto: "Let us put aside the techniques which consist of setting up ordinary materials," Matta admonishes, rallying for an "architecture of time":

> We need walls like damp sheets which lose their shapes and wed our psychological fears . . . To find for each person those umbilical cords that put us in communication with other suns, objects of total freedom that would be like psychoanalytic mirrors.[12]

Le Corbusier's notion of an anthropomorphic architecture was tied to its idealized form in the modular man—mathematical, reasoned, vertical, proportional. By contrast, Matta's architecture invokes the sticky vicissitudes of the human body, a surrealist analogue to the psychic contingencies of the unconscious. His sensitive architecture is thus motivated by a decidedly non-rationalized subject. A malleable, ever-changing subject, its every psychic turning was mirrored by an architectural transformation.

With its "walls like damp sheets" and "umbilical cords," this ever-changing place functions as a kind of intra-uterine safehaven, an observation Anthony Vidler makes in brilliantly treating the space through the Freudian trope of the uncanny.[13] The sensation of unease founded upon the doubled, shifting implications of the German *heimlich* and *unheimlich*—at once "native, belonging to the home"[14] and shaded

by an almost palpable feeling of dread—the uncanny is freighted with both architectural and spatial implications. At one and the same time, it is of the home and it is not, comfortably domestic and yet alienating. For although the terms *heimlich* and *unheimlich* would seem at odds with one another, Freud's account enumerates a number of examples in which they are semantically coincident. "What is *heimlich,*" he ultimately argues, "comes to be *unheimlich.*"[15]

As the literal birthsite of the domestic order, the womb is among the most uncanny of places. Representing an impermeable retreat from everyday life, it is also haunted by a deeply sinister affect, explained partially by the uncanny's link to Freud's subsequent formulation of the death instincts.[16] Matta's intrauterine apartment can be understood as a doubled place of absenteeism in this regard. As womb, it is both the very precondition of life—the place from which one is expelled into being—and the retreat or escape from life to the subject's imagined death.

It is tempting to consider Matta's perspective on space as directly arrogated by his son Matta-Clark. Judith Russi Kirshner argues that there is much of Matta's "Mathématique Sensible—Architecture du Temps" to be seen in Matta-Clark's later architectural investigations;[17] and, surely, strong parallels exist between the two artists' relation to architecture. Like his father before him, Matta-Clark opted to study architecture before becoming an artist; and he, too, would reserve particular venom for the modernist architectural program, with the figure of Le Corbusier subject to an especially dismissive critique.[18] In a letter of December 1973, for instance, Matta-Clark offered a blunt inversion of one of Le Corbusier's best-known theses, as if to reproduce the same critique as his father. "A Machine for not living," he wrote, ". . . with an extract from Le Corbusier's *Vers un Architecture* showing the virgin machine he wants us all to live in."[19]

But crucial differences between the two approaches also exist, as if no direct vector of influence connected father to son. To state the most obvious distinction, one's model is painterly, representational; the other's mediates the play between the sculptural and the architectonic. If Matta's version of architecture was conditioned by

1.2 Roberto Matta Echaurren, illustration, "*Mathématique Sensible–Architecture du Temps,*" *Minotaure*, 1938. Courtesy Artists Rights Society (ARS) 1999.

the “changing states of inwardness”—romanticizing the space of interiority—Matta-Clark reflected critically on the temporality of the built environment, a materialist recoding of an “architecture of time.” For the presence of his work within both the urban and suburban sphere demanded that it be encountered as a socialized thing; and its imminent demolition ensured that it not be elevated to the rank of transcendent art object.

The artist’s investigations of the home offer a suggestive case study in these principles, particularly his best known work, *Splitting* (figure 1.3), a project staged at 322 Humphrey Street in Englewood, New Jersey. Its history tells us much about the way the home—in this instance, a suburban home—cannot sustain the interpretations of Matta-Clark’s father, nor allow for a ready equation between place and formation.

THE HOME AS LEAVE TAKING: ON SPLITTING AND SUBURBAN HOMELINESS

In the spring of 1974, Matta-Clark approached his dealers Holly and Horace Solomon with a strange proposal. He wanted to cut a house in two and would they happen to know of any buildings available for this purpose? An odd request to be sure, but Horace Solomon happened to own such a house. It was purchased not for the sake of the building, a banal thing in a decrepit neighborhood, but for the value of its lot. Solomon’s, in short, was an act of real estate speculation dramatized by the fate of the building itself: the house was to be demolished in a few months’ time. Thus Matta-Clark was granted the use of the building, but with the knowledge that his work would be impermanent.

The Humphrey Street cutting bore precedent in a project from the fall of 1973 that also dealt implicitly with the home. While traveling in Italy with Caroline Goodden, who was performing there with the Trisha Brown Dance Company, Matta-Clark undertook his first officially sanctioned cutting of an entire structure. Titled *A*

1.3 Gordon Matta-Clark, *Splitting,* 1974, 322 Humphrey Street, Englewood, NJ.

W-Hole House, it was sponsored by the art dealer Paolo Minetti, whose Galleriaforma exhibited Matta-Clark's work later that year. Earlier, in Milan, the artist had made a cut called *Intraform* in an abandoned warehouse. Now in an industrial neighborhood of Genoa, he set about "defunctionalizing" an office for engineers, with whom Minetti had personal connections—rendering it literally workless because no longer functional.[20] Owned by a steel plant, this simple one-story structure, organized around a rigid central plan, was scheduled to be demolished. But Matta-Clark was taken in by its disposition of space, for the engineers had divided this "small, square primitive hut" in half, creating a large drafting room on one side. One of the remaining quarters was left as a large office space while the other quarter was divided in half again for a coatroom and a bathroom. Finally, one of those quarters was divided once more. "Everything" Matta-Clark noted, "was progressively divided so that the remaining last piece was 1/32 of the whole."[21]

The notion of a central, seemingly stable plan shored up by division fascinated Matta-Clark. His subsequent cutting revealed how the totality of the building, initially experienced as blunt and indissoluble, was predicated on the progressive cutting of space. As the pun of his title suggests, the "wholeness" of the building was organized around its "holes," which he conveyed in two parts of the project. In the section *Atrium Roof* (figure 1.4), the artist chiseled out the center of the pyramidal roof, which he then removed through the use of the company crane. Hence, the "structure was cored, walls and doors, roof and ceiling were united by a centralized opening," and the office was "no longer a building to separate owners from workers but a hub around which nothing but light worked."[22]

In the artist's desire to remove the architectural barriers between owners and workers, suggesting that "nothing but light worked" in the building, a paradox about the building's worklessness presents itself. Here, it is the structural integrity of the building—its seeming opacity and totality—that is read as alienating and divisive; whereas its dissection by the artist opens onto the communal horizon of its audience,

1.4 Gordon Matta-Clark, *A W-Hole House: Atrium Roof,* 1973, Genoa, Italy.

1.5, 1.6 (pages 14, 16) Gordon Matta-Clark, *A W-Hole House: Datum Cuts,* 1973, Genoa, Italy.

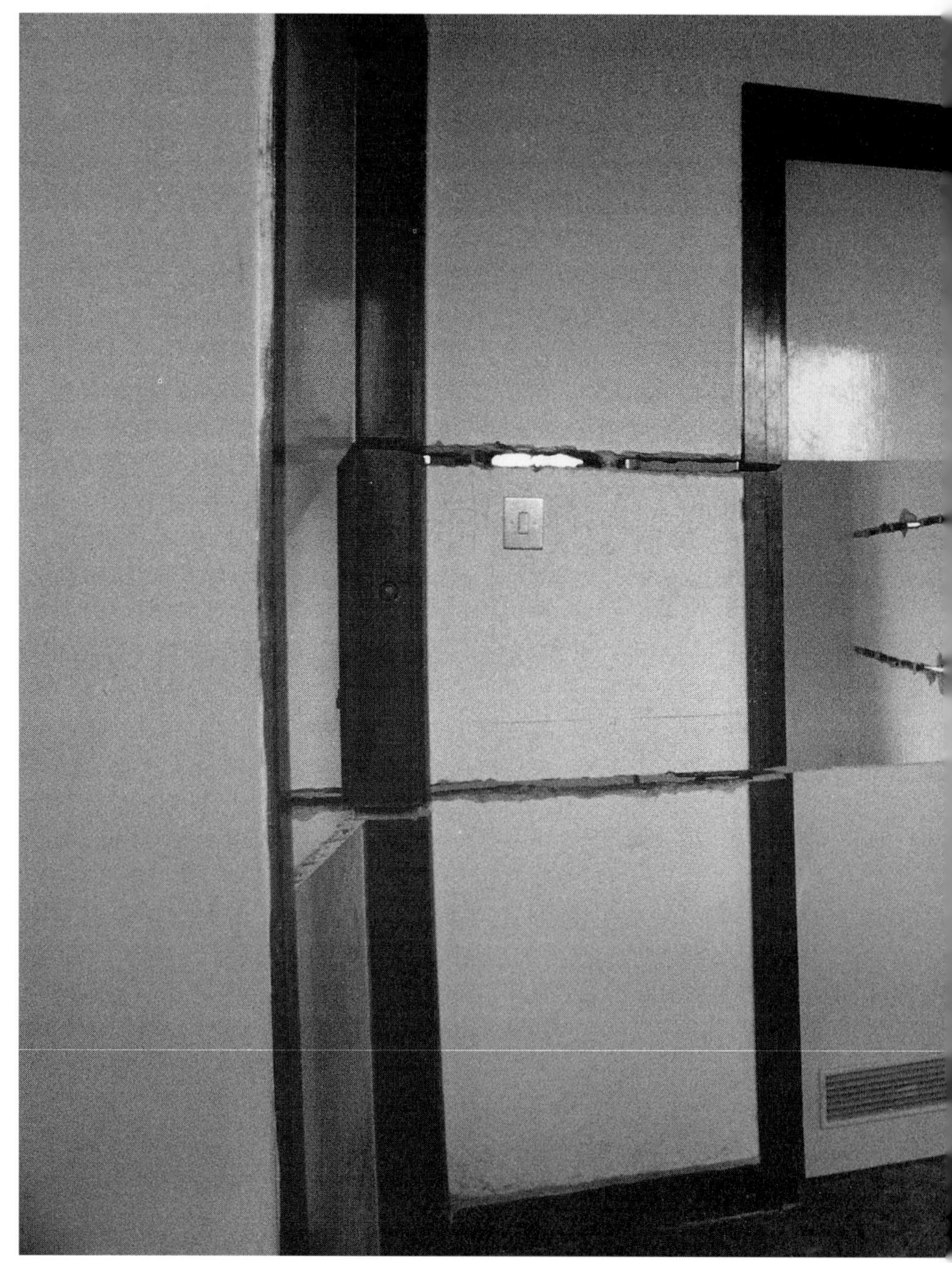

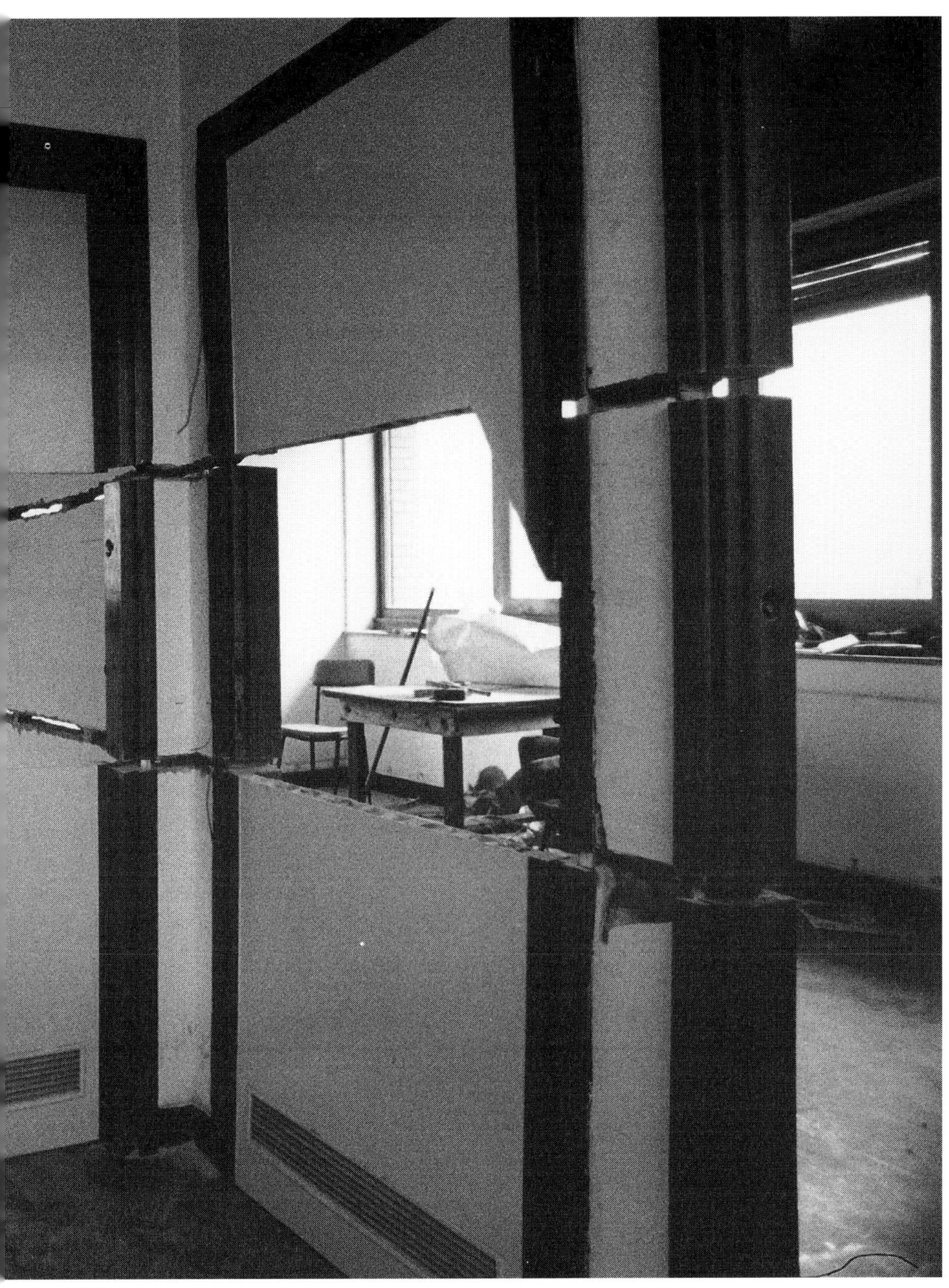

heterogeneous and no longer separated. In the second part of the project, titled *Datum Cuts* (figures 1.5 and 1.6), Matta-Clark continued this analysis, cutting a "horizontal line three feet from the floor around the center of the interior, with another parallel line eighteen inches above it." A dense imbrication of the surfaces of remaining walls and the gaps registered by the cuts, the walls appeared to be woven into three intersecting bands, as if braided.

Although the building used for *A W-Hole House* was not designed as a house, it is instructive that Matta-Clark described it as one, finding a cogent parallel to the Humphrey Street project, which was begun in late March of the following year. Like its Italian counterpart, the Englewood house was prosaic in its design. A two-story, single family home with porches at the front and back, its plan was as rigid and symmetrical, its appearance as blunt and box-like, as the Italian building was centralized. It was the stolid objectivity of both—the apparent immediacy of their gestalt—that seemed the crux of Matta-Clark's interventions. Yet what the economy of cuts in both *A W-Hole House* and *Splitting* revealed was the very emptiness at the center of the two structures, a centerless center, so to speak.

As for *Splitting* itself, Matta-Clark cleared the house of the debris left by its former occupants and placed it in the basement, suggesting a refusal to sort through "a fragmented biographical garbage heap" and denying the work any anthropomorphic associations.[23] He then cut two parallel, vertical lines through the middle of the building with a chainsaw, an act he documented on film (figures 1.7 and 1.8). With the assistance and knowledge of Manfred Hecht, who had assisted in the construction of a number of lofts, Matta-Clark set to tipping the house back on its foundations:

> I beveled it at an angle dictated by one course of cinder block. First we scored and chiselled away all the block reinforcing the foundation as we worked, until the rear half of the house was standing on four points at the corners. Then, using building jacks, we transferred the load, about fifteen tons of it, from the final blocks and just lowered it.[24]

1.7 Gordon Matta-Clark, *Splitting* (in process), 1974, 322 Humphrey Street, Englewood, NJ.

LIVERPOOL JOHN MOORES UNIVERSITY
Aldham Roberts L.R.C.
TEL. 0151 231 3701/3634

Matta-Clark and Hecht thus "set down the rear half of the house onto a slightly lowered foundation, creating a wedge-shape that bisected the house"[25] (figure 1.9). Removing the material from the middle, they also extracted the eaves of the building, which exist today as the sculptural work *Four Corners* (figure 1.10).

In an interview with the critic Liza Bear, Matta-Clark made clear that the production of the work was "anything but illusionistic . . . It's all about a direct physical activity, and not about making associations with anything outside it."[26] Nevertheless, he recognized that people would inevitably make such readings, and reception of the work has tended to follow suit. Some critics have remarked that Matta-Clark's work comments upon the "split" character of American life in the seventies, as if the "house divided" spoke to the nation's collective woes.[27] Others read the work as potentially misogynistic, a violent attack against the domestic order gendered as feminine.[28] The artist himself received a number of angry letters about the project, one of which accused him of performing an "out and out rape" on the house.[29]

But in such readings the symbolism of the house is accepted at face value, its meaning uncontestable, immutable, and transparent. If the house divided speaks to the unhealthfulness of the contemporary scene, its unsplit form would seem to represent its security. If the building cleaved suggests a threat to the space of domesticity, coded as maternal, the house uncut represents the integrity of that sphere as feminized. A longer narrative of the house lays bare the dangers in treating it as a metaphor for stability, permanence, security—as if the metaphor itself were not ideologically embedded, free of its own constructedness. To subscribe to this iconography is to defer, however implicitly, to the myth of the suburban home—the dream of middle-class America.

A necessarily brief detour of American suburbia is called for, coordinated largely around the twinned ideologies of privacy and retreat. Dating back to the time of the colonies, the first American suburbs were not considered entirely separate from metropolitan life, but were deemed as "second" cities, a notion that finds parallels in more recent accounts of suburbia.[30] The second historical fluorescence of the Amer-

1.8 Gordon Matta-Clark, *Splitting* (in process), 1974, 322 Humphrey Street, Englewood, NJ.

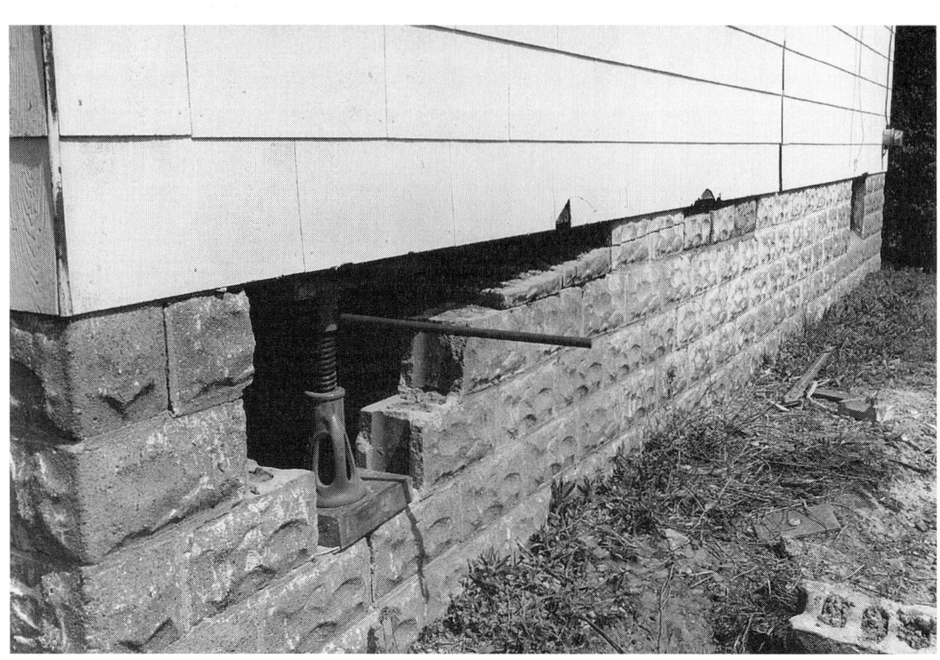

ican suburb began in the mid-nineteenth century, when affluent citizens began to move to outlying areas of the city. If not wholly a causal reaction against industrialization and the swelling populations of laborers who fueled the city's growth, this movement was certainly a partial function of these phenomena. New transportation and building technology facilitated (if hardly determined) the exodus of the wealthy and, later, the middle class. But it was in the aftermath of World War II that the American suburb underwent its most infamous explosion, represented by the sprawls of Levittown and other housing experiments. If the mass-produced boxes of popular stereotype crystallized the image of the suburbs as a cultural wasteland for many, they generated a powerfully seductive myth nonetheless: the cult of privacy.

Political philosophy describes many versions of privacy—the privacy of religious belief, the privacy of economic freedom—but its commonplace usage centers around the terms of private property, specifically the "intimate sphere" of domestic life and the home.[31] Formulated in dialectical relation to the idea of the public, the term generally privileged in that binary, privacy is defined negatively for our purposes. To follow Jürgen Habermas's classic thesis, the bourgeois public sphere emerged as an Enlightenment category against the intimate sphere of domesticity in the eighteenth century, as well as against the state and the marketplace. Opposed to the hermetic realm of domestic space, one function of the public sphere was its spatialization of civil society. Its claim, if hardly its reality, was the democratization of free exchange, to which the emergence of new institutions—coffee houses, salons, reading groups, and newspapers—served notice.

The intimate sphere of privacy, by contrast, idealizes the nuclear family and its hierarchy and lays claim to its autonomy, bracketed off as it is from the demands of civil society. By virtue of its distance from the city, the privacy of the suburb would seem to literalize this conceit. And the suburban home symbolically condenses this leave taking, acting as a spatio-temporal retreat from a public sphere now regarded as debased by class, ethnic, and racial influences.[32]

1.9 Gordon Matta-Clark, *Splitting* (in process), 1974, 322 Humphrey Street, Englewood, NJ.

1.10 Gordon Matta-Clark, *Four Corners,* 1974.

That such privacy ever existed has been deeply contested within political philosophy; indeed, the maintenance of the public sphere itself is at the nexus of a long debate surrounding the terms of modernity and postmodernity.[33] For what constitutes publicness in the late twentieth century—with its new modes of communication, its heightened technology, and its revised notions of community—stands in sharp contrast to gentile modes of Enlightenment discourse, or, more to the point, the faith placed in that discourse. At bottom, the private interests of economic gain could hardly have remained at a distance from the public sphere, assumed largely to be "urban" and "metropolitan." Thus, what many have uncritically described as a "flight" to the suburbs is far more complicated than a mere retreat, as much as the growth of these areas inaugurated a socioeconomic shift in late capitalism. This is not the place to rehearse that argument, but it bears saying that the growth of the suburbs as settlement space was not simply a reaction to the growth of the city; instead, the allegedly peripheral status of the suburb dialectically conditioned the city's status as "center." But the privacy of suburban living came at another price historically. It came at the expense of excluding many—namely, low-income families and African-Americans—while virtually imprisoning others.[34]

What this gloss on the privacy of the American suburb reveals is that its facade of stability and autonomy masks the deep-seated *insecurity* of its most treasured icon, the suburban home. Matta-Clark's own grasp of the chasm between class and domestic space spoke well to this. "Social mobility," he wrote, "is the greatest spatial factor . . . how one manouevers [sic] in the system determines what kind of space [one] works and lives in."[35] He also suggested that the result of these spatial principles was expressed at all levels of the socioeconomic ladder. "I would not make a total distinction between the imprisonment of the poor," he declared, "and the remarkably subtle self-containerization of higher socioeconomic areas."[36]

The suburban home is no less than a cipher of the pretension to class mobility, now given a highly "objective" form. In the Niagara Falls site project *Bingo X Ninths* (1974) (figure 1.11), sponsored by Art Park, Matta-Clark made use of a condemned

1.11 Gordon Matta-Clark, *Bingo* (or *Bingo X Ninths*), 1974, 349 Erie Avenue, Niagara Falls, NY.

DED WHEA

suburban house as if to comment on this "objectivity." He progressively removed sections of its facade as a Bingo game in reverse—a negative grid extracted by ninths—with the stark geometry of the excisions recalling his treatment of both *A W-hole House* and *Splitting.* Some of the fragments were then dumped at the site of Artpark, a debris slide of a ruined building. One large section of a wall was later displayed in the John Gibson gallery (figure 1.12) as a kind of architectural relic, dead because condemned. As Matta-Clark wrote,

> These projects took most of their energy from the object-like treatment of the suburban home. Buildings are fixed entities in the minds of most people. The notion of mutable space is taboo, especially in one's own house. People live in their space with a temerity that is frightening. Home owners generally do little more than maintain their property. Once an institution like the home is objectified in such a way, it does understandably raise moral issues . . .[37]

He recognized that the faith placed in the home's objectivity carried pervasive sociological implications, the effects of its alienation felt equally in both the suburban and urban context.[38] "By undoing a building," he wrote "there are many aspects of the social conditions against which I am gesturing . . . first, to open a state of enclosure which had been preconditioned not only by physical necessity but by the industry that profligates suburban and urban boxes as a context for ensuring a passive, isolated consumer—a virtually captive audience."[39]

The fate of the "passive, isolated consumer" took on a specific character in *Splitting.* The changing status of Englewood as a city underscored the imaginary divide between city and suburb, public and private. Founded during colonial times, Englewood was later developed as a "bedroom" community for commuters to New York City, a prewar suburb whose growth was facilitated by the founding of the Northern Railroad in 1859.[40] The Humphrey Street house itself was built sometime in the thirties, but by the 1960s a different turn in its fortunes had taken place.[41] That

1.12 Gordon Matta-Clark, *Bingo,* 1974 (building fragment displayed at the John Gibson Gallery, New York, NY).

Solomon purchased the house for speculative reasons suggests that its real estate values were already depressed—the result of the "white-flight" patterns typical of other suburban communities in the postwar era.[42]

By the time the artist invited his friends to see the cutting, the mythical split between the alleged privacy of the suburbs and the publicness of the city became all too egregious. On a sunny day in June, a bus from downtown Manhattan brought visitors to the site like school children on a class field trip.[43] Exploring the suburban exotica, they became uneasy witnesses to the ruin of this division, an act that bore parallels to Matta-Clark's peculiar interest in voyeurism. Recalling his childhood in New York, the artist spoke of the proximity of living spaces and high-rise apartments as encouraging voyeuristic acts, a gesture in which the sphere of privacy takes on a semipublic dimension as permeable, open to spectacle.[44] Now, within the suburban environs of *Splitting,* Matta-Clark had collapsed a very public activity—the collective viewing of art—onto a space conventionally regarded as private; and the categories of urban and suburban, center and periphery were likewise "defunctionalized" by the artist's intervention.

But how is one to read Matta-Clark's cutting more specifically? This was not by any means a vandalized space, nor can the effects of its cutting be universalized. Matta-Clark's gesture might be thought of as a destructive act, but it could just as easily be read as a "liberating" gesture, a freeing up of the box-like form of a common frame house. Time and time over, Matta-Clark emphasized the non-monolithic nature of his cuttings; in part, this ambiguity was a function of his indissociable braiding of positive and negative space. "I don't know if you read the negative space," he offered in reply to an interviewer, "you read through the negative space to the edges of the building."[45]

Analogously, while the house on Humphrey Street represented one of Matta-Clark's more gestalt cuttings when viewed from the outside, the encounter within it questioned its totalization as secure. He described the process of cutting the house as akin to "juggling with syntax," and this was an apt metaphor, for the conventional signs of mediating architectural experience were scrambled to a considerable degree.[46] Because *Splitting* was cut down its middle and set back on its foundations, the perpendicular axes that organize most domestic architecture could no longer contain the perceptual horizons of the spectators. To reinforce this, various architectural elements that once marked its structural integrity—the carriage of its stairs, the four corners of its roof—were also cut by the artist (figures 1.13–1.16). The cleaving of the staircase in particular emphasized this disintegration. "Starting at the bottom of the stairs where the crack was small," Alice Aycock remembers, "you'd go up, and as you'd go further up, you'd have to keep crossing the crack. It kept widening as you made your way to the top, the crack was one or two feet wide. You really had to jump it. You sensed the abyss in a kinesthetic and psychological way."[47]

The viewer's faith in the groundedness of these architectural conditions was besieged further by the vagaries of shadow, light, and weather admitted into the house by the cut. Functioning like a sundial, the house clocked the passage of the day, internalizing light to enact the most pressing sense of its incongruities. Thus, the encounter within *Splitting* became most destabilizing at the moments of its illumination, its breaks and fissures dramatically lit. By the same token, the light could be thought to clarify and enlighten the hermetically sealed "container" of the suburban home, restoring air and light to this space of social isolationism.

The limbic quality of Matta-Clark's work suggests an alternate mode of reception to his father's example, refusing conventional verities of the home. In an equal but opposite fashion, to suggest that *Splitting* is a metaphor for the "split" character of his family life is deeply problematic, as is the parallel claim that the work signifies the crisis underlying the "flight" to the suburbs. Both readings suggest, if negatively, an iconographic model of homeliness against which they are dialectically posed. But the undecidable character of Matta-Clark's space does not so much work in opposition to these terms as it works around them, or perhaps even *after* them. For what are the ideological stakes in describing the "context" and, by implication, "meaning" of the suburban home as secure when it is anything but? Matta-Clark's notion of "leave taking" demonstrates the force of the places that came too late.

1.13–1.16 (pages 30–33) Gordon Matta-Clark, *Splitting,* 1974, 322 Humphrey Street, Englewood, NJ.

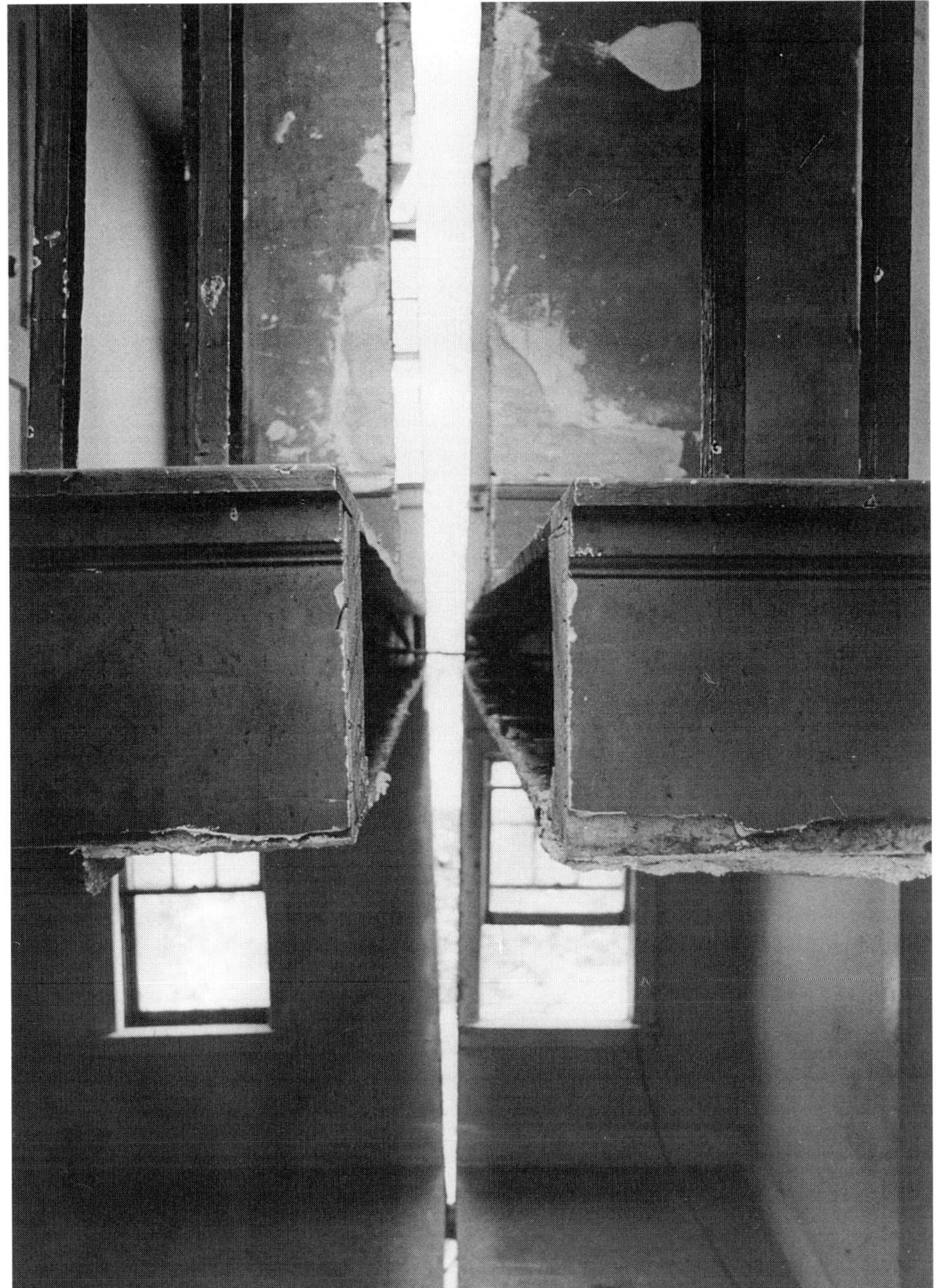

MONUMENTS TO ENTROPY: ROBERT SMITHSON'S PLACE FOR MATTA-CLARK

CORNELL AS "CONTEXT"

Matta-Clark's first place—his encounter with Matta—allegorizes a specific thinking about site conditioned by, if not reflective of, his absenteeism. It was the figure of Robert Smithson, whom Matta-Clark met at Cornell University in 1969, that revealed such places to be entropic at their origin.

Attending the college from 1962 to 1968 (he enrolled in the fall of 1962 and spent fall and spring of the following year studying literature at the Sorbonne,) Matta-Clark continued to live in Ithaca for the remainder of 1968 before settling in New York (he also reports to have worked on an urban renewal project in Binghamton, New York, at the time.[48]) A student in the School of Architecture who trafficked socially with art students, his transcript reveals that he performed miserably in the classes considered the basis of an architect's education receiving "D's" in no less than three (of four) semesters of "Structural Principles."[49] Surely, Matta-Clark resented his architectural training enormously, a sentiment that would infamously resurface throughout his career as an artist. As he once complained, "[T]he things we studied always involved such surface formalism that I never had a sense of the ambiguity of a structure, the ambiguity of a place . . . the quality I'm interested in generating in what I do."[50]

What was Matta-Clark referring to in this rather elliptical statement? What doctrine or studio, what professor, aesthetic, or charette was the object of his generalized dismissal? Although his transcript reveals he took the requisite span of undergraduate courses in architecture and urban planning (Architectural Design, Building Materials and Construction, Building Installations, Principles of City and Regional Planning), one is hard pressed to determine just what he meant by "surface formalism." A review of Cornell's School of Architecture in the sixties allows for some speculation, though. Regardless of Matta-Clark's hostility, this was a redoubtable institution in the sixties, progressive in its pedagogy and unimpeachable for the importance of its contributions to contemporary architectural theory and practice.[51] The full-time as well as visiting faculty and critics included Colin Rowe, Robert

Slutzky, John Hejduk, Werner Seligmanm, and many of the other so-called "Texas Rangers," the extraordinary faculty of architects that had taught at the University of Texas at Austin in the fifties.[52] Of the younger generation, many of whom were visiting critics, one counts the likes of Peter Eisenman and other figures historically associated with the "New York Five."[53]

As Kenneth Frampton has written, the internal politics within the department were confrontational in the late sixties, and its pedagogy was accordingly complex.[54] On the one hand, a certain socio-populist platform was supported by the German architect O. M. Ungers, who was named chairman of the department in 1968. On the other hand, like so many other American universities in the sixties, the program brought to the fore an acute concentration on the works of Le Corbusier and has often been caricaturized as "Académie Corbu" as a result.[55] The publication of the fifth volume of Le Corbusier's *Oeuvre complète* in 1957, followed by his death in 1965, implicitly called for a new institutional assessment of the architect in the sixties; and in the heated pedagogical climate in which one "sided" with either Corbu or Wright (or perhaps even Mies,) the teaching of the master assumed a doctrinaire resonance. At Cornell, however, the figure of Le Corbusier cut a different profile as interpreted by Colin Rowe. For Rowe, Le Corbusier was "seen as the sole modern practitioner to establish a methodology for the systematic de-construction and elaboration of a Neo-Humanist architecture."[56]

In the seventies, Rowe's appraisal of Le Corbusier was not to be understood as an isolated phenomenon, but was related fundamentally to the urban philosophy of what has come to be known as "contextualism."[57] Broadly put, contextualist notions of urban planning are conceived of as anti-deterministic and anti-utopian, at once informed by Karl Popper's formulations of the Open Society—an "incremental, fragmentary and contingent" account of historical knowledge—as well as Rowe's own neo-humanist formation at the Warburg Institute.[58] As William Ellis writes, contextualism was intended "to mitigate two received architectural images of the city: the traditional city, with its open spaces 'carved out of a solid mass,' and Le Corbusier's 'City in the Park,' with its isolated buildings standing free in open space."[59] Thus it envisioned architecture's relationship to the city through the notion of type and context, or the analogous gestalt model of the figure-ground relation, acknowledging the "place making" capacity of architecture and its embeddedness at a given site. In contrast to what was regarded as the "placelessness" of much modernist architecture and the universalizing imperatives of the avant-garde, contextualism recognized the mutually constitutive relationship between building and context, and was deeply skeptical of totalizing architectural solutions to urbanism. Its most famous metaphor, later published in Colin Rowe and Fred Koetter's *Collage City* of 1978, was that of the collage. Now the city was less a *tabula rasa* awaiting the great plan of the architect/demiurge, than a kind of urban bricolage, a "whole range of *axes mundi*" that took account of the historicity of place as a network of overlapping, architectural tissues.[60]

How does this figure into Matta-Clark's formation—or anti-formation—as an architecture student? The artist's transcript reveals that he did take a course with Rowe (Rowe's history of Renaissance and Baroque architecture), a suggestive if hardly conclusive piece of information. One might also imagine that Matta-Clark's notion of the "ambiguity of a place"—or its perceived lack in his training—might refer retrospectively to Rowe's contextualist imperatives, in which the figure-ground relationship between building and site spoke to a gestaltist grounding of place by architecture.[61] Another hypothesis considers Matta-Clark's aggravation with "surface formalism." Perhaps the artist was reacting, if unspecifically, to the formalist concerns many of the faculty were espousing—principally, planarity, surface, thinness, and transparency in architecture—versus the social "solutions" to architecture championed by other members of the faculty.[62] Ultimately, it is impossible to determine what Matta-Clark was specifically reacting to in this debate; and we should take care not to be swayed by some generalized notion of an architectural *Zeitgeist.* Nonetheless, his later work will be seen to move against some of these architectural presumptions, much as it challenged similar conceits about site-specific art in the sixties.

Indeed, the two models might be bridged in a number of crucial respects; for beyond the strengths of the School of Architecture, the Cornell of the late sixties was also considered a meeting ground for a number of artists who would gain significant recognition in the following decade. There, under the partial guidance of J. B. Van Cleff and the sculptor Will Insley, who taught a class significantly titled "Sculpture as Architecture," a group of students seemingly emerged from the university's mantle as a readymade community.[63] A quick survey of those individuals contributes further to the mystique of that place, including Alan Saret, Louise Lawler, and Susan Rothenberg, all of whom graduated within one or two years of each other in the late sixties, and all of whom traveled broadly within the same social milieu as Matta-Clark.

The romanticization of Cornell as a virtual *Ursprung* for early seventies art practice was also a function of the staging of the *Earth Art* show there in February 1969. While not the first museum or gallery show to display the works that have come to be known as "earth art" or "land art,"[64] the exhibition is broadly recognized as seminal in the critical formation of site-specific art and conceptualist practices in general. The show was the brainchild of Willoughby Sharp, the New York-based critic and editor of the influential conceptual art magazine *Avalanche.* Choosing the Cornell campus as its site partially for its unique topography and partially for its academic and bureaucratic embrace by Andrew Dickson White Museum director Thomas Leavitt, Sharp invited ten artists to the campus to construct works in situ, including Robert Morris, Michael Heizer, Dennis Oppenheim, Hans Haacke, and Robert Smithson.

The curatorial innovations of the show included Sharp's encouragement of the artists to take advantage of "the richness of [Ithaca's] raw materials, almost unsurpassed in the eastern United States."[65] Attention given to the placement of the work, both within the confines of the Andrew Dickson White Museum and in the environs of the Cornell campus, represented a further contribution to the normative mechanics of the group exhibition. Sharp's invitation to the artists was unorthodox as well. Its inclusion of a map of the Ithaca topography was a solicitation to produce work that ranged throughout the landscape.

In all of these respects, the exhibition was very much keyed to the generalized discussions on site-specific art that emerged in the mid-sixties.[66] The conventional wisdom dictates that a work's siting demands a reception correllative to the properties of its environs or terrain—its topographical contingencies, its seasonal and diurnal fluctuations, its larger environmental conditions. In her important genealogy of site-specific practices, Miwon Kwon describes this reading as the phenomenological model of this art, a notion of site dependent upon a chiasmatic intertwining of body and space.[67] Two related models of spectatorship derive from this account. One suggests that the subject placed before the object maintains a degree of self-presence, the capacity to rationalize intellectually his or her relationship to thing and place; to equate the object with place; and to participate in a model of "place making" held under the sway of absolute space as a result.[68] The other, related reading sees the production of works for a specific site appealing to a local and totalized constituency, a thinking about place co-extensive with a generalized notion of community.[69]

Shortly, we will see how Smithson's model implicitly departs from this interpretation, with his own theorization of the Site and the Non-Site among his most formidable contributions to contemporary practice. For all intents and purposes, the complex dialogue between Site and Non-Site is that of the work made in situ, in a spectrum of outdoor places, and its synechdochal displacement as an "indoor" earth work framed within the space of the gallery: photographic documentation and maps of the site itself, or geological specimens take from each place. "Both sides are present and absent at the same time," Smithson notes, giving voice to the mutual embeddedness of Site and Non-Site within that space.[70] While the site remains beyond the purview of the museum or gallery, it finds its fragmentary reference, or more probably the entirety of its public reception, within such spaces. And yet the Non-Site derives its meaning fundamentally from a place where it is not. It accrues significance only in relation to a situation that is held outside of its immediate surroundings.

Not all of the works in the *Earth Art* show abided by Smithson's premises, but they did fall under the mantle of site-specific work. The fact that the work was made specifically for the exhibition guaranteed that the roster of participating artists congregated around the Cornell campus at least for the amount of time required to conceptualize and later install the work.[71] As a result, the *Earth Art* show did not simply inspire Matta-Clark for the artistic models it proposed, but served as his veritable entry to the New York art world. Under the auspices of the exhibition, he met and befriended the influential conceptual artist Dennis Oppenheim, and actively participated in the installation of Oppenheim's *Beebe Lake Ice Cut*—a project that involved cutting an undulating line into the frozen surface of Cornell's famous lake with a chain saw.

But of all the contacts Matta-Clark made at Cornell, the encounter with Robert Smithson is considered the most important. Although Matta-Clark's actual participation in the making of Smithson's piece may have been negligible (Louise Lawler suggests that his usefulness to the older artist extended to the possession of a much-coveted pickup truck[72]), his meeting with Smithson is perpetually thematized as influential nonetheless.[73] The artist Nancy Holt, Robert Smithson's widow, remembers

Matta-Clark's presence at the couple's studio, describing a young artist listening to her husband's creeds on the conditions of contemporary art making, not to mention his eagerness to "connect with older, more established artists."[74] But perhaps more than anything else, she recalls the long discussions on entropy Smithson subjected every willing ear to, including Matta-Clark.

Along with his concerns for the dialectical nature of Site and Nonsite, the notion of entropy remains among the most important critical category in Smithson's thinking.[75] Its seemingly obscure theorization by Smithson is best understood against the historical backdrop of "process art." Beginning in the late sixties, artists such as Robert Morris, Carl Andre, Richard Serra, Mel Bochner, Eva Hesse, and Smithson began to formulate, in their respective ways, a theory and practice of art that concentrated less on the making of an art object that was formally proper and finished than on an art that revealed the processes of its making, or "unmaking," as the case would have it. Composed of materials considered impoverished by the traditional hierarchies of artistic media (rubber, foam, rags, asphalt, thread), the work bore a markedly "disintegrative" aesthetic by internalizing the pull of gravity in its design.

Smithson's own peculiar formulation of process art stemmed from his reading of entropy, which assumes an eschatological, even apocalyptic value within the popular imaginary.[76] As developed in the physics of the mid-nineteenth century, however, the category of entropy fell under the Second Law of Thermodynamics, which followed the First Law of Energy Conservation. The First Law states that energy is materially constant, and that it can neither be created nor annihilated. The Second Law of Thermodynamics regards entropy as a dissipating force within the universe, driving the physical world from a system of order to maximal disorder. Whereas energy is constant, entropy either remains at the same measurable state or increases its distribution of thermodynamic, chemical, and material processes. The nature of temporality is likewise affected by entropy, described as either static, cold, and lethargic, or dissipative in its chronological unfolding. In both instances, the temporal dimension of entropy is understood as irreversible, correlative to the progressive disintegration of form.

Once a subject best conceptualized through complex equations in physics, by the time Smithson published his essay "Entropy and the New Monuments" in 1966,[77] the topic had shed its arcane scientific origins. Already its millenarian implications had gripped fin-de-siècle Europe.[78] By the period spanning the late fifties to the early seventies, it enjoyed a second coming of sorts, widely discussed by figures ranging from Claude Levi-Strauss to the young Thomas Pynchon.[79] And in 1971, four years after Smithson's contribution, Rudolf Arnheim published his popular *Entropy and Art.*

Smithson's reading had little to do with Arnheim's perceptualism, and his article is mentioned only dismissively in Arnheim's book. Yet the artist's formulation was far more complex than Arnheim would admit. Discussing the entropic tendencies within sixties art making, Smithson was as concerned with the temporal nature of the entropic as its surface effects. Emphasizing objects that appeared to configure "an inactive history" or an "energy drain,"[80] recent art is described by Smithson as embodying a "systematic reduction of time," whereby "the value of the notion of action" in art was progressively annihilated. The result of this apparent nihilism was work which revealed its own "time decay or de-evolution,"[81] which coincides well with the themes of process oriented sculpture. Hence, minimalist objects by Morris or Sol LeWitt were cited as examples of art that "helped to neutralize the myth of progress."[82] Their repetitious or serial dimensions, Smithson argued, undercut the possibility of attributing a teleological impulse to them.

Matta-Clark's art would seem to share little formally with the minimalist program, at least at first glance. Yet the broad concerns with material attrition in process art and Smithson's reading of entropy, find marked confirmation in his work. This appears glaringly self-evident in a number of works dating from the late sixties to the first two years of the next decade, particularly the obscure, gift-like object known as *Photo-Fry.*

In late 1969, a small beige package, no bigger than a cigar box, arrived at the Smithson/Holt loft on Greenwich Street (figure 1.17). As a component of Matta-Clark's project *Photo-Fry,* it contained a Christmas greeting from Matta-Clark. The upper half of the box bore a virtually illegible picture of a Christmas tree, a Polaroid whose cracked and welted surface took on the appearance of charred skin. Its excrescent finish served to distort and nearly efface the image, so much so that its photo-

1.17 Gordon Matta-Clark, *Photo-Fry,* 1969.

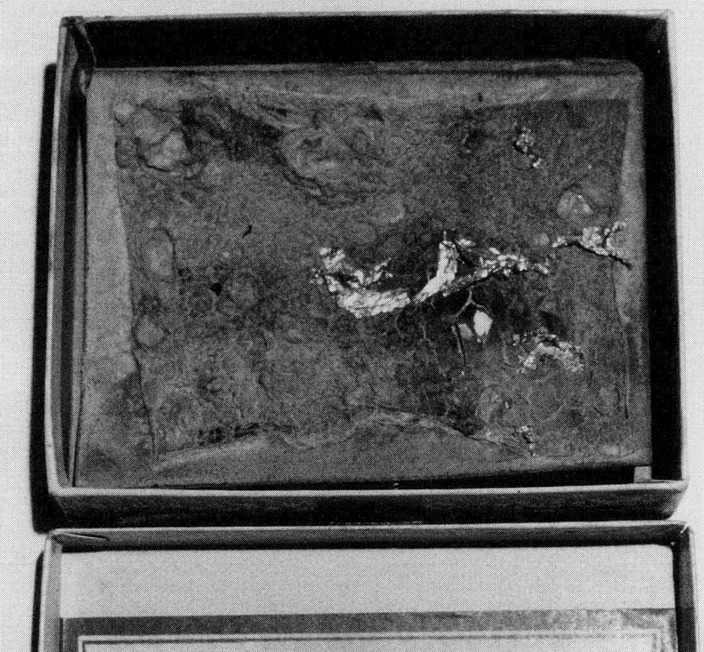
A
GOLD LEAFED PHOTO-FRIED XMASS
TREE
& BEST LATED
WISHES
GORDON

graphic properties were rendered irrelevant in considering the object. As if to underscore this further, some desiccated flakes of gold leaf were strewn randomly over its surface. Metaphorically rich, the propriety of the material did less to illumine the browning image than to dramatize its implacable baseness.

The structural tension between such a formal element and the photographic dejecta unfolded in the lower half of the box as well. For even the inscription that accompanied the picture provided little in the way of legislating the image through language. "A Gold Leafed Photo-Fried XMass Tree & Best Lated Wishes" it read, a typically convoluted message from an artist renowned for his violations of syntax and his love of word play.[83] Rather than adequately explain the image, the clarity of the artist's hand belied the rhetorical involutions of the message itself.

A memento of sorts, *Photo-Fry* stands as a testament to a relationship that Matta-Clark sought to forge upon his return to New York in 1969. As part of a group exhibition called *Documentations,* hosted by the John Gibson Gallery, the artist set about literally cooking Polaroids of Christmas trees in an iron skillet atop an old-fashioned stove, applying the gold leaf as the images reached their "boiling point." "He dropped the Polaroid into the hot oil," his friend Tina Girouard recalled, "and as it fried the emulsion bubbled up. He then tossed the gold leaf over the bubbles, and as the photo cooked the gold and emulsion bonded."[84] Leaving the photographs in the pan until the show ended, Matta-Clark then housed the images in boxes, which he sent as Christmas cards to a number of friends, including Smithson.

One can only speculate about the experience of entering the gallery at the time *Photo-Fry* was produced, or even shortly thereafter. The fumes emitted by the photographic emulsion, mingled with the heat, noise, and smell of frying grease, could hardly have created the most pleasing of aesthetic encounters, a fact confirmed by John Gibson's summary review of Matta-Clark's contribution: "it smelled terrible."[85] And one can only wonder further about being the recipient of such a thing, an object which, over the course of its lifetime, has virtually decayed before the eyes of its owners, the image of the tree growing dimmer as the once-unctious sheaf of gold paper dries and withers and cracks over the scorched photograph. The pathetically residual quality of the object, little more than a blackish smear overlaid by a film of gold leaf, is very much a paean to entropy and process art.

Smithson's formulation of entropy thus appears a theoretical springboard for many of Matta-Clark's early works, particularly those involving the processes of cooking, dating from 1969 to 1971. Frequently, these gestures were described as relating to the processes of alchemy;[86] and the gold leaf involved in *Photo-Fry* confirms that model on a superficial level. But the particularly disintegrative character of the early work shares more with an entropic tendency to fall apart than an alchemical transmutation of turning base matter to gold; and so the historically specific discussion of process art must be addressed in historicizing objects from that period.

Above all, the installation work *Museum* (figure 1.18) and the series *Incendiary Wafers* (1970–1971) (figure 1.19) represent an unintentionally humorous demonstration of the entropic. A mixture consisting of agar agar, a gelatinous derivative of saltwater algae, and other various organic and non-organic materials was brewed by the artist in a cauldron, which he then poured into trays roughly a meter long. When the base matter began to ferment, drawing nameless moldering cultures to its surface, it also began to shrink and crack, forming what Matta-Clark described as "skinlike fabrics of dormant life."[87] *Museum* was displayed in the Bykert Gallery in 1970; and in keeping with the moribund resonance of its title, became progressively moldier over the course of the exhibition. Another incident literalizes the entropic dimensions of this body of work. On January 1, 1971, one of the "skins" actually exploded for reasons not fully explained. This event forced the artist to ignite the remaining objects outside as a protective measure against any other accidents of this nature.

As much as the explosive character of that work fulfills its entropic dimension, Matta-Clark's relation to Smithson and process art can also be understood through the terms of site specificity. It is a connection that Nancy Holt readily identifies when she "remembers vividly"—that is to say, with audible disgust—the initially gelatinous and then moldering pieces Matta-Clark made with agar agar in the early seventies. They brimmed with all matters of purplish organic stuff, including materials such as "chocolate flavored Yoo-Hoo, V-8, yeast and *Mucors-Racemosus*."[88] Matta-Clark installed one of these pieces outdoors near the Smithson/Holt loft. The homage was fit-

1.18 (page 44) Gordon Matta-Clark, *Museum,* 1970.

1.19 (page 45) Gordon Matta-Clark, *Incendiary Wafers,* 1970–1971.

ting. It announced an era in which the issues of both entropy and site-specificity could be seamlessly melded together in one work.

To be sure, the laws of entropy were expressly bound to the question of architecture and site for no less of an authority than Smithson. In an interview with Smithson titled "Entropy Made Visible," he gave voice to a "kind of entropic architecture" illustrated with various photographs of buildings on the verge of collapse.[89] That the artist's lengthiest treatment on entropy is called "Entropy and the New Monuments" is also telling. It devotes at least half of its argument to the idea of the monument—an object purposefully made to ground a historical figure or event at a place, mark the very site of that event, or to be preserved to such ends.

Matta-Clark's building cuts would seem such monuments to entropy, but he was clear as to the distinction between his own art and earth work. "The choice of dealing with the urban environment in general, and building structures specifically," he remarked, "alters my whole realm of reference."[90] Still, the implications drawn from the production of his work resound with Smithson's sensibilities. The notion that the object is made at the moment of the building's ruination—the work's simultaneous self-effacement as it comes into presence—suggests that it actually "rises into ruin," to borrow an expression from Smithson.[91] Thus, Matta-Clark's work shares much with Smithson's more architectural projects, primarily his *Partially Buried Woodshed* (1970) (figure 1.20), an abandoned woodshed installed on the campus of Kent State University. Covered by a mountain of dirt, which cracked the central beam of the structure, the work's slow progression into ruin emblematizes one of Smithson's terms of pronounced relevance for Matta-Clark, the building's capacity toward its own "de-architecturization."[92]

From Matta-Clark's production of moldering objects to his building cuts, Smithson's influence on the younger artist seems secure. Somehow, though, the précis through which it is accorded place reads as a little too neat for both artists' entropic preoccupations, as if Smithson's lessons were missed altogether. Is there another way to think Matta-Clark's encounter with Ithaca and Smithson, one that takes seriously

1.20 Robert Smithson, *Partially Buried Woodshed,* 1970, Kent State University, Kent, OH. Estate of Robert Smithson. Courtesy John Weber Gallery, New York, NY.

their respective readings on temporality and place? An interpretation that does not suggest such a causal relation between subject and site, that supports the younger artist's concerns for the "ambiguity of place?"

I would argue that there is. It requires a method that veers paradoxically toward the literal. It takes Cornell University as a place so seriously that some remarks of a seemingly touristic nature are occasioned. Shading into observations of a far more exigent nature, it ends with some speculations on the nature of place and causality, and Matta-Clark's radical inversion of the monument.

SITELESS MONUMENTALITY: BEYOND PLACE AND FIRST PRINCIPLES

Situated on a plane overlooking the Cayuga River Valley, the campus of Cornell University presents itself to a most impressive vista, a landscape left in the wake of a glacier's crushing mass. So pervasive is the almost alien or prehistoric quality of this terrain, that it would be difficult for even the university's students to become innured to the school's dramatic setting. With its vertiginous topography, its sweeping panoramic view of the valley below, and its pliant leafiness set against hauntingly primordial rock formations, the siting of the campus appears better suited to a national park than an academic institution.

But when Ezra Cornell broke the ground for the college in 1866, both he and first president Andrew Dickson White understood well the importance of the landscape for imparting a peculiar aura to the university. In a gesture not without relevance for the concerns of both Smithson and Matta-Clark, Cornell hired Frederick Law Olmsted as one of the college's chief designers. The founder of the profession of landscape architecture in the United States, Olmsted is best known as one of the chief designers of Central Park in New York City.

For artists of the 1970s, however, Olmsted's reputation was reinvigorated and secured through another means. As the subject of Robert Smithson's last published essay, "Frederick Law Olmsted and the Dialectical Landscape,"[93] Olmsted achieved the status of an earth artist *avant la lettre.* Published in *Artforum* in 1973, Smithson's essay lauds Olmsted's presentation for the effects of its decrepitude, not the clean, planometric geometry of the Italian picture garden. The effusive comingling of decay and growth in Olmsted's designs drew Smithson to his example, described by the artist as "a dialectical materialism applied to the physical landscape . . . a way of seeing things in a manifold of relations, not as isolated objects."[94] It was precisely the condition of irregularity and contrast that Olmsted attempted to internalize in his own designs.

Abrupt vistas, meandering pathways, topographies both overgrown and restrained, architectural order threatened by natural chaos: Smithson's identification with Olmsted seems obvious enough. Informed as it is by romantic aesthetics, Olmsted's formulation seems no less than proto-entropic: a dialectic in which the rationalizing bodies of architecture are wedded to the progressive disintegration of its site. To consider Smithson's reading of Olmsted through the Cornell campus, then, is to reveal this dialectic played out in the struggle and realization of its plan. Andrew Dickson White may have had the insight to hire Olmsted, but the two soon came to blows over the quadrangle plan that White preferred for the university.[95] For Olmsted argued that the quadrangle structure could in no way accommodate the inevitable expansion of the university. He regarded it as repressive, binding, reigning in the explosive force of the university's growth.

Olmsted failed ultimately in his attempts to dissuade White from that plan. Yet the interpenetration of architectural and natural space, and the sharp contrast of vistas that marks the picturesque, does exist on the Cornell campus to some degree. With the Cayuga Valley rising dramatically into view, neither the irregularity of its topography nor the landscape's horizon is forced or contained by the school's plan. And in this juxtaposition of the controlling bodies of architecture with a landscape both stark and precipitous, a tension mounts between a rational impulse and an entropic force. It is a tension that goes to the heart of the question of Smithson's place for Matta-Clark.

The implications of this entropic landscape might be pushed to an even more extreme point, for another dimension of the campus topography sheds light on considerations of origin and place. Jacques Derrida, in his essay "The Principle of Reason: The University in the Eyes of its Pupils,"[96] treats the Cornell campus as an extended meditation on the conceptual intertwining of reason—that is to say, causality—and the thematics of place. Discussing the history of the campus, Derrida cites James Siegal's remarks about the troubled character of the university's setting: how its dizzying terrain inspired romantic thoughts about solitude, melancholy, death—topics that lead to questions of pedagogy and personal cultivation.[97] Seizing upon the sublime character of the Cornell topography, with all its associations of cowering subjectivity in the face of a violent terrain, Derrida relates these observations to the startling, even terrifying gorges that gird the campus (figure 1.21). One needn't be well versed in deconstruction to grasp their significance for the relationship of place to being. An unofficial history of the university would be incomplete without acknowledging the steady number of suicides that have occurred at these sites.[98]

The reality of these tragedies notwithstanding, Derrida's consideration of the Cornell site focuses upon how the metaphysical tradition links the thematics of place to the essence of the university, its *raison d'être.* "To have a *raison d'être,*" he notes,

> is to have a justification for existence . . . but also to have a cause, to be explainable according to the principle of reason . . . a footing and a foundation, ground to stand on.[99]

The Leibnizian as well as Heideggerian implications of the account needn't be examined here.[100] To be gleaned from this passage is the linkage between the principle of reason (*nihil est sine ration*—nothing is without reason) and the language of ground or foundation to which it is attached. Thus, if reason or causality is bound to place, the reason or essence of the university becomes increasingly vexed at the Cornell site. Teetering at the limit of ground, literally abysmal at its base, the university becomes an allegory for a peculiar kind of universal reason, suspended, as Derrida notes, "above a most peculiar void."[101]

How is this formulation brought to bear upon Smithson's relation to Matta-Clark, to say little of the latter's art itself? For one, it suggests that the circumscription of the first place—that is, a first principle or cause—enacts a condition of endless *dissipation,* an observation that shares much with Smithson's reading of entropy. For just as a system of order proceeds to disorder, following the Second Law of Thermodynamics, Derrida likewise suggests that the progressive attempt to situate causality—to give it a foundation—can only flounder in a certain groundlessness.

1.21 View of gorge running through Cornell University campus, Ithaca, NY.

LIVERPOOL JOHN MOORES UNIVERSITY
LEARNING SERVICES

The spatial and causal implications of this thinking are crucial in considering the terms of influence between Smithson and Matta-Clark. A piece routinely designated as Matta-Clark's "first" work, erected around the environs of Cornell University, provides a litmus test of sorts for this conceit. College friends have alluded to other works from the time—notably, an inflatable tunnel-like structure produced in memory of Marcel Duchamp—but the piece *Rope Bridge* (1968) (figure 1.22) is claimed by two major catalogues as Matta-Clark's first work. The one published photograph of the work pictures a heavily knotted piece of rope strung somewhere across the Ithaca gorge, like an outsized cat's cradle hovering above the landscape. Appropriately enough, it bears all the earmarks of the earth works in the Cornell exhibition that followed it by a year. Its medium recalls one of Hans Haacke's contributions to the show, a rope allowed to accumulate icicles in the frigid Ithaca air. Even more than this, the configuration of *Rope Bridge*—a tenuous material thing dangling over a gaping rift—shares properties with one of Smithson's Site/Non-Site pieces in the exhibition, his *Mirror Wedge* or *Mirror Displacement,* a part of the larger *Cayuga Salt Mine Project.* In the sited configuration of the piece, a mirror, a singularly fragile object, was wedged at an angle between the precipitous walls of a chasm. Smithson then photographed the object and displayed it within the White Museum as a Non-Site, along with some geological specimens he gathered within the salt mines.

The structure of Smithson's *Mirror Wedge* seems evident in Matta-Clark's *Rope Bridge.* But when we ascribe primacy to *Mirror Wedge,* we become increasingly mired in a morass of conflicting dates and histories, personal recollections and tautological footnotes. Installed in February 1969, Smithson's *Cayuga Salt Mine Project* is thought to have been conceived at the site either in October or December 1968.[102] Matta-Clark's piece is consistently if ambiguously dated 1968. In short, there seems to be little or no material evidence about the installation of *Rope Bridge;* the exact place of its siting; the specific time of its making; or the formal meeting of the two artists themselves.[103]

Such disparities unwittingly testify to both the situational and temporal logic of Matta-Clark's art. For out of this bottomless pit of failed chronologies and lost ori-

1.22 Gordon Matta-Clark, *Rope Bridge,* 1968, Ithaca Reservoir, Ithaca, NY.

gins emerges the problematics of reception—specifically, the issues of the place and timeliness of reception, the twin pillars upon which site-specific work is erected. While this may seem informed by the canonical thinking on site-specific art, the historiographic insecurity that surrounds the treatment of *Rope Bridge* challenges the logic of that model. For if entropy subtends reason and place at the Cornell site, it conditions the temporality of spectatorship for Matta-Clark's work as well. The discontinuities in its reception should be taken seriously, for they question the givenness of a work's relation to place, and rethink the terms of the monument in the process.

As such, the lessons of Smithson for Matta-Clark demand a certain reassessment. In the dialectic of Site and Non-Site, the site-specific work is coordinated as much around its indoor displacement as its outdoor display. The work's reason for being, in other words, cannot be linked uncritically to a place regarded as cohesive and whole. Its siting is founded on an act of dissipation, a removal that locates entropy at its origin.

In this regard, Smithson shares something with Alois Riegl's classic account of the monument. In his essay "The Modern Cult of Monuments: Its Character and Its Origin," Riegl writes how the monument was conceived through a range of methodological categories, among which the "intentional" monument—the object specifically erected to commemorate an event or moment or person—was its "oldest and most original" form.[104] But Riegl spoke as well of its modern "historical" manifestation. "Every work of art is at once, and without exception, a historical monument,"[105] he observed, a thing that implicitly bears its historicity. Thus he makes plain that all "historical" monuments are ultimately contained under the category of "age value"—an object of history whose various signs of age guarantee its function as such a valued thing. No matter how mundane or formally uninteresting, anything might attain the status of a monument by these terms.

Ranging from the degenerative sites to the detritus of the suburban "ruin," Smithson's engagement with the monument confirms the litanies of Riegl's types. Because the value placed on Riegl's historical monument was in part dependent upon that thing's ruination, Smithson's notion of the monument fulfills the terms of that condition as well as ironizes it. Now harnessed to the rhetoric of entropy, his monuments signify less the substantiation of a historical place than a critically self-conscious commemoration of "age" value.

Matta-Clark's site-specific works engage an even more extreme relation to the logic of the monument. In their to-ing and fro-ing between a past that continuously underwrites itself, and a future that cannot be built on such historical aporias, they radicalize the entropic monument, render it a "non-ument," to borrow the artist's term. They do not aspire to the fantasy of historical stability as conventional monuments do; if anything, these works embrace the impossibility of inhabiting that moment. Counterintuitively, they do this in the marking of such a place, only to be removed or destroyed, acknowledging the historicist presumptions around which the conventional monument is established. Somehow, this notion seems to haunt Riegl's thinking. He writes:

> . . . even a violent human intervention into the natural life of the monument may over time strike us as evocative. . . . Seen from a distance, the effect of human destruction, which appears so violent and disturbing at close range, can be experienced as the orderly and necessary workings of nature itself.[106]

Because Matta-Clark's work presupposes its own destruction, it internalizes this historical loss, this entropic remove. In doing so, it is a monument to the very pretensions of the monument, becoming itself siteless in the process.

2 IMPROPER OBJECTS OF MODERNITY

To appropriate something means basically only to manifest the supremacy of my will in relation to the thing and to demonstrate that the latter does not have being for itself and is not an end in itself. . . . This manifestation occurs through my conferring upon the thing an end other than that which it immediately possessed. I give the living creature, as my property, a soul other than that which it previously had; I give it my soul.
—Hegel, *Elements of the Philosophy of Right*[1]

The metapsychology of Gordon's art was to embrace the abandoned. He worked in old buildings, neighborhoods in a state of rejection. He would nurture a building that had lost its soul.
—Les Levine[2]

What does it mean to have property? In what ways does property have a soul? And what are the theoretical convergences between the artist, the art object, and property, here loosely understood as real estate and architecture? In 1971, Matta-Clark inaugurated a process of art making that spoke to the progressively fraught relationship between art and property in the sixties and seventies. Using a crude method that would soon evolve into his more complex building dissections, he would cut and then extract a small section from a given building using hammers, chisels, and a variety of saws. Earning the name of "building fragments" these morcellated pieces of architecture provide an object lesson in the ways architecture and, by association, property assume a constitutive function in the reception of art, and vice-versa.

2.1 Gordon Matta-Clark, *Food,* 1971.

One of the earliest of these remnants is *Food* from 1971 (figure 2.1). Composed of the blunt intersection of two wooden beams, it is a coarse, even dumb object, a veritable sampler of architectural accident. Displaying nails, hinges, and pencil marks across its overlapping surfaces of spackled green and scumbled white paint, it bears characteristics similar to modernist assemblage, if little of its compositional complexity. Rather, if *Food* succeeds as a *discrete* object at all, it is paradoxically because the specific elements that lend it its peculiar plastic interest—its artless drips of paint, twisted hinges, and the tired, brittle warp and weft of its support—are deeply evocative of phenomena that stand in excess of the thing proper. Indeed, its interest accrues around something that is outside of it, improper to it: the architectural setting that literally supported the fragment in its former life.

The history of that setting will be discussed shortly; for now, consider the following. *Food,* like other building fragments, allegorizes an important formulation in seventies art practice and criticism: that the object's seeming autonomy is actually underwritten by its provenance, the *property* from which it is extracted or produced, exhibited, and preserved. By the same token, Matta-Clark's work provides a dialectical reversal of this idea. For such property only emerges from—is thrown into stark relief by—the fragment itself, which lays claim to the site in its absence.

The proper and the improper; property and appropriation; inappropriate: this litany evokes the ambiguous registers of meaning that obtain between the thematics of property and Matta-Clark's art. First, it positions the notion of a fragmented and therefore "improper" thing against a classicist conception of the work of art, coherent in its composition and internal relations, seamless in its finish, and "autonomous" in the way it allegedly signifies. It recalls also the historical specificity of the property with which Matta-Clark was involved. This chapter attends to Matta-Clark's early investigations into buildings and architecture, works that are deeply inscribed in the history of property in lower Manhattan, and the larger "problem" of the city in the sixties and seventies. But my concern for the topic does not stop there. What constitutes property for Matta-Clark moves beyond historical discussions of SoHo and the spaces in which he worked. His project *Fake Estates* and his investigations with the group Anarchitecture open onto broader historical and philosophical questions about the nature of social space and property—how property and identity are deeply intertwined; how property constitutes a relation and not just a thing; how the notion of property is bound to the terms of its use, its consumption, and, most important, its waste.

ART IN PROPERTY: 112 GREENE STREET, FOOD, AND THE AESTHETICS OF FLOORS, DOORS, AND BASEMENTS

What conditions of possibility were at play when Matta-Clark arrived at the seemingly random activity of cutting up buildings, extracting and preserving their various elements like some obsessed urban archaeologist? After moving to Manhattan in 1970, the artist found himself living in and constructing a number of different places, which over the years included lofts on Fourth Street, Chrystie Street, and Wooster. But in a 1974 interview with Liza Bear, who with Willoughby Sharp co-founded the important conceptualist art magazine *Avalanche* in 1970, Matta-Clark was explicit as to how his artistic work with architecture began: "One of the things that is clearest in my mind," he said, "is how the interest in working in buildings originated."

It evolved out of that period in 1970 when I was living in the basement at 112 Greene Street and doing things in different corners. Initially, they weren't at all related to the structure, I was just working in a place, but eventually I started treating the place as a whole, as an object.[3]

Although self-reflective about the degree of his own involvement with buildings, Matta-Clark is nevertheless opaque about its historical surround. Speaking to the contemporary readership of *Avalanche,* a magazine devoted to the most experimental forms of seventies artistic practice, there was no need for him to explain just why he was living in that specific basement or to discuss the address to which he so casually alluded. Embedded within the artist's comments is a history of sorts, one that implicitly articulates the links that emerged between art and property at the time. On its surface, it is that of the non-commercial gallery or alternative space. More fundamentally, though, it is a strangely wrought, even byzantine narrative about SoHo, the area in lower Manhattan bounded by Houston and Canal Streets to the north and south, and Lafayette and West Broadway to the east and west.

Regarded by some as the *locus mundi* of the international art market (or, to judge by recent demographic changes, its former locus) the early history of SoHo as an artists' community is in many ways crystallized through the history of 112 Greene Street. As a metonymy of this history, the formation of 112 Greene Street as an art space—and Matta-Clark's activities within its walls—sheds light on its beginnings.

The period of the early seventies has commonly been described as the era in which the alternative space first flourished in New York. Among the most important of these spaces was Holly Solomon's 98 Greene Street loft (which Matta-Clark helped to construct and also exhibited in frequently); Alanna Heiss's space at 10 Bleecker Street, which grew into the Institute for Art and Urban Resources, and then bifurcated into Public Space 1 (P.S. 1) and the Clock Tower; and Artists Space, founded in 1973.[4] Yet of the dozen or so alternative galleries that sprang up in New York then, 112 Greene Street remains of particular note for its historical longevity, the importance of the work and performances it staged, and its reputation as a social gathering place. The records of its earliest participants are an impressive roster of 1970s artists and performers, including Alice Aycock, Vito Acconci, Chris Burden, the Grand Union Dance Company, Susan Rothenberg, Trisha Brown, Phillip Glass, Mel Bochner, Laurie Anderson, Juan Downey, and William Wegman, among others. Now known as the non-profit gallery White Columns (and now something of an *eminence grise* among New York's many alternative spaces), 112 Greene Street opened in 1970 and continued under the directorship of its founder, Jeffrey Lew, until 1975. The site of a former rag-salvaging operation, the actual building was constructed in 1884 and designed by the architect Henry Fernbach.[5] In the seventies it was bought by Lew, who conceived of the space in conjunction with Alan Saret.[6]

Open "twenty-four hours a day and never locked,"[7] 112 Greene Street was a raw and unfinished space, bearing little if any resemblance to the blue-chip galleries of today's SoHo. Striking in scale, it measured 33 feet in width by 110 feet in length, with a sixteen-foot ceiling. A row of corinthian columns, seven in all, divided the gallery, serving as the only formal elements in the otherwise crudely finished room. Yet, however decrepit its appearance, 112 Greene Street was never acclaimed as an alternative space, at least not to the extent that such jargon was in use at the time. Instead, it was as much a social space as an artistic one, a place in which artists, dancers, and performers could work and collaborate with little restriction, a place "that wasn't pristine, that we could knock around in," as the late Suzanne Harris recalled.[8] The sculptor Jene Highstein remembers the atmosphere of the early 112 Greene Street in similar terms, emphasizing its alternately democratic or chaotic nature. "It was a constant kind of social scene," he notes, ". . . a way for people to meet and exchange information, almost as though you were living as a family." Highstein also muses on another aspect of the space, an informality that for some bordered on the intimidating, perhaps because it lacked apparent organization or authority. "Actually," Highstein admits, "some people were afraid of going into 112 Greene Street."[9]

The casual and inclusive character of 112 Greene Street conveys its aspiration to provide a putatively socialist model of exhibiting art. Commentary from many of its early participants suggests that it tacitly (if not dogmatically) represented a distinct shift from a previous generation of New York based artists, many of whom were associated with minimalism and the commercial interests of the midtown galleries that represented the older artists.[10] This was hardly a novel sentiment of course, as the desire to break from the midtown galleries finds ready precedent in the Tenth Street cooperatives of the late fifties, among many other examples. Yet the challenge to rethink the mechanics of the commercial gallery took on a renewed exigency by the late sixties and early seventies.[11] In part a result of theoretical developments in earth art and conceptualism, a certain exhaustion with the parameters of the traditional exhibition space was widely expressed.

Lew's idiosyncratic approach to directing 112 Greene Street seemed to hinge on these dual concerns. Deeply aware of the logistical difficulties contemporary artists and performers faced in exhibiting their art, he did not so much orchestrate exhibitions as he allowed them to happen.[12] "There wasn't really a first show there because everybody just arrived," he notes.

> They would say, Jeffrey, could I have a show here? My answer would be "No!" but then of course they would have their show. They would just walk in and do it. That's what I liked about it—the fact that there was no administration. None . . . I was the head administrator. And, of course, nobody listened to me.[13]

One of the "nobodies" who never listened to Lew—and one of the first participants in Lew's "non-existent" first show at 112 Green Street—was the director's

LIVERPOOL JOHN MOORES UNIVERSITY
Aldham Roberts L.R.C.
TEL. 0151 231 3701/3634

close friend Gordon Matta (as he was still known), whom he had met the previous year through Alan Saret. Matta-Clark's first work with buildings and property is virtually contiguous with the early history of the site. The documentary history of the space reveals that he performed and displayed work in or organized some eleven exhibitions and performances from 1970 through 1974 alone.

Lasting roughly from October through December 1970, the opening exhibition included works by Bill Beckley, Alan Saret, Marjorie Strider, Barry Le Va, Richard Nonas, Brenda Miller, George Trakas, Lew himself, and Gordon Matta. While the works Matta-Clark produced for that show are undocumented, three site-specific pieces (*Winter Garden: Mushroom and Waistbottle Recycloning Cellar, Cherry Tree,* and *Time Well*) shortly followed. In their deep fascination with material, organic (and, ultimately, architectural) refuse, all three represent something of a theoretical continuum of the artist's earliest works, objects produced out of moldering or ruinous materials, entropic in their disposition.

Begun on New Year's Day 1971, *Cherry Tree* involved planting a sapling in a hole dug through the floor of the basement. Measuring eight feet long, four feet wide, and six feet deep, the hole was cavernous enough to engulf a good part of the tree, as only its crown remains visible in the photographic documentation (figure 2.2). The tree died some three months after it was planted—a casualty, presumably, of the dank, airless environment and its failure to take root at the site. Soon after, the artist planted a colony of mushrooms around its empty cavity, a telling display of his interest in the less salubrious forms of botanic life.

But the original site in which *Cherry Tree* stood had not been exhausted by the artist: about six months after he had planted the sapling, watched its minimal growth and death, and then installed a bed of fungus in its place, he belatedly memorialized its presence with a work titled *Time Well* (figure 2.3). A ceramic chimney pipe six feet in length was placed into the hole, which in turn housed a bottle containing the "remains" of the original cherry tree. Crowned by a one-foot by one-foot well cover made of zinc, the pipe was then set in concrete that filled the remaining space of the hole. Around the edges of the bed, "molten lead was poured into the expansion joints

2.2 Gordon Matta-Clark, *Cherry Tree,* 1971, 112 Greene Street, New York, NY.

of the concrete to delineate the original cavity."[14] The flat, anthropomorphic dimensions of the piece evoke a tombstone, a quality of the work that Matta-Clark confirmed with his usual convolutions intact. Serving as a temporal index of the tree that came before it, *Time Well* was at once a "permanent non-structural sub-basement burial," and a means to "extend a room beyond its common limits."[15]

The shaft-like cavity around which both *Cherry Tree* and *Time Well* were organized also structured the subsequent *Winter Garden* (figure 2.4), which consisted of a large bin placed at the bottom of a disused elevator shaft, also located in the basement. Hundreds upon hundreds of old glass bottles were stored in the area by the artist, so that the sculptural installation grew in direct proportion to the proliferation of garbage. Collected from around the city by Matta-Clark and his friends, this accumulation of bottles enacted visual effects that were surprising in the murky space. The more bottles the artist amassed, the more the piece refracted the dim light admitted into the basement.[16]

Matta-Clark's insistence on placing these works in the basement seemed a function of two interrelated phenomena. First, there was the roughshod character of the space, matched only in unrefinement by the crudeness of the artist's interventions. "In most galleries, you can't scratch the floor," Jeffrey Lew recalled, "here you can dig a hole in it. Gordon Matta even dug up the basement."[17] Richard Nonas's humorous recollections on such activities go beyond Lews's, as he notes: "it was basically about tearing apart Jeffrey's building."[18] But aside from these claims—which appeal strongly to the spirit of collective anarchy prevalent at 112 Greene Street—the recessive quality of that place, its symbolic and structural associations, also offered an appropriate arena for Matta-Clark's progressively focused relationship to architecture.

Two parallel interpretations arise from this. The first reading, loosely metaphorical in its implications, stems from the associations of working in such subterranean conditions.[19] The planting of a tree in a hole dug deep into the basement, and the subsequent installation of its ersatz headstone, does much to confirm a sensibility taken in by the atavistic, the entropic, and the uncanny.[20] *Winter Garden,* too, considered the production of art in analogous terms, equating art making with refuse.

2.3 Gordon Matta-Clark, *Time Well,* 1971, 112 Greene Street, New York, NY.

In both works, the basement is regarded as a place where the growth of things is congruent with the death of things, a place in which the proliferation of less than salutary objects—mushrooms, bottles, refuse—commingles with their imminent fatigue.

The second, more rigorously architectural reading is founded around the same dialectical logic. Describing the motivations behind *Cherry Tree,* Matta-Clark voiced a strong curiosity about the building's foundations:

I dug a deep hole in the basement of 112 Greene Street. What I wanted to do I didn't accomplish at all, which was digging deep enough so that a person could see the actual foundations, the "removed" spaces under the foundation, and liberate the building's enormous compressive, confining forces simply by making a hole.[21]

The liberating if necessarily failed enterprise of carving out a hole from underneath the basement demonstrates a paradoxical approach to the building's ostensible support. Matta-Clark's desire to go beneath the building, to subtend it, conveys that what is *foundational* to the architecture is a virtual *absence,* here represented by the "figure" of the hole. Impossible as this goal may be, the impossibility is instructive. For what virtually holds up 112 Greene Street can neither be contained nor articulated by the architecture proper, as if site were always conditioned by something deeply inaccessible, *offsite* even.

The basement projects distill something fundamental about Matta-Clark's investigation of art and architecture. Removed from the more socialized spaces of domestic and commercial architecture, they provide an analogue to the ways that architecture is perceived in its structural relation to art. As much as the obscure setting of the basement acts as a framing device for his art, so, too, does architecture recede into the background in the service of art's display, like ground to figure in representational painting. "Why hang things on a wall when the wall itself is so much more a challenging medium?" Matta-Clark once asked when questioned about the "flat" arts. "It is the rigid mentality that architects install the walls and artists decorate

2.4 Gordon Matta-Clark, *Winter Garden: Mushroom and Waistbottle Recycloning Cellar,* 1971, 112 Greene Street, New York, NY.

them that offends my sense of either profession."[22] Accordingly, he treated the basement in a manner to confuse the distinction, so that the basement emerges *out of* its traditionally recessive role by becoming the place of art's encounter. But of equal if not even greater importance in this economy is that architecture is rendered visible *only* in its supporting relation to art.

This phenomenon is also in evidence in the artist's activities at the restaurant Food, representative of still another example of the strange filiations between art and property in the seventies, as well as the deeply social, communitarian ethos of the young community of SoHo. Located at 127 Prince Street on the corner of Wooster (figures 2.5 and 2.6), Food was founded and run by artists cooperatively, but was the principal enterprise of the dancer and photographer Caroline Goodden (now Caroline Goodden Ames), who was Matta-Clark's partner at the time. Along with the artists Tina Girouard, Suzanne Harris, and Rachel Lew, all of whom were deeply involved in the activities of 112 Greene Street, Goodden opened the original restaurant in the fall of 1971 (leaving it to other management by 1973). It quickly became a meeting ground for the burgeoning SoHo community, a place where artists could eat inexpensively during its flexible open hours ("11:30 am until midnight, and until 3 am on Saturdays, closed on Mondays"),[23] work part-time jobs, or, as we shall see, engage in art making.

Goodden recalls the beginnings of Food in 1971.[24] Hosting a party for Richard Nonas, she struck up a conversation with Matta-Clark, whom she had recently met. He encouraged her to open a restaurant in which he would serve as contractor and designer; soon after, the two found such a space in SoHo, a Criollos restaurant that had formerly served local workers. Perhaps it seems inconceivable that one could simply stumble upon such a place today, and it is no less difficult to imagine the depressed character of the neighborhood, its light manufacturing lofts, sweatshops, and rag factories deserted by their previous tenants. Partially funded by Goodden's inheritance, it was at this site that Goodden, Girouard, Lew, Harris, and Matta-Clark opened Food on September 25, 1971. Robert Prado, a former army cook and musician with

2.5 Exterior view of Food, corner of Prince Street at Wooster, New York, NY, with Tina Girouard, Caroline Goodden, and Gordon Matta-Clark, 1971.

DORIS' Restaurant
COMIDAS CRIOLLAS
DRINK
Pepsi-Cola

the Phillip Glass ensemble, was the managing chef of the restaurant. Richard Peck washed dishes. Ned Smythe also cooked. Cajun cuisine was served frequently, as was organically raised produce.

There was more to the business of Food than the mere act of cooking and eating, though, for the restaurant also served as a backdrop for art-related events, catalyzing SoHo's social horizon. In a manner not unlike Daniel Spoerri's Eat Art Gallery in Dusseldorf, or artist Les Levine's New York restaurant, the activities at Food were much in keeping with that minor form of art peculiar to the performative seventies: food art. Matta-Clark was no stranger to the "genre": certainly, his works produced with agar agar, chocolate Yoo-Hoo, and other incongruous materials were a kind of cooking, however disgusting the results. And other events, "performances" of a sort, were evocative of the communal sensibility that took place around the activity of eating. For a group show curated by Alana Heiss under the Brooklyn Bridge in May of 1971, he roasted an entire pig as part of his contribution. Several years later in Paris, alongside his major site work *Conical Intersect,* he repeated this gesture, this time with roast beef.

At the restaurant itself, Matta-Clark organized a series called the Sunday Night Guest Chef Dinners, which saw artists take on the role of cook to produce meals of a decidedly artistic bent. Among the people who are said to have cooked there were Keith Sonnier, Robert Rauschenberg, Richard Landry, Italo Scanga, and Donald Judd, although many of the proposed events were probably more fabulous than actual, or at the very least, more visual than edible. Mark di Suvero's idea to serve dinners through a window with his crane never came to fruition, unsurprisingly. And in an equally improbable request sent to the artist Lee Jaffe, Matta-Clark wrote of the cannibalistic impulses repressed within Christianity: "I am writing because I feel you are the chosen one," he wrote in mock serious terms, "the perfect subject for a culinary communion as the modern world has long forgotten." He then suggested that Jaffe become the ultimate sacrifice, imploring, "just imagine what a fabulous treat you would make."[25]

2.6 Interior view of Food with Gordon Matta-Clark, New York, NY, 1971.

The sense of playful, at times parodic communion at Food became the stuff of early SoHo mythology, as did Matta-Clark's own contributions to the restaurant. One of these "meals," served on February 20, 1972, consisted of piles of bones, arrayed and stuffed with various ingredients. Another performance, titled *Alive,* included the serving of live brine shrimp hidden away in the recess of a hard-boiled egg. To follow Carole Goodden's account, the "reception" of these "works" ranged from horror to amusement: Liza Bear screamed in disgust at the sight of the shrimp, while Jackie Winsor was reported to have blithely (or perhaps bravely) downed the live crustaceans.

But there was another more serious way that "art into life" took shape at the site of Food, a question of the broader uses of that space altogether. When Goodden and Matta-Clark appropriated the restaurant, Matta-Clark was made its general contractor, responsible for reconstructing its walls and floors, techniques garnered from his experience in the construction of lofts. Goodden recalls a formative moment in this process of reconstruction: "While we were putting Food together," she notes, "there was a piece of wall that had to come out." She then remembers, "Gordon decided to cut himself a wall sandwich . . . he cut a horizontal section through the wall and door and fell in love with it."[26]

Food, architecture, sociability: the strange conjugation of these terms in the history of SoHo parodically evokes Henri Lefebvre's call for a "social space . . . that emerged in all its diversity . . . with a structure . . . reminiscent of flaky *mille-feuille* pastry."[27] Goodden's reference to a "wall sandwich" suggests a conflation of the architectural specificity of the cut (the wall), the alimentary function of the site (a restaurant), and its reclamation as a social space by artists. As one of a number of Matta-Clark's first building fragments, the object *Food* thus serves as an architectural metonym for the non-extant restaurant Food, restituting the history of that place in abbreviated form. For however much a discrete object, the fragment *Food* refuses to be understood as an autonomous thing, reminding us of Rodolphe Gasché's words, when he observes of the thematics of literary "fragmentation": "Such a fragment is a piece of an ensemble, possible or constituted at one point. It receives its very meaning from that ensemble that it thus posits and presupposes rather than challenges."[28]

The fragment is at once constituted by and posits the ensemble out of which it emerges, a relationship Matta-Clark began to consider actively in other buildings at the time. Two months before the opening of Food, he wrote a letter to the assistant commissioner in the Department of Real Estate in New York, inquiring about the uses of abandoned buildings in the city. The letter is instructive not least for its demythologization of the image of the artist as reckless iconoclast, an anarchist in the most vulgar understanding of the word. It is also one of the artist's first programmatic statements on his artistic relationship to buildings, resounding with a preservationist sensibility. "In regard to the many condemned buildings in the city that are awaiting demolition," Matta-Clark wrote,

> it seems possible to me to put these buildings to use during this waiting period . . . As an artist, I make sculpture using the by-products of the land and people.[29]

Clearly, Matta-Clark did not receive a timely enough response to his letter, for shortly after he sent it, he began to seek out buildings that were abandoned or condemned as raw material for his art. In some respects, the process had already begun at home: that same year he extracted a section of a sauna at his loft on Fourth Street. Now, however, his interests were to take him much farther afield. With the assistance of Goodden and Manfred Hecht, Matta-Clark began to remove pieces from buildings illegally, scoring sections of floors, walls, and ceilings in potentially dangerous situations in ever more depressed neighborhoods (figure 2.7). In a gesture that recasts Smithson's formulation on the Site and the Non-Site within the urban sphere, he would then photograph the spaces left in the wake of these removals.[30]

The most important series of fragments and complementary photographs from this period were those Matta-Clark made in the Bronx from 1972 to 1973. Under the general title of *Bronx Floors,* the series consists of rectangular, squarish, or L-shaped extractions that were taken from the floors and walls of each site (figures 2.8 and 2.9),

2.7 (page 74) Gordon Matta-Clark, *Bronx Floors* (in process), 1972–1973, building fragment.

2.8 (page 75) Gordon Matta-Clark, *Bronx Floors: Floor Above, Ceiling Below,* 1972–1973, building fragment.

along with black and white photographs documenting the location of the removals (figure 2.10), and paired or grouped images that show these extractions from a variety of perspectives (figure 2.11). There seemed to be minimal guiding principle in extracting the fragments other than their portability as objects and the ease with which the artist could perform his removals without complicated equipment. Crude and blunt in their extraction, they appear less like found objects aestheticized for the gallery than architectural debris randomly deposited there.

Yet when the *Bronx Floors* fragments were first displayed at 112 Greene Street in 1972 (figure 2.12), they begged the question of their status as works of art. Displaying the floor extractions vertically, Matta-Clark partially enabled the fragments to begin to read as sculpture—and yet not quite. The garish linoleum surfaces that covered the floorboards, intended less to be studied than stepped upon, were now made the object of a certain visual scrutiny, each layer a kind of historical stratum to be discerned and parsed by the careful spectator. The interior system supporting the floor was now exposed to vision as well, revealing the heavier joists and a section of the ceiling below. In preserving these structural elements along with the linoleum surface, the apparently flat dimensions of the floor fragment expanded outward, so that what was once architecturally oriented along a horizontal axis was now flipped within the space of the gallery. And in this expansion or rather extension into a new social space, the fragments provided an incisive recoding of minimalist sculpture. They literalized the quotidian dimensions of architectural space by submitting its ground—the residue of its floor plan—to artistic appraisal.

Comparing the *Bronx Floors* to minimalist work suggests an object lesson as to why Matta-Clark's appropriation of the floor was not simply an elevation of the fragment to the traditional terms of sculptural object. At once clumsy and inassimilable, threaded with the "seams" of their former architectural life, they neither obscured the

2.9 Gordon Matta-Clark, *Bronx Floors: Floor Above, Ceiling Below,* 1972, building fragment.

2.10 (page 78) Gordon Matta-Clark, documentary photograph of *Bronx Floors,* 1972–1973.

2.11 (page 79) Gordon Matta-Clark, *Bronx Floors: Threshole,* 1972–1973.

ground upon which they stood nor concealed their former use. Hence they established a dialogue with the floor itself, so that the categorical porousness between the two objects—floor and floorpiece—further homologized the sliding between the terms of architecture and art.

A similar logic underwrites the serialized, colored photographs of distressed walls, titled *Walls Paper* (figures 2.13 and 2.14), taken in the Bronx over the course of several months in 1972. Picturing the exposed walls of lower income housing, the photographs present the buildings' ruinous state as a gridded, blank-faced visage. In one version of the work, Matta-Clark developed the images on newsprint, which he then bound into books with the help of his college friend, Joan Simon. At 112 Greene Street, however, he let the pictures hang loosely from the walls like strips of film cascading from ceiling to floor. In this peculiar mode of display, Matta-Clark registered an acute correspondence between walls and wallpaper, not unlike the floorpieces exhibited before.[31] Its effect was to throw the still functioning site of the gallery into a certain relief, locating the outmodedness of a building elsewhere by reproducing the structures of its walls on another building's surface. As such, the relationship between the respective sites was not conditioned simply by the place of art and architecture, but by the uneven temporalities of both. The timeliness of each building—one now "alive," the other now "dead"—spoke to the virtual "speed" of the built environment, the endlessly fluctuating historicity of its architecture.

The elision between art and architecture, floor and floorpiece, walls and wallpaper, presentness and outmodedness, is reflected in a number of photographic works surrounding *Bronx Floors*. A group of images titled *Threshole* plays on the thematics of liminality as if to graft a passage through something onto a passage over a place. But to insert the word "hole" in place of the customary "hold" is to suggest that the movement toward such a place remains radically indeterminate, a paradox the pho-

2.12 Gordon Matta-Clark, *Bronx Floors,* 1972, installation view, 112 Greene Street, New York, NY, October 21–November 10, 1972.

2.13 (page 82) Gordon Matta-Clark, site of *Walls Paper,* NY, 1972.

2.14 (page 83) Gordon Matta-Clark, *Walls Paper,* 1972, installation view, 112 Greene Street, New York, NY, October 21–November 10, 1972.

tographs themselves embody. One *Threshole* image, for instance, sets an L-shaped cavity nearly flush with the picture plane, appearing first as a strong gestalt against a largely white ground, but tipped slightly to reveal its architectural disposition (figure 2.15). Quickly, though, this "figure" is understood as an absence or a hole: a "threshole" through which to enter into the photographic image. Yet what first reads as a parodic treatment of Albertian space, a literalizing of the perspectival window as hole, is complicated upon further viewing. Rather than represent a deep space contiguous with the horizontally set cavity, the space behind the hole enframes part of the jamb of a door; and a glimpse of a doorsill that delimits the hole set within the image. A conflation of the vertical with the horizontal, a flattening of plan and section, it is a threshold lodged within a threshole.

Still, the picture conflates more than this. It generates a metaphor of visual transparency—an optical reference to the perspectival window—for the contortions of an embodied viewer in architectural space. Taken by the artist by craning his neck back toward the ceiling above, it locates the spectator, empathetically, in a position at odds with the pictorial orientation of the image. And in this collapse of architectural space within pictorial space, Matta-Clark suggests how the two point to one another, even underwrite one another, a dizzyingly contingent relationship contained within the photograph.

The quality of Matta-Clark's work "pointing to" the conditions of its production has been famously considered by Rosalind Krauss in her central essay of 1977, "Notes on the Index, Part 2," in which she discusses, among other works, Matta-Clark's cutting *Doors, Floors, Doors* (1976).[32] Drawing upon the theories of the semiotician C. S. Peirce, she identifies a pervasive structural phenomenon in the art of the seventies: that much work from this time turns around the logic of indexicality. Opposed to the notion of the symbol or icon—signs that are coded by means of convention or resemblance—the index registers the process or conditions of its own inscription, "the physical manifestation of a cause."[33] A fingerprint, then, stands as the classical model of the index, acting as a literal "clue" to its making.

2.15 Gordon Matta-Clark, *Bronx Floors: Threshole,* 1972.

But Krauss is clear that the indexical operations of seventies art are not "a means of establishing presence," as in, for example, the criticism surrounding abstract expressionism and its existential rhetoric of artistic selfhood. Instead of relying upon pictorial models of the index, dependent on the notion of the artist's gesture, the trace-like quality of these works affirms its connection to the properties of photography and the testimonial powers attributed to its images. Acknowledging Roland Barthes on the subject, Krauss discusses the quality of something "having-been-there" in this work, a trace that registers its temporal remove from the set of conditions that gave rise to it. Thus the cutting by Matta-Clark "is able to signify the building—to point to it—only through a process of removal or cutting away," so that "the process of excavation succeeds therefore in bringing the consciousness of the viewer in the form of a ghost."[34]

The indexical operations Krauss describes in the building cuts cannot be precisely applied to the *Thresholes,* the *Walls Paper,* nor many of Matta-Clark's projects at 112 Greene Street. In *Walls Paper,* a photograph of a site is mapped onto yet another site, so that the set of external and internal relations it lays bare does not enact the same circuit of signification Krauss describes. Yet the heuristic value of her argument is unimpeachable for this particular body of works, for without resorting to her vocabulary, popular contemporary accounts of Matta-Clark's art externalize (or generalize) its situational logic.

A photograph from the *Village Voice* taken in 1971 of the *Winter Garden* literalizes how "art takes on the character of its environ," juxtaposing Matta-Clark's work against "an unintended art work in the street," a garbage can brimming with trash.[35] As if to triangulate both images, a heading from the same page alerts us to the terms of that surround. "Legal lofts nearing ok," it reads flatly, and in the stilted economy of this caption, another means to consider Matta-Clark's practice emerges. Bluntly, elliptically, its language anticipates the threshold between the work of art and property in the seventies. A phenomenon that was hardly unique to SoHo, it confirms the historical exigency of Matta-Clark's interests.[36]

PROPERTY IN/AS ART

A body of art from the period, associated with the work of Michael Asher, Daniel Buren, Dan Graham, and Hans Haacke, reflects upon the maintenance and evaluation of the work of art through the channels of its distribution—or, in specific instances, the ideological interface between art and the institutions in which it circulates. Taking its lineage in earlier site-specific practices, it has fallen under the broad rubric of "the critique of institutions" or, in more popular cant, the critique of the "white cube."[37] It makes plain that the museum and gallery, as particularized manifestations of the social relation, participate in shaping the reception of the work of art through a dense if often imperceptible weave of political, cultural and economic interests. Often, the peculiar architectural character of these places is addressed, as if to convey the value architectural space accords to its objects.

Such ideas have long assumed the status of art historical fetish, at once institutionalized by curators as museological practice, taught as method in art schools, and appropriated by artists as a kind of style, allegedly transparent and self-reflexive. But the moment at which these tendencies emerged in the sixties and seventies—a type of postwar solution to earlier models of defamiliarization—suggests something about the timeliness of these gestures. The French artist Daniel Buren has been especially articulate in attending to such concerns, and while his formation is clearly different from Matta-Clark's, his observations bear acute relevance still. Buren offers a cogent analogy between the internal architecture of the work and the architecture that in turn supports the work when he writes:

> We can speak of the internal architecture of a painting, or of any work of art . . . However, the work of art only exists, can only be seen, in the context of the Museum/Gallery surrounding it, the Museum/Gallery for which it was destined and to which however no special attention is paid.[38]

The implied relationship between the internal support of the picture and the architecture that remains outside requires demystification by the artist, a notion implicit to Buren's practice of applying generic, prefabricated material of alternating white and colored stripes to various sites within and outside the institution (figure

2.16). Begun in 1966, Buren's project establishes that the legibility of the art work *as work* is always contingent upon the institution's structuring of that legibility, or, conversely, its seeming invisibility.

Questions of legibility, of visual access to the work of art, are also at the crux of Michael Asher's practice. The very apogee of inexpressiveness, it is so subtle in its interventions that it threatens to pass into invisibility for the casual observer. A project staged at the Lisson Gallery in London in 1973 witnessed Asher's working in the basement of the site (figure 2.17), an area that had "originally been described as being 'unsuitable for any kind of installation.'"[39] There, he cut "an architectural reveal ¼ inch wide and 1½ inches deep, into the wall at floor level, around the perimeter of the room," a gouging so slight that "the floor line became instinguishable" from where the wall originally joined it.[40]

In both Asher's and Matta-Clark's work, there is a literal inscription between art and the particularities of its site—at once a cleaving and a conflation of art and architecture—whether in the basement of the Lisson Gallery in London or its analogue at 112 Greene Street in New York. Of course, to claim some intrinsic relationship between Asher and Matta-Clark would be to risk a pseudomorphism, as if their basement-bound works were one and the same thing. Matta-Clark's cuts were decidedly cruder, more obtrusive than Asher's; and however banal the observation, it distills something central about the mechanics of art and architecture addressed by both. The extreme quietude of Asher's work is a function of its institutional placement, in which the legibility of the object to the spectator is tantamount to declarations of aesthetic value. By contrast, the place of art making for Matta-Clark cannot be described as an institutional given. Matta-Clark could hardly proffer a critique of such places as *institutions*, then, because none of the sites he worked in had yet to assume such a mantle, wielding none of their cultural purchase.

And so, in a manner that may seem to contradict the critique of institutions, but which dialectically compliments its conceptual sensibilities, Matta-Clark's art demonstrates that the terms of art making may, in fact, shape the terms of property,

2.16 Daniel Buren, *Through the Room,* 1987. Courtesy John Weber Gallery, New York, NY.

2.17 Michael Asher, Lisson Gallery installation, London, 1973. Courtesy Michael Asher.

even facilitate its constitution as such. If architecture acts as the support or the ground to the "figure" of the work of art, his work announces the ground in turn. Not only is this notion confirmed at a structural level, but through the longer history of SoHo.

SOHO: THE SLUM INCUBATOR

. . . New York has never learned the art of growing old by playing on all its pasts. Its present invents itself, from hour to hour, in the act of throwing away its previous accomplishments and challenging the future. A city composed of paroxysmal places in monumental reliefs.
—Michel de Certeau[41]

New York's Oldest Cast Iron
Facade
Dismantled, Laid Out
and Waiting
—Gordon Matta-Clark[42]

Thus far Matta-Clark's early practice has been situated in relation to the specific histories of 112 Greene Street and Food, as well as to other artists whose work concerns art and property. But this represents a limited view of his engagement with the built environment, suggesting that 112 Greene Street was an already established institution and that its environs were definitively "built." Instead, Matta-Clark's relation to 112 Greene Street and Food should be understood as at once presaging and refracting the history of SoHo, as well as larger debates on the virtual "health" of the city at the time. Finding its apparent beginnings in the early sixties, it is a history in which architectural refuse—a "slum" in the complex jargon of urban politics—was appropriated and transformed to assume the status of an economically important site.

A longer account of the area serves notice to the ostensible patterns of valuation, devaluation, and gentrification to which it was historically subjected. A posh residential neighborhood in the late 1700s, its reputation as an important commercial hub was solidified in the mid-nineteenth century, a partial function of the cast-iron building technology introduced into the area and the construction of light manufacturing lofts that followed. While this necessarily drove its former residential population away from the neighborhood—and then secured for it the profile of a red light district—it remained a thriving center of industry nonetheless. But the area's industrial growth accelerated to the point of its own nullity, as it fell into serious decline after the Second World War. Now, the once flourishing cast-iron lofts were considered too small for the demands of mass production in the years after the war.[43] Close to six hundred loft spaces in lower Manhattan were destroyed from 1959 to 1962 as a result; in 1963, an entire block of cast-iron manufacturing lofts between Broadway and Church Street was razed to build a parking lot. By 1967, all but one of the complete cast-iron lofts of James Bogardus, one of the primary developers of the cast-iron technique in lower Manhattan, had been destroyed.

Perhaps this pre-history of SoHo reads like so much technological determinism, as though the neighborhood's slide into decrepitude was solely a function of shifting technologies and their deadening impact on industry. Shortly, we will see that the changes wrought in the area were a fragment of a much larger phenomenon in Manhattan, involving land speculation and zoning laws. Yet the urban phenomenon described in this brief does bear a structural dimension, one theorized by Henri Lefebvre as the "double process" of urbanization. The process is "double" because it revolves around twinned, even parasitic axes, conflictual and necessarily uneven in their development. Discussed in Lefebvre's *Right to the City* (1968), the double process speaks to the destruction of the city as it simultaneously extends the urban, destroying the conditions of everyday life in the process. While it brings with it "industrialization and urbanization, growth and development, economic development and social life," it also admits to a "clash between urban reality and industrial reality."[44] For if the "city played an important role in the *take-off* of industry," industry returns the favor by "constituting agglomerations in which urban features are deteriorating."[45] And it does this with a certain violence. It "attacks the city, assaults it, takes it ravages it." It "appropriates this network and refashions it according to its needs."[46]

But just as the "double process" bespeaks a discontinuous and uneven account of urbanism, an alternate formulation of the city by Lefebvre suggests other fortunes, attesting to the deeply contradictory impulses of urban development, and the possibility of moving beyond a functionalist (or economist) vision of urban space as the topographical mirror of economy, politics, and ideology.[47] For Lefebvre, the city is also a *work.* Not a work in the classicist or aesthetical conception of the term—a thing born and rationalized through the logic of *techne* or the "city-state" as imagined in antiquity—but a work as an open-ended *oeuvre.* It can be playful, subject to the imminent use of its citizens, a center of knowledge; that "which contrasts with the irreversible tendency towards money and commerce."[48] The city as *oeuvre,* in other words, is at the same time *la fête*—a "celebration which consumes unproductively."[49] Which is to say, a notion of the city that generalizes its economy rather than rationalizes it; or that emphasizes its use value by its citizens as opposed to its exchange value by the state.[50] A city, in other words, of non-instrumental play.[51]

Each city is its own *oeuvre* as it is also subjected to the peculiarities of its own double process. Thus to read Lefebvre's model through the specific history of SoHo and New York in the sixties and seventies is to confirm this push-pull dynamic among industry, land speculators, and the city's inhabitants. A certain claim was laid to the spaces left in the wake of its "double process," spaces that may well have been the product of the claimants themselves.[52] But the double process also opens onto the dialectical reading of space Lefebvre would later discuss as alternately social and abstract, a model that bears marked implications for discussions of early SoHo. Social space, for Lefebvre, complicates the notion of space tied unilaterally to the means of production, appealing instead to its use value, and rejecting its representation as necessarily functionalist. Social space is determined conflictually—it is riven at its foundation, heterogeneous and structured around difference. It is "not a thing among other things, nor a product among other products": rather,

> it subsumes things produced, and encompasses their interrelationships in their coexistence and simultaneity—their (relative) order and/or (relative) disorder . . . Itself the outcome of past action, social space is what permits fresh actions to occur, while suggesting others and prohibiting yet others. Among these actions, some serve production, others consumption (i.e., the enjoyment of the fruits of production). Social space implies a great diversity of knowledge.[53]

Social space also has a decidedly temporal dimension. "Space is a use value," Lefebvre writes, "but even more so is time to which it is ultimately linked, because time is our life, our fundamental use value."[54] Abstract space, by contrast, is alienated space, universalized and therefore without time. Reified as exchange value by the state, by planners, by capitalist interests, it is an object of instrumentalization, a way to condition and contain its inhabitants. Its terrain is neither sociability nor everyday life but real estate, zoning, property.

A brief litany, necessarily selective and abstract, attests to this dialectical phenomenon in New York, centered largely around the question of housing and the "deconcentration" of cities.[55] Indeed the sixties mark the beginnings of urban renewal in the United States on a sweeping scale, an observation that finds its acute manifestation in New York.[56] In 1961, for instance, New York was rezoned for the first time since 1916, facilitating the apportionment of federal monies to the city's "reconstruction." In 1963, the destruction of Penn Station generated heated controversy, inspiring the architectural historian Nathan Silver to publish *Lost New York,* a document of buildings that fell victim to the wrecking ball.[57] In 1965, New York passed its first Landmarks Preservation Law, as if to acknowledge the loss, perhaps to atone for culpability. In 1969, Mayor John Lindsay inaugurated his "Lindsay Plan," an effort to shore up Manhattan's central business district, build the notorious "Westway," clear the West Side of its outmoded ports, introduce new construction in the downtown Lower Manhattan area, *and* manage to maintain some of the city's manufacturing areas—at least to follow the final version of their plan.[58] And throughout the decade, the efforts of Robert Moses, head of the Mayor's Committee on Slum Clearance, crucially altered the face of the city.

The examples are numerous, going far to support Sharon Zukin's observation that "by the early 60's, urban renewal plans and private redevelopment had destroyed—or threatened to destroy—so many landmarks, that people began to speak of a sense of loss."[59] On the one hand, this sense of loss was addressed through architectural proposals. If, for example, Colin Rowe's contextualist platform called for a peculiar assessment of the city through the figure-ground relationship in the years that followed, other architectural programs focused even more acutely on the value of the streetscape or neighborhood, regionalist sensibilities that verged critically (and in some instances, conservatively) on the anti-modern or postmodern.[60] On the other hand, many suspected architectural solutions were at the root of the problem itself. The "physicalist" fallacy entertained by architects—the notion that "living and working arrangements could be easily manipulated through architectural practice"—was held as deeply suspect by urban planners, who understood their concerns to be at odds with the demiurgic impulses of many architects.[61]

Beyond this, the question of urban renewal also had a markedly grassroots dimension. In fundamental ways, it was crystallized by the publication of Jane Jacobs's *The Death and Life of Great American Cities,* a generalized manifesto around which many New Yorkers rallied. Published in 1961, Jacobs' book was a call to resuscitate American cities and neighborhoods just as they reached their apparent death through urban planning. Declaiming against modernist notions of the megalopolis, among which Le Corbusier's *Ville Radieuse* is especially vilified, she attributes a biological character to the city in crisis, desperately in need of medical attention. Particular neighborhoods are called "amputated areas [that] typically develop galloping gangrene," so neglected that "all the art and science of city planning are helpless to stem decay."[62] In spite of the language of urban decay she helped popularize, her prognosis was ultimately optimistic. The "death" of the city was challenged only by its "rebirth," founded in community-based efforts to preserve the diversity of mixed-use neighborhoods and the local character of their streets. The family operation, the mom and pop store, and the ethos of small business were her partial solutions to this end. "Time makes certain structures obsolete for some enterprises," she observed, "and they then become available to others."[63]

In this statement alone Jacobs anticipated the events that were to unfold in SoHo in the next two decades. Certainly, her language resonates within Matta-Clark's own claims over ten years later when he wrote:

> Work with abandoned structures began with my concern for the life of the city of which a major side effect is the metabolization of old buildings. Here, as in many urban centers, the availability of empty and neglected structures was a prime textual reminder of the ongoing fallacy of renewal through modernization.[64]

The inverse relationship between urban development and the attrition of historical site Matta-Clark identifies found its object lesson in SoHo. The area was known not as SoHo back then, but as the far less glamorous South Houston Industrial Area; and far from the seamless loft spaces and gleaming boutiques of today's SoHo, it was then the very embodiment of urban decay, replete with abandoned buildings, a progressively deplenished work population, and streets shadowless for lack of illumination. In spite of its decrepitude, artists had come to inhabit the area illegally in the mid-fifties, living in lofts not zoned for residential use. Renting directly from owners with commercial leases and obscuring signs of their tenancy from building inspectors, they understood fully that they could be evicted at a moment's notice.[65]

While this is certainly a large part of the historical narrative, too often it is romanticized as the only part, as if the transformation of the area to present-day SoHo was simply one of artists appropriating abandoned buildings, like squatters staking a claim for property.[66] But to accept this abandonment at face value is to pay homage to a myth: the belief in the transparency of the natural cycles of urban decay and renewal, a myth Jacobs inadvertently confirmed in the organicizing rhetoric of her own account. The history of SoHo is anything but natural, its development less a matter of biology than a protracted contest among local government and city planners, corporate speculators, and citizens who may have unwittingly facilitated government efforts. Artists may have tacitly contributed to the area's economic development as property, but they were not alone in their efforts. The conditions of this appropriation were partially established in advance of their tenancy.

In 1955, for instance, David Rockefeller formed the Downtown Lower Manhattan Association (DLMA), a group whose purpose was to decentralize Lower Manhattan in concert with the City Planning Commission (CPC) of New York. Their collective aim was to transform the area from an industrial "slum" to an expanding corporate and financial center, of which the new headquarters for the Chase Manhattan Bank (owned by the Rockefellers) would be the centerpiece.[67] The demolition this called for was soon met with resistance from many of the area's inhabitants, not to mention from local politicians whose constituencies might lose their jobs as a result of dislocation. As a result, in 1963 the CPC hired the city planner and economic consultant Chester Rapkin to undertake a massive study on the uses of obsolete property in the neighborhood. Surveying close to 650 firms in the South Houston Industrial Area,[68] Rapkin bestowed the title of an urban "incubator" upon the area, suggesting that its primary function was transitional, a kind of economic way station. Its role as incubator was to enable fledgling companies to operate on a relatively limited scale before leaving the city for larger facilities or dying as unsuccessful businesses.

There is something rather Darwinian to Rapkin's narrative. It appeals on its surface to a pioneer mentality—as if property were there to be claimed and settled—but it also concedes to the possible loss of that property, an evacuation of its tenants should their businesses die an early death or be exiled because of the outsized scale of their operations. In this regard, the evolutionist strain of Rapkin's rhetoric is not unlike Jacobs's, as the language of survivalism permeates both accounts. This is not incidental, as both were indebted, however tacitly or inadvertantly, to the school of "urban ecology" first associated with the "Chicago School" in the prewar era, and the work of Amos Hawley after the Second World War.[69] Both subscribed to the ideology of the small business and its "symbiosis" and survival in a diversified and competitive environment.

Of course, the ends to which Rapkin and Jacobs made use of this jargon were distinct: Rapkin represented the interests of the "city" and Jacobs its inhabitants. Indeed, just who had the right to the city was a different matter altogether, as witnessed in the struggle by artists to occupy lofts legally and the uses to which those spaces (and their occupants' identities as artists) were institutionally put. In 1961, the same year Jacobs's book was published, a group of artists formed the Artists Tenants Association (ATA), an organization devoted to attaining legal residency in Lower Manhattan through changing the zoning laws that forbade residential occupation of the buildings. One important outcome of their efforts was the passage of the New York State Multiple Dwelling Law, Article 7-B (chap. 939, sec. 276), in 1964. The article recognized that artists were an "enhancement to urban life who deserve special housing provisions,"[70] and so were permitted to live in manufacturing lofts.

Superficially, the rhetoric of the law is affirmative, even celebratory: artists were now recognized as an "enhancement" to urban life and they deserved "special housing" as such. But as Zukin and others have written, there was much to dislike about Article 7-B in spite of its apparent embrace of the profession. Chief among the objections was that it legislated that artists, and only artists, had the exclusive right to live in manufacturing lofts, a notion that would seem to generate little complaint from that sector of the population.[71] What this demanded, however, was a bureaucratized definition of the artist, stipulating an implicit connection between artists and arts institutions, which required sanctioning by the state. "As used in this article," Article 7-B stated:

> the word artist means a person regularly engaged in the fine arts, such as painting and sculpture on a professional fine arts basis, and so certified by an art academy, association or society, recognized by the municipal office of cultural affairs or the state council on the arts.[72]

Article 7-B did not just bureaucratize the artist's identity as organized around the terms of institutions and property. It effectively barred a large sector of lower-income residents (largely non-white) from inhabiting the area.

Not surprisingly, a number of artists protested this section of Article 7-B as being little more than an authoritarian gesture, preferring illegal habitation instead. When the definition of "artist" was expanded in 1968 to include the non-plastic arts and newer professions in visual culture, the colonization of artistic identity seemed that much more acute. By 1971, when it was self-evident that the area was beginning to reestablish its cache as property of some value, the terms of admission into the loft market had softened considerably; indeed, the transformation from slum incubator to real estate oasis was completed that year, with artists attaining legal residential rights in the district, and landmark status granted to its cast-iron architecture.[73] Along the way, the South Houston Industrial Area assumed the catchy acronym SoHo, befitting the population of galleries and alternative spaces that had begun to settle there and recalling the residential neighborhood in London of the same name.[74]

This history makes plain an ambivalence. It speaks first to the communitarian sensibility advocated by Jane Jacobs: the will of artists to live in the area and to salvage, preserve, and "recycle" the once decrepit neighborhood from the totalizing schemes of urban planners; to render the city an *oeuvre* or, in Matta-Clark's words, to "put it to use" as a space of social praxis in excess of its alienation as zoned property and real estate. But what we know now of the area—that its commercialism has driven many of its original settlers away, resulting in its current manifestation as an outdoor shopping mall—suggests something about the use of the artists to the advantage of property. Artists had inadvertantly "incubated" the area, facilitated (however unknowingly) by a corporate and governmental effort to decentralize Lower Manhattan. And, however problematic this decentralization (or however beneficial to artists), the shift in the area was likewise burdened with historiographic connotations: how a certain effacement of history took place in the attempt to reclaim place itself. Matta-Clark addressed this directly. "The loft experience," he wrote, "denies the history of the building."[75] This statement recognizes the extent to which artists contended with property issues in a fundamentally quotidian way, as if their identity as artists and the modes of their sociability were imbricated in questions of urban space, zoning, city bureaucracy, and real estate.[76] And it underscores further the complexities of urbanism and preservation at the time, a kind of fallout of the "double process" first, but something that might not be so inexorable and final, something that might be put equally to playful use. But if all this reads like so much contextualist art history, recall that Matta-Clark's art critically anticipated these events. Tacitly acknowledging its indexical relationship to each site, it also conditioned the role of architecture in its display.

Even more so, two of Matta-Clark's projects from the time, his *Fake Estates* and the "collaborative" investigations of the group *Anarchitecture,* move beyond the historical and spatial conditions of early SoHo to think more broadly about the question of property altogether. Implicitly, they understand that the matter of property is not just about the world of things—of objects to use and places to rent—but an acute notion of selfhood and its constitution, and that which refuses ownership outright.

THE SOUL OF PROPERTY

Return, then, to the seemingly mysterious proposal articulated by Hegel at the outset of this chapter, that property might actually have a soul. How does one attribute a soul to property, particularly buildings? And how, if at all, does this formulation resonate within the recent history of SoHo and, more specifically, in Matta-Clark's art?

In 1973, Matta-Clark embarked on two projects that complemented each other in their implications for the question of the "soul of property." One, titled *Fake Estates* (or *Reality Properties: Fake Estates*), was organized principally around a business transaction, the purchasing of "surplus land" through auctions sponsored by the City of New York. Better known as "gutterspace" or "curb property," these tiny slivers of land were actually "leftover" parcels from lots drawn by architects and city planners for buildings and property. They had now become city property because their owners had failed to pay taxes, and were available for around $35.00 apiece.

Never exhibited during Matta-Clark's lifetime, the first part of *Fake Estates* consisted of the purchasing of five parcels of gutterspace property in Queens and Staten Island (later totaling fifteen pieces); "written documentation of the piece of land, including exact dimensions and location, and perhaps a list of weeds growing there"; and "a full scale photograph of the property."[77] As originally envisioned by the artist, the property and the deed would become available to anyone who might actually buy the work.

Recorded with a surveyor's banality, the *Fake Estates* afford no visual pleasure. Evoking works by Hans Haacke, Douglas Huebler, and Edward Ruscha, the deadpan character of the images and documentation recalls the rhetoric of bureaucracy, of contracts and property rights, deeds and lot numbers. Here property is reduced to the most basic of plans and the most mundane black and white photographs (figures 2.18–2.20). A stretch of crabgrass, a curb, a dimly lit alley framed by a chain-link fence: these pathetic images of modern real estate constitute one third of the project, an ironic *punctum* of the suburban imaginary.

The plans of the sites themselves are schematic grids upon which property lines govern the real estate; and they share much with other grids—that modernist sign *par excellence*—in their impulse to rationalize the space that falls within and around them. But they also reveal that Matta-Clark's "fake estates" fall between the borders of property because they are "leftover," confirming the intractability of this model as they underwrite it.[78] Thus they serve notice to the ambivalence (or even double ambivalence) of the grid, a phenomenon which Rosalind Krauss importantly discusses

2.18 (page 100) Gordon Matta-Clark, *Fake Estates,* detail ("Jamaica Curb," Block 10142, Lot 15), 1973.

2.19 (page 101) Gordon Matta-Clark, *Fake Estates,* detail ("Little Alley," Block 2497, Lot 42), 1973.

SEE PAGE 11

53RD LEDERER ST. ROAD

2497

53RD VAN DYKE ST. DR.

RAMSEY ST.

ST.

SEE PAGE

when she speaks of the grid's "schizophrenic" impulses: how its autoinscriptive capacities—its seeming retreat from the real—are positioned against its implied expansion outwards, towards a field potentially construed as materialist or scientific.[79] Matta-Clark's work furthers the ambivalence of the grid by suspending it between the registers of art and architecture. If modernism's artistic grid mythically affirms the autonomy of the picture plane and its security as self-reflexive object, the architectural grid speaks to the rationalization of space, its colonization of something outside and beyond it. The very model of abstract space, in this respect.

Yet what the seeming rationality of the grid belies is the principal gesture of the *Fake Estates:* the purchasing of property so useless and irrelevant, so pathetic in its claims to appropriate space, that the absurdity of real estate is laid bare as a bad pun. One piece measured three feet square, hardly a livable environment. Another piece, the most improbable and tortuous of corridors, bore the odd proportions of one foot wide by ninety-five feet long, set between buildings, "utterly landlocked." The inaccessibility of the space intrigued the artist. "There's no access to it which is fine with me," Matta-Clark remarked, "that's an interesting quality; something that can be owned but never experienced."[80] He noted of the project:

> When I bought these parcels at the New York City Auction, the description of them that always excited me the most was "inaccessible." . . . What I basically wanted to do was designate spaces that wouldn't be seen and certainly not occupied. Buying them was my own take on the strangeness of existing property demarcation lines. Property is so all pervasive. Everyone's notion of ownership is determined by the use factor.[81]

Something that can be owned but never experienced; certainly not occupied; the strangeness of existing property lines: the paradox of buying this unusable land, of submitting something without use value to the registers of exchange value, presents a contemporary attenuation of Marx's early thinking on property, when he notes that "private property has made us so stupid and narrow-minded that an object is only ours when we have it, when it exists as capital for us or when we can directly

2.20 Gordon Matta-Clark, *Fake Estates,* detail ("Little Alley," Block 2497, Lot 42), 1973.

possess, eat, drink, wear, inhabit it, etc., in short, when we use it."[82] Matta-Clark's reformulation of this statement in *Fake Estates* is that one cannot actually use or inhabit the gutterspace property, but that humanity's overall drive to possession is so rapacious, "has made us so stupid," that the function of the property is actually rendered irrelevant under capital.

In *Fake Estates,* the unusuability of this land—and the reification of space through the laws of property—is Matta-Clark's principal object of critique. At the same time, that which cannot be used, that which is inaccessible and therefore *non-productive* or *workless,* may also be a potential source of social space. Another means to think the possibility of unlegislatable space in non-instrumental terms was found in the loose, informal "collective" or social gathering of artists known as Anarchitecture. (*Fake Estates* seems to have found its conceptual origins with the group: a letter addressed to Caroline Goodden and the group in 1973 names the project as one of many "anarchitectural" ideas.[83]) Initially formed by Matta-Clark, Suzanne Harris, and Tina Girouard, Anarchitecture was a "work session," to borrow Jene Highstein's characterization of it, that included among its participants, Highstein, Bernard Kirschenbaum, Laurie Anderson, Richard Landry, and Richard Nonas. Jeffrey Lew and Goodden attended the meetings on occasion.

In 1973, the group met for a period of about three months, every couple of weeks, in various bars, restaurants, and studios, to discuss the ambiguous character of space and to think about the transitional, or transpositional, in architectural practice.[84] As conveyed by the name of the group, Matta-Clark observed that their musings were not limited to concerns of architecture proper, but were meant to investigate the idea of places outside of architecture, without architecture, or extra-architectural. Building and design were to be worked against, for Anarchitecture "attempts to solve no problem."[85] If anything, "cosmetic" design (cosmetic because at the surface of things) was itself the problem. As Matta-Clark wrote:

> A response to cosmetic design
> completion through removal
> completion through collapse
> completion through emptiness[86]

To counter the notion of design, which at once implies good taste and universalizing, timeless imperatives, Anarchitecture considered "improper" models of space: the space of collapse or removal. In another instance, Matta-Clark referred to such places as "interruptions":

> The group's architectural aim was more elusive than doing pieces that would demonstrate an alternative attitude to buildings . . . We were thinking more about metaphoric voids, gaps, leftover spaces, places that were not developed. . .for example, the places where you stop to tie your shoelaces, places that are just interruptions in your daily movements. These places are also perceptually significant because they make a reference to movement space. It was about something other than the established architectural vocabulary, without getting fixed into anything too formal.[87]

A place that is an "interruption" or a "movement space" is a liminal space, unbounded by the restrictions of real estate. "Leftover" because not legislated for use, these spaces refuse ownership because they are illegible, ambiguous, kinetic even.

The sense of this spatial ambiguity led the group to play innumerable word games with the word "anarchitecture." "Anarchy Torture," "An Arctic Lecture," "Anarchy Lecture," "An Art Collector"; the phrase anarchitecture was punned upon endlessly as if to suggest that the ever-shifting nature of this space could no more assume a static linguistic position than a fixed spatial one. For, like the word "anarchy" to which it is etymologically close, to be "anarchitectural" is to be without first principles or foundations—an organizing principle that would rationalize the space through its buildings.

In March 1974, the "findings" of the Anarchitecture group were displayed at 112 Greene Street (figure 2.21). Deciding to work anonymously, the members chose a uniform photographic format with slight deviations in composition from Nonas, Highstein, and Anderson. A few months later, a two-page spread appeared in *Flash Art,* in which the group presented puns and images that illuminated their theoretical interests. Photographs of holes, horizon lines, fallen monuments, and other images served to emphasize a thinking about places that stood outside the readily demarcated

ANARCHI
TECTURE
GROUP
112 GREENE ST

and legislatable. The image of a train derailed (figure 2.22), its tracks collapsed beneath its weight, underscored the notion of a "movement space" as uncontainable.

While little documentation exists of the exhibition, written and photographic materials reveal the breadth of Matta-Clark's anarchitectural ideas. Sometimes the photographs attest to the loss of space through the theme of mortification. Three tombstones, for instance, appear to descend into the earth progressively, as if absorbed by the passage of time (figure 2.23). Another recurrent interest is the issue of private space and the attendant tropes of accessibility and inaccessibility that both fascinated the artist as well as haunted his reception.[88] Under a sketch of a ring of keys he once wrote, "a catalogue and apology of locked spaces to be carried in the pocket."[89] The notion of a "catalogue" of space, closed down and carried off through a set of keys, recalls the suburban isolationism explored in his cuttings and the progressive rationalization of space the isolation implies. But to refer to this as an "apology" of locked space is to invoke the culpability implied in its closure, not to mention the possibility of redemption in its acknowledgement. A photograph dating from 1974 reiterates this interest (figure 2.24). Picturing a post from which two heavy locks dangle in relief against a brick wall, the image is closed, tight, airless. No doubt this effect results partially from the wall's proximity to the viewer, but the presence of the locks thematically confirms the claustrophic sensibility.

If the "apology" of locked space engaged Matta-Clark at one level, an equal but opposite anarchitectural interest concerned the seemingly extensionless scale of space wrought by the vertical city and its high-rises, which the artist opposed to the limitless span of the horizon. Responding to his own call for "the perfect structure," Matta-Clark wrote elliptically, ". . . erase all the buildings for a clear horizon."[90] To illustrate this "perfect structure," he sketched twinned skyscrapers, ideograms of a sort, on a horizon line complete with the half disc of the sun. But the perfect structure—or structures—was not so much the skyscrapers as the condition of their erasure, indicated by the two blunt "X's" that violently mark the images of the buildings. Where

2.21 Anarchitecture, invitation to "Anarchitecture," 112 Greene Street, New York, NY, May 1974.

2.22 Anarchitecture, image from "Anarchitecture," published in Flash Art, June 1974.

once the vertical trajectory of the skyscrapers suggested a certain colonization of space, their erasure to a horizon line—itself extensionless—acknowledged the space negatively framed by the buildings. It recognized the impossibility of reaching and thus appropriating the horizon line as well, a thing that always slips beyond grasp as a headlong, forward trajectory and a lateral spread at once.

It is clear what Matta-Clark was referring to in this erasure of buildings to the horizon. Yamasaki's World Trade Center had been formally dedicated in April of 1973, and the artist was alternately attracted and repulsed by its gigantism.[91] To borrow from Michel de Certeau, perhaps the Center represented for the artist "a gigantic rhetoric of excess in both expenditure and production," as it dramatically refigured Lower Manhattan along a vertical axis.[92] As the symbolic figure of private interests in the city, the towers also represented Late Capital's newest and most profligate of monuments. Matta-Clark, however, regarded its existence as an anarchitectural opportunity. In a letter to the Graphic Consultant for the Art and Design Program at the World Trade Center, he identified himself as "representative" of the Anarchitecture group and offered his creative services on their behalf. "In our response to highly determined spatial conditions," he wrote, ". . . we believe we could contribute some positive and interesting insights into the new scale and complexity of the World Trade Center."[93] Matta-Clark's language is purposefully ingratiating, but as implied by his desire to "erase" the buildings, his motivations were by no means utopian. His photograph of the twinned buildings features the monoliths positioned against a skyscape of drifting cumulus (figure 2.25). Set against the monumental slabs of the towers, the clouds offer a glimpse, however fleeting, of a space held outside of the buildings—a movement space.

Improper, useless, and inaccessible places, "something that can be owned but never used": Matta-Clark's places contravene the traditional wisdom surrounding property. As he observed of Anarchitecture, such concerns were "more elusive than doing pieces that would demonstrate an alternative attitude to buildings"; and this is appropriate, given the genealogy of the term itself. For property is not so much considered a thing at all but a right: a relationship between object and subject structured

2.23, 2.24 Gordon Matta-Clark, from Anarchitecture, 1974.

around the terms of personality and consumption. Treating the notion of the modern individual as constituted around his possessiveness, C. B. Macpherson argues that the notion of property as "a thing to be owned" is a relatively recent phenomenon, beginning as late as the eighteenth century.[94]

To be sure, when one speaks of a thing as a property *of* something else, one refers not only to the object's distinction from one's person, but implies (through the genitive "of") an internal relation by way of possession or predication. Hence, things in the world are typically identified by their properties: whiteness is regarded as a property of snow; blackness a property of the night; hardness of wood, hotness of fire. Property, then, is less the *extension* of one's person than the *constitution* of one's being. The accumulation of these attributes, resulting in a bundle of properties, configures the identity of the subject in question.[95]

Legal theory describes this as the "personhood perspective" of property, and its argument is that "to achieve proper self-development—to be a person—an individual needs some control over resources in the external environment."[96] The thesis seems a banality at this point: issues of conspicuous consumption, of links between property and social status, are among its most obvious (or perhaps its most troublesome) contemporary manifestations. Well before such ideas were commonplace, however, Hegel articulated the confluence between persons and their property as structured further around property and use. "I give the living creature, as my property, a soul other than that which it previously had," he notes. "I give it my soul."[97] Hegel is writing about the most reprehensible form of property in this instance—slavery—but the formulation suggests that possessions become a repository for the subject's very being, as if property assumed its owner's character or soul.

But a paradox governs the maintenance or possession of property and those who would lay claim to it, a paradox Matta-Clark's work brilliantly ventriloquizes and dialectically criticizes. Property's "essence," Hegel writes, "consists in its being used and in vanishing."[98] The use of the thing demonstrates the very moment of its fullest possession as property, for it reveals the subject's capacity to *negate* the thing, to enact the full power of the subject's control over the object.[99] Distant as these re-

2.25 Gordon Matta-Clark, from Anarchitecture, 1974.

marks may seem from the purview of seventies art making, the virtual bestowing of a soul or identity to property finds its enactment in the history of SoHo, in which one's identity as artist served as bureaucratic guarantor for a peculiar claim to property. But Matta-Clark's focus on obsolete buildings, on the one hand, or inaccessible, ambiguous places on the other, theatricalizes the notion of property organized around the conjunction of personhood and use. If Hegel argues that property's "essence" consists in its use and "vanishing," Matta-Clark parodizes this idea through literalizing it. For him, property's essence consists equally in its *attrition;* it is accorded value as property only when it passes into a state of uselessness or ruin. As a dialectical reversal of this, the inaccessible spaces of *Fake Estates* and the ambiguous spaces of Anarchitecture demonstrate the radical uselessness of things demarcated as property: the impossibility of these things to be used and the non-instrumental sense of play they might bring about.

The history of SoHo is no less than a narrative of this repressed attrition, the destruction of the built environment that opens onto the possibility of its later reclamation. What this suggests about the identity of the artist in question is salutory; and the anti-nominalist interests that motivated the Anarchitecture group facilitate this understanding. Concerned as they were with unnegotiable things and equivocal experiences of perceptual space, no doubt they imagined the same for the status of the artist as well. An artist, "unfixed to anything too formal," to borrow Matta-Clark's own words, is not so much powerless in commenting upon the situation of property; rather, he questions his use for property's ends.

3 ON MATTA-CLARK'S "VIOLENCE"; OR, WHAT IS A "PHENOMENOLOGY OF THE SUBLIME"?

Cutting, shattering, fragmenting, dissecting, mutilating, even decapitating: to consider the reception of Matta-Clark's art is to survey a language riven by violence—of gestures at once trenchant and brutalizing. A language that reads the artist's cuttings as a virtual dismemberment of the human body, the rhetoric of violence has long been a critical trope in discussions of his art. As Maud Lavin has argued, "the destruction process is begun by the artist, and it becomes an act of sovereignty":

> . . . I would argue that to emphasize the act of possession of property through a violent and private manipulation is actually to confirm and extend prevalent codes of private ownership—and that Matta-Clark's *autopsied* buildings are as immutable in their forms and as autocratic in their presentation as in conventional architecture.[1]

Lavin then suggests that Matta-Clark's art is complicit with a "violation" of the feminine order:

> Matta-Clark's wounding of a house can be seen as a male violation of a domestic realm with female associations. I am not making a case for Matta-Clark's work as a whole to be read as anti-female, but certainly it is concerned with male virility . . .[2]

Lavin's critique of Matta-Clark is among the more truculant in print. Her attack is to be taken seriously, though, for it is argued on historiographic grounds, linking the criticism surrounding his practice to the hallowed tradition of the individual master, the mythos of the romantic genius pitted against the world. Charges by other critics were less considered. In 1975, Matta-Clark wrote a letter to Melvyn Kaufman of the Wm. Kaufman Organization, to whom he was referred by the City Planning Commission of New York. Having heard of Kaufman's "innovative design attitudes," he contacted him about the possibility of "collaboration." "My idea is to secure a building awaiting demolition," he wrote, "and 'restructure' it. . . . Since you may now have or will have such a building it may be of interest to you to be involved with an adventurous 'unbuilding' design statement."[3]

Kaufman's rather sanctimonious response was less than positive, misinterpreting Matta-Clark's gesture as an uncritical celebration of urban demolition. "Someone said that dying gracefully is an art," his memo to the artist began:

> Perhaps it is. But I do not like funerals either as sad occasions or as celebrations.
>
> I believe in the great demise but I believe in life more and I resent the infringement of death processes prolonged as a devitalization of the living.[4]

For his part, Matta-Clark was deeply frustrated by the charges that his art was violent and destructive. What some read as decadent or sensationalistic, he felt to be necessarily regenerative. "The people who have attacked me in the past," he remarked, "see it [the work] not [for its] potential but as a collusion with the forces of destruction and [urban] renewal."[5]

In spite of his objections, Matta-Clark could hardly deny that the production of the work was literally violent, nor could he refuse the "clean-line brutality" he once claimed for one of his cuttings.[6] One infamous gesture seems to confirm this violence, so blatant is it in its attack on the profession of architecture. In December 1976, Matta-Clark was invited by Andrew MacNair to participate in the exhibition *Idea as Model,* a show that included three members of the so-called "New York 5": Michael Graves, Charles Gwathmey, and Richard Meier. The exhibition was hosted by the Institute for Architecture and Urban Studies (IAUS), which was among the most progressive forums for the study and discussion of architecture during its existence from 1967 to 1985. Founded by Peter Eisenman and located on West 40th Street, the Institute itself was something of a bastion of "Cornelliana": Eisenman had graduated from the Cornell School of Architecture before the "Texas Rangers" made their move to Ithaca, and many of the School's students and esteemed faculty taught at the Institute as well as published in its seminal journal *Oppositions.* Certainly Colin Rowe's mentorship of Eisenman at Cambridge played some part in the Institute's foundation (though Eisenman would later reject Rowe's ideas).[7]

Yet no matter how theoretically progressive the Institute was, it recalled Matta-Clark's prejudices against his Cornell education. Still, he agreed to participate in *Ideas as Model.* He originally proposed for the show a small-scale cutting for one of its seminar rooms—a windowless box of sheetrock. On the afternoon of the opening, however, Matta-Clark appeared with a BB gun borrowed from Dennis Oppenheim and asked MacNair permission to shoot out a couple of the windows of the Institute instead. The windows were already cracked, he reasoned, and he would use their empty casements as a frame for photographs of housing projects taken in the South Bronx.[8] Titled *Window Blowout,* the group pictured anonymous, derelict buildings with their windows fractured, gridded walls in brick punctured by star-shaped bursts of shattered glass (figure 3.1).

MacNair agreed conditionally to Matta-Clark's proposal, but it was a decision he would come to regret. Describing the artist as "incredibly wrecked," he watched horrified as Matta-Clark proceeded to shoot out all the windows on the floor of the Institute, all the while raging against its esteemed members and the architectural ideologies they supported. "These were the guys I studied with at Cornell," the artist reportedly vented, "these were my teachers. I hate what they stand for."[9] For Matta-Clark's attack linked the abstract tendencies of modern architecture—the very notion of "idea as model"—with the degeneracy these models wrought in the urban environment, witnessed in the failed housing projects of the Bronx. Not surprisingly, the fellows of the Institute were enraged by the gesture; and while the windows were boarded up before the opening, the incident had clearly struck a nerve, recalling historical traumas in excess of Matta-Clark's action. According to MacNair, Eisenman compared the event to *Kristalnacht,* as if Matta-Clark's commentary on modern architecture was akin to the shattering of glass by the Nazis.[10]

Matta-Clark's action was unquestionably aggressive, reckless even. What is questionable, however, is the way that violence is metaphorically figured in the encounter between artist and building in his works, an encounter metaphorized as rape,

3.1 Gordon Matta-Clark, *Window Blow-Out,* 1976.

LIVERPOOL JOHN MOORES UNIVERSITY
Aldham Robarts L.R.C.
TEL. 0151 231 3701/3634

say, or as parallel to the acts of a stormtrooper. Such totalizing interpretations have been rejected in chapter 1, yet the stark, at times brusque physicality of the works remains, as do the questions regarding their physicality. In sum: if violence is such an unavoidable reference in Matta-Clark's reception, might it be understood as the *object* of critique in his work, refusing the notion of the artist as merely decadent? A way to read the artist's gesture beyond the avant-garde's creaking tradition to *épater le bourgeoisie?*

My claim here is, yes, Matta-Clark's "violence," to use the term provisionally, bears critical consequences that reject the willful nihilism commonly ascribed to his art. This chapter reads two major site projects closely to understand the specific mechanics that structure the terms of experience in his work. Two disparate bodies of thought commonplace to the criticism of the time will be used as heuristic devices: the discourses of phenomenology, on the one hand, and the lessons of the sublime, on the other. Their applications to the building cuts—and the way they figure into recent sculpture—open critically onto the troublesome logic of this "violence."

AT THE END OF EXPERIENCE: DAY'S END

A reader even marginally well-versed in philosophy might be disturbed by the conjunction of the terms "phenomenology" and the "sublime" that open this discussion. Their pairing would seem to engender a conceptual oxymoron. If the former is generally understood as a cognitive bracketing of sensory perception—an elevation of the phenomenal world to the status of philosophical principle—the latter would seem to be the opposite: the failure of the mind to comprehend an excess of sensible phenomena, the unattainability of which results in a feeling of pleasure and pain for the subject. Considering two of Matta-Clark's most ambitious site projects (*Day's End* and *Circus*), however, these seemingly competing strains of thought are brooked, and their linking provides an incisive critique of recent sculptural practices and urban space.

Questions of the phenomenological and the sublime will be put aside for the moment to discuss the cutting that took place at the abandoned Pier 52 near Gansevoort Street and West Street in Lower Manhattan. Titled *Day's End* or *Day's Passing* (1975) it was staged in one of the many outmoded warehouses on the lower West Side waterfront of the Hudson River (figure 3.2), a short distance from the meat-packing plants that continue to occupy the area today. The work was situated at the rear of a marine transfer station still in use by the Department of Sanitation; and while the walls and floor where the cuts were made have long been removed, replaced now with plastic siding, its skeleton remains.[11] The former warehouse was an enormous steel-truss and corrugated tin building, measuring roughly six hundred feet long and seventy feet wide (the "clerestory" level of the structure ranged around fifty feet up). The pier appears to have been built in the 1870s, as it was first registered in the 1879 Annual of the New York City Department of Docks and Ferries. Leased by a number of companies, including the Cunard Steamship Co. and the Hudson River Navigation Corporation, the Baltimore and Ohio Railroad came to occupy its space after the Second World War.[12]

Long since abandoned by the time Matta-Clark got to it, the status of Pier 52 had been subjected to changing economic priorities, new shipping technologies, and the decentralization that shaped urban planning in New York in the postwar era. The fate of Manhattan's piers was especially charged during John Lindsay's tenure as mayor from 1965 to 1973: his 1969 plan included the steady conversion of the piers to urban reserves for sunbathing and recreation. But if this was the official narrative of the Chelsea waterfront, two other faces of that narrative, marginalized in their respective fashions, figured just as prominently in the piers' historical reckoning. One was labor-oriented in its implications, witnessing the transformation of the piers from sites of labor to sites of real estate speculation. The other concerned the use of the abandoned piers by gay men living in the neighboring West Village.

On the one hand, the progressive abandonment of the piers in the sixties spoke partially to the international trend toward containerized cargo ships. Although this was hardly the only reason for the disuse of the Westside waterfront, it impacted critically on its fortunes. Now freight was increasingly stored and shipped in containers far too large to be accommodated by these nineteenth-century wharves, leading to the closure of shipping operations in the area and the subsequent loss of 1,400 longshoreman jobs in the late sixties.[13] Beyond this, a number of the deserted spaces had been reappropriated by gay men as cruising sites, a "sexhunter's playground" as one former denizen recalled. When some journalists complained of the growing crime

BALTIMORE AND OHIO

that took place around the piers, a "muggers' paradise" as one writer called it, they implicitly (and homophobically) criminalized the victims' behavior.[14]

Who had the right to the piers and what constituted their proper use? Acknowledging Pier 52's fall into decrepitude, Matta-Clark described his intervention as "making a mark in a sad moment of history."[15] Certainly, the artist was no stranger to the piers as sites for his art making. As part of a group show staged at Pier 18 in 1971 (organized by Willoughby Sharp), Matta-Clark produced an untitled performance in which he hung from the ceiling by a rope above a pile of debris. And the object *Pier In/Out,* a rectangular sheet of metal illegally excised from Pier 14 (figure 3.3), was displayed as a building fragment in 1973.

Yet no project up to that time was as ambitious as the one he envisioned for Pier 52. From early July to August of 1975, Matta-Clark secretly worked on the building with the help of Manfred Hecht and two other assistants, whom he paid with monies from a CAPS grant. "During the months of July and August," he wrote to a friend,

> . . . I totally devoted myself to a working vacation by the water on the Hudson. My "studio retreat" consisted of appropriating a nearly perfectly intact turn-of-the-century wharf building of steel truss construction having virtually basilical light and proportions. A beautiful shape for such an industrial "hangar." Once [I had] secur[ed] the space from other intruders, mainly S & M cruisers, I . . . spent the next two months working out—that is cutting and working out sections of dock 10–18″ thick, roof, walls and heavy steel trusswork.[16]

While the production of the work was physically demanding, its reception was enmeshed in an equally trying bureaucratic scenario. A few days prior to the completion of the piece, Matta-Clark's illegal activities were discovered by a city worker, most likely from the Department of Sanitation. Efforts to lock up the space were repeatedly transgressed by the artist and his assistants, but when Matta-Clark finally held an opening at the pier on August 27 (figure 3.4), the event was closed down by

3.2 Gordon Matta-Clark, *Day's End,* 1975, Pier 52, Gansevoort Street and West Street, New York, NY.

authorities from the New York City Economic Development Administration. In the months that followed, an investigation against the artist was launched by the EDA, with the threat of litigation mounting. In his defense, Matta-Clark and his supporters claimed the work to be a part of the "public domain" and suggested further that it represented an artistic contribution to a "decaying city."[17]

The complications that arose at this level were matched only by the complexity of the space itself. While *Day's End* was the most difficult cutting that Matta-Clark had made up to that point, it appears, at least at first glance, to be relatively simple in its configuration. A schematic drawing of the project (figure 3.5) reveals that most of the activity was concentrated at the west facade of the building, but the artist accounted for the enormity of the space with several well-placed cuts. Unlike the blunt, rectilinear excisions that shaped his earlier building projects, most of these were circular or ovoid, totaling five cuts in all. The first of these was a nine-foot wide cut in the floor that ran seventy feet in length, bisecting the width of the space (figure 3.6). Admitting a view of the water below, a drop of at least ten feet, it was echoed by a "sail-like" shape carved out from the roof above (figure 3.7). Perpendicular to the north end of this channel stood another semi-circular shape that functioned as a kind of door opening the rigidly planned building to the flow of the Hudson River (figure 3.8). And at the southwest corner of the warehouse, the artist carved out a quarter circle that was also open to the water.

The most prominent of the cuts was an enormous almond-shaped form, set askew on its acute edge, that pierced the west wall of the building (figure 3.9). A gargantuan, misplaced occulus, it was clearly visible when one approached the warehouse from the water, and was the main source of light in the building's dark interior.

3.3 Gordon Matta-Clark, *Pier In/Out,* 1973.

3.4 (page 124) Opening of *Day's End,* August 27, 1975, with Gerry Hovagimyan, William Wegman, and Holly Solomon.

3.5 (page 124) Gordon Matta-Clark, schematic drawing of *Day's End,* 1975. Private collection, Antwerp.

3.6 (page 125) Gordon Matta-Clark, *Day's End,* detail, 1975, Pier 52, Gansevoort Street and West Street, New York, NY.

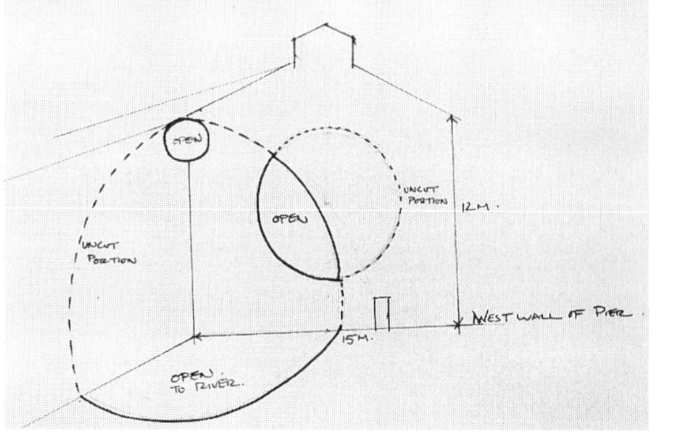
OPEN
OPEN
UNCUT PORTION
UNCUT PORTION
12M.
WEST WALL OF PIER.
15M.
OPEN TO RIVER.

This "cat-eye," as the artist called it, charted the course of the sun throughout the passage of the day, beginning with a thin arc of light around noon that gradually swelled into full radiance by dusk. The manipulation of light was manifest also in the small cut made in the roof above the building's "channel;" it allowed "a patch of light to enter which arch[ed] over the floor until . . . captured at noon within the watery slot."[18] Seen in conjunction with the effects of the larger window, the shifting plays of light within the cavernous pier served as a crucial component to the viewing of the work.

In the vastness of its interior and its tenebrous choreography of shadow and light—a shifting from murky blackness to utter refulgence—the work functioned as a kind of late capitalist pantheon, charting the time of one's experience within the building as measured by the inexorable drift and spread of light across its darkened surfaces. And yet just as Matta-Clark harnassed light to somewhat contradictory effects within *Splitting,* here, too, he reversed its signifying capacity. Paradoxically, it was at the *end* of the day—at the day's exhaustion, so to speak—that the work was most vibrant, most suffused with light. Thus the falling of light in the space was allegorically charged as well. For its passage within *Day's End* was structurally coincident with the building's historical passage into outmodedness, illuminating the twilight of the pier itself.

Some observed that the pronounced use of light within *Day's End* imbued it with a sacral character, an effect the artist stressed when he described the pier as "looking like an enormous Christian basilica whose dim interior was barely lit by the clerestory windows fifty feet above."[19] Along similar lines, Matta-Clark referred to the cut in the west wall as functioning like a "rose window." These statements are metaphorical, but what they ultimately convey is the awesomeness of the kinaesthetic experience within the space. Indeed, those who attended the opening testified strongly to its simultaneously sacral and fearful associations. As Holly Solomon noted:

3.7, 3.8, 3.9 (pages 126, 128, 129) Gordon Matta-Clark, *Day's End,* detail, 1975, Pier 52, Gansevoort Street and West Street, New York, NY.

I remember when I saw the piece for the first time, it reminded me of the first moments of seeing a Michelangelo, of being in a cathedral with flying buttresses and light-stained glass. Yet I was also afraid. I was afraid to cross the cut he made in the floor; I'm afraid of heights. He made a small handrope for me and other people who were fearful.[20]

Solomon's reflections are valuable precisely because they are so impressionistic. Likening her experience to that of being in a cathedral, she then lapses unreservedly into a discussion of her fear of the work—a fear that is registered as a threat to the body in its movement across the nine-foot wide channel. Similarly, Joel Shapiro's account of *Day's End* speaks to the perceptual unwieldliness of his encounter within the building:

The pier was probably the most successful of the pieces I saw. It was a mysterious, decrepit place–a huge space–and the cuts had a certain scale. It was frightening. I recalled thinking, whose building is this? It is dangerous . . . To go into an abandoned place and chop it up–I don't know what I thought about that. The destructive aspect, I mean . . . The willful aspect, I don't know. The piece was dangerous to the viewer. It was large; it had scale. He was creating some kind of edge–flirting with some sort of abyss. It wasn't like the earthworks of the same time.[21]

Characterizing the project as "the most successful of the pieces" he saw, Shapiro nonetheless inveighs against its "destructive aspect." In spite, or, perhaps, because of his rhetorical grappling, the sculptor's observations are instructive on a number of counts. Foremost among them, he is able to locate the general source of his fear experienced within *Day's End:* its scale, the cuts, and the scale of the cuts. He alludes first to the "cuts . . . as having a certain scale," followed by the pronouncement, "it was frightening." This point is reiterated—if in a more thematic way—when he speaks about the work's "edge." A claim for the overall experience of the work is then made when he offers, "The piece was dangerous to the viewer . . . it was large; it had scale."

The cut or the edge, the scale of the cuts, and the scale of the piece: in and of themselves, Shapiro's observations tell us little about the "violence" specific to Matta-Clark's work. But when these reactions are situated within the terms of the art and art criticism of the time—and in light of Matta-Clark's oblique references to current architectural practice—the "violent" experience of the building cuts assumes a fundamentally different texture.

ON SCALE, THE CUT AND THE MINIMALIST BODY

Dealing with nothing more
Complex than the limits
of human scale
—Gordon Matta-Clark[22]

Begin, then, with the problem of scale. While the discussion of scale would seem to be one of the organizing principles in analyses of *all* art works, frequently it is mistreated in the art critical literature as little more than a question of *largeness.* As Yve-Alain Bois observes, "[A]ll too often, scale is confused with size, which is always absolute." He notes that "scale . . . is relative and is only concerned with proportions, whether it is a question of internal relations, or of external relationships."[23] Scale is, in sum, a matter of *relative quantity* and the dynamics that transpire between elements within and without the art object. *Quantitative difference,* deployed both within the body of the work of art and its disposition in space, is that which enacts the experience of scale.

That scale is such a relative principle and not the provenance of magnitude as such links a discussion of it fundamentally to minimalist sculpture and its critical reassessment in the art that followed.[24] For to consider a work of art in 1975 primarily through the terms of scale, as Shapiro does, is historically resonant. In part, this focus resulted from the manner in which the question of scale shifted radically for the minimalist sculpture that preceded Matta-Clark's work. Dramatized by the minimalist object's effacement of any hierarchizing or relational elements, scale was arrogated to external, rather than internal relations, and, by extension, to a viewing public.[25]

Scale issues were necessarily issues of beholding. In his canonical dismissal of minimalism, "Art and Objecthood," Michael Fried implicitly remarks upon the escalation of space within minimalism and the effects on its audience. He condemns "literalist work" on the grounds of its "theatricality"—the sense in which it "is concerned with the actual circumstances in which the beholder encounters the literalist work."[26] "The experience of being distanced from the work in question seems crucial," Fried notes, "for the beholder knows himself to stand in an indeterminate, open-ended—and unexacting relation as subject to the impassive objecthood on the wall or the floor."[27] What Fried addresses is the way that the object fundamentally shapes spectatorship itself as artistic experience, coordinated around the object's scale in relation to its surround.

Scale thus became something of a critical trope in the writing of that decade. "Scale is not just the extent of surface or mass," Judith Wechsler noted of its "elusive" quality, "it is also the interaction with space."[28] "The sculptor's sense of scale is particularly to be communicated as a sense of place," Lucy Lippard observed.[29] Museum exhibitions devoted themselves to the topic, as if "scale" was a formal attribute of the object, something to be grafted onto the work—a kind of mannerism or style.[30]

Nonetheless, if the particular scale of minimalist sculpture coordinated space for the viewing body, or coordinated the body in that space, it was the form of the thing—and its delineating cut or edge—that served to foreground that relation to its viewer. At once limning its surroundings and articulating its place within it, the contour of the minimalist work enacts a kind of cutting into space, implicitly addressed by two strains of minimalist criticism.[31] The first treats gestalt psychology in relation to art, and is organized around the figure-ground paradigm; the second shifts the terms of its critique to the phenomenological, emphasizing the contingency of the object in its environment.[32] Both are described in two consecutive accounts on sculpture by Robert Morris. In the first of these essays, "Notes on Sculpture, Part 1," dating from February 1966, he notes:

> Characteristic of a gestalt is that once it is established, all the information about it, qua gestalt, is exhausted. . . . Furthermore, once it is established, it does not disintegrate. One is then both free of the shape and bound to it.[33]

The apprehension of the work's gestalt is immediate in the minimalist object. The form of the object would seem to emboss itself clearly, definitively on its audience's perceptual horizon: once it is "got" by the viewer, he can also be "free" of it. Like a stamp on a piece of paper or, more pointedly, a figure impressed upon its ground, the edge or *the cut* of the minimal object secures the ontological givenness of the work and the space into which it is set.

Yet, for all the apparent stability of the gestalt position, the terms of minimalist criticism shifted rather quickly. In the second installation of "Notes on Sculpture," the primacy of the gestalt reading was undermined by the contingency of the embodied viewer now subjected to "various positions and under varying conditions of light and spatial context."[34] "Some of the best of the new work," Morris notes,

> being more open and neutral in terms of surface incident, is more sensitive to the varying contexts of space and light in which it exists. . . . In some sense it takes these two things into itself, as its variation is a function of their variation. Even its most patently unalterable property, shape, does not remain constant. For it is the viewer who changes the shape constantly by his change in position relative to the work.[35]

Hence, the traditional security of the subject/object, viewer/viewed relationship is thrown into radical doubt; and space, likewise, is considered less a transparent integument into which objects are universally deposited than a kind of elastic membrane, conditioned, shaped, and intertwined by and with bodily experience.

The phenomenology of Maurice Merleau-Ponty took on pronounced relevance to the art of this period, as his work served as a critical apparatus for historians, critics, and artists of minimalist art and of the sculpture that was shortly to follow.[36] From *The Phenomenology of Perception* to the posthumously published *Visible and the Invisible,* there was perhaps no other philosopher as rigorous and eloquent as Merleau-Ponty in his discussion of the chiasmatic relationship between objects and subjects within space. "The body [is] no longer conceived of as an object of the world," Merleau-Ponty notes, "but as our means of communication with it, to the world no longer conceived as a collection of determinate objects, but as the horizon latent in our experience and itself ever-present and anterior to every determining thought."[37]

The body, then, was a kind of phenomenal "tissue" for Merleau-Ponty, measuring the apparent perspectivism of objects it encountered in space, as it was measured by these objects in turn. Described as "the problem of the body," the circumnavigation of the perceiving subject in, around, and about the object shored

LIVERPOOL JOHN MOORES UNIVERSITY
LEARNING SERVICES

up the sense that the thing existed "in-itself," resistant to the singularizing perspective of a viewer. But this only led to the contradiction that this apparently independent thing might represent all perspectives at once, effectively dashing the notion of its apparent "objectness." Crucially, Merleau-Ponty drew upon the figure of the house in discussing this "structure of perception:"

> I see the next-door house from a certain angle, but it would be seen differently from the right bank of the Seine, or from the inside, or again from an aeroplane: the house itself is none of these appearances . . . But what do these words mean? Is not to see always to see from somewhere? To say that the house itself is seen from nowhere is surely to say that it is invisible! . . .
>
> . . . [T]he house itself is not the house seen from nowhere, but the house seen from everywhere. The completed object is translucent, being shot through from all sides by an infinite number of present scrutinies which intersect in its depths leaving nothing hidden.[38]

Thus the house opens up to "an infinite number of scrutinies" while also serving as the "spectator to the hidden aspects" to other objects that constitute the phenomenal field. "Seen from everywhere," the house becomes an object of "translucency," a cipher in Merleau-Ponty's rhetoric for a thing that makes legible spatio-temporal experience to its viewer.

The appeal of such thought for minimalist criticism is evident enough, narrating as it does the subject's mobility around the object as registering the contingent relation between subject and thing. How this relates to Matta-Clark's work and the violence ascribed to it may not seem so evident. The buildings' very profusion of cuts and vistas and scale would seem the stark antithesis of the primary structure: cool, linear, mute, rational. Yet such associations were not lost on Matta-Clark's contemporaries. As John Baldessari notes:

> This might sound strange, but he was both a Minimalist and a Surrealist . . . Gordon was a second-generation Minimalist in that some of the dissatisfaction and restlessness, not with the ideas but with the execution of Minimalist art, are evident in his work. He made

the transition between Minimalist concept and a kind of expressionist execution. You could say he was a messy Minimalist; he liked big rough edges.[39]

Susan Rothenberg similarly describes the experience of *Splitting* through a comparison to minimalism:

It showed more about volume than any Minimalist work—it had psychological and formal punch. Robert Morris' box piece made you walk around the edges of the room, but he forced you out of participation, while Gordon invited you into some very macabre participation.[40]

And when Matta-Clark voiced his admiration for his contemporaries, he singled out the figure of Sol LeWitt as "an artist he truly admired." Tellingly enough, he was drawn to LeWitt's "wonderful line."[41]

What is one to make of these statements, with their curious phrasings of "messy minimalist," "formal punch," "macabre participation"—statements riven with contradictions, tendering the refined and the aggressive all at once? To understand their implications, the question of Matta-Clark's own phenomenology arises, by fits and starts presaging the sublime.

MATTA-CLARK, PHENOMENOLOGIST?

"The eye lives in this texture of the visible and invisible as a man lives in his house."[42] When Merleau-Ponty penned "Eye and Mind," the last essay he saw published before his death in 1961, he offered a succinct revision to his earlier thinking on the "problem of the body" and the perspectivism of the house. Always embedded in the corporeality of one's body, the mechanics of vision are homologous to the inhabitation of the house by a subject. Architecture comes to represent the structure of incarnate subjectivity, the locus at which space and object and subject necessarily intertwine.

Following these formulations, it seems almost too convenient to claim that Matta-Clark's work functions by similar principles. The house would appear to be the connecting thread between the artist's interventions and the philosopher's interests, a space in which Matta-Clark proffers an acutely embodied experience of vision. For a demand is built into the encounter with Matta-Clark's art, the demand that the subject move about within it. Scaled up to the dimensions of architecture, the experience of the work reinforces Merleau-Ponty's larger conviction that vision is such an embodied, kinaesthetic experience.

The kinaesthetic—indeed, performative—dimension of Matta-Clark's production (and later reception) was explicitly acknowledged by both artist and peers. When Jackie Winsor spoke of the shared references between her own sculpture and Matta-Clark's, she emphasized the physicality of the work, which she likened to the movements of dancing, among Matta-Clark's favorite pastimes. In a beautiful passage, she recalls:

> The commonness was our shared sense of physicality. There was something I could trust about his physicality, how he physically related to objects in the universe. I got to know that a bit through dancing. He was my special dancing partner. I completely trusted him—he was one of the very few people in my life I could trust so thoroughly that way. He would throw me over his shoulder into all sorts of strange contortions—and I never once got hurt.
>
> He had a fine-tuned language and logic of the body and that fine physical sensibility, that comprehension in his body, was very evident in his work. When you cut a house in half to get a few inches between the parts, or you gymnastically tumble someone around safely, there is such a refined understanding of mass, weight and delicacy. There's an enormous amount of physical understanding necessary to be able to gently move mass just a little bit.[43]

Winsor is ostensibly speaking about Matta-Clark's production, but her comments reveal that reception is tantamount to the making of art. Considering his art through a memory of dancing, of a physically embodied intelligence, she emphasizes the quality of its movement and the roles of two parties in its formation. The artist leads the dance and the viewer completes it.

Thus Matta-Clark's art fulfills the minimalist proposition that the object necessarily implicates a movement around it, literally internalizing that movement. As Matta-Clark himself noted:

You have to walk—this is one of the big issues which I've brought up before: the difference between a kind of anecdotal piece—I don't know how you would classify it—and this sort of internal piece. There are certain kinds of pieces that can be summarized from a single view—at least characterized. And then there are other ones which interest me more, finally, which have a kind of internal complexity which doesn't allow for a single or overall view, which I think is a good thing. I like it for a number of reasons, one of which is that it does defy that category of a "snapshot" project or a sort of snapshot scenic work. The other thing is that it defies the whole object quality that is [implicit] with all sculpture, even with people who have escaped the so-called sculpture habit by going into some landscape or extra-gallery, extra-museum type of territorial situation.[44]

Given the imperative to walk through the work, the artist articulates his primary interest in a "sort of internal piece" which "doesn't allow for a single or overall view." An art that announces its resistance to a singularized viewing point, it revisits Merleau-Ponty's observation that the building is not so much the thing seen from nowhere, but the "thing seen from everywhere." The quality of "everywhereness" implicit in the experience of building cuts serves to elude the "snapshot" category of the traditional art object.

That Matta-Clark's work stages this kind of encounter does not logically square with the other model of its reception: its apparent "violence." Here, then, the phenomenological engagement with the art object merges with a peculiar reading of the sublime, principally Kant's second analytic in the *Critique of Judgment*.[45] I have noted the apparent contradiction that arises in pairing issues of phenomenology and sublimity and this contradiction will be preserved in what follows. For in returning to the problems of scale and the cut in the project *Circus* (also known as *The Caribbean Orange*), Matta-Clark's treatment of phenomenology prefigures a certain reading of the sublime: the question of an object in its presentation, the limits of experience itself.

MATTA-CLARK'S SUBLIME LIMIT

To speak of Matta-Clark's art in relation to the sublime is to step into a long, seemingly bankrupt art historical tradition, one that would attempt to apply Kantian aesthetics to necessarily art critical ends. While the roots of the sublime tradition are classical and appeal to the rhetorical arts, its commonplace associations are largely romantic and pictorial. But the images conjured by its uses within art history—towering peaks, belching volcanoes, icebergs, and other extravaganzas of nature—have done less to clarify the philosophical formulations of the sublime than to reproduce the worst order of romantic clichés. Here considerations of Matta-Clark's art as sublime are heuristic, as they lead to a closer analysis of the mechanics of his work.

Some preliminary notes, though, first on the sublime and then on its place in recent art historiography, are occasioned. Too often characterized as the affective condition of overblown landscapes and the power of nature, the sublime is described in banal superlatives, absolutes: the marvelous, the powerful, the overwhelming, the monstrous or terrifying. Yet in the *Critique of Judgment,* Kant is quite clear that the sublime cannot be adequated to the object of nature, nor art, nor the ontic at all for that matter: "We may describe the sublime thus: it is an object (of nature) the representation of which determines the mind to think the unattainability of nature regarded as the presentation of ideas."[46] The sublime is a question of the mind's struggle to grasp the supersensible—a question of presentation and, hence, representation.[47] It "may be regarded as quite formless or devoid of figure"[48] bringing about "a feeling of pain arising from the want of accordance between the aesthetical estimation of magnitude formed by the imagination and the estimation of the same formed by reason."[49]

The sublime, then, is not so much the province of aesthetics as of ethics, freedom, subjectivity—the relationship between reason and the imagination. For many readers of Kant, it constitutes a mode of deep reverence in the face of awesome phenomena, enabling the subject to bridge the gap between understanding (the faculty of natural philosophy) and reason (the faculty of ethics). But the sublime also stages questions of temporality: the extent to which one's experience of the sublime can be delimited as a matter of presentness, of the "Instant."[50] The question as to whether the sublime "is happening" underscores the extremity of its defamiliarization.

Philosophical subtleties of this nature were hardly taken up by art historical accounts of the sublime, however; but just as the work of Merleau-Ponty assumed an elevated status in discussions of sixties art, so, too, did the sublime figure prominently in the art criticism of postwar America.[51] Barnett Newman's "The Sublime is Now" (published December 1948) undoubtedly stands as the inaugural text, but this interpretation gave way to a different understanding by the late sixties and seventies.[52] Apart from some treatments of the "minimal sublime" and the "abstract sublime," it was now the category of earth work that became subject to a rather commonplace notion of sublimity, linking the forms of that work to "Bold, overhanging, and as it were threatening rocks; clouds piled up in the sky, moving with lightning flashes and thunder peals; [and] volcanoes in all their violence of destruction."[53] In sum, nature's *terribilitas* was claimed for the more dramatic and wrenching forms of earth work.[54]

Beyond such spectacular displays, the question of scale in land art also seemingly recommended it to the sublime. The notion that the sublime exceeded perceptual consciousness was commonly linked to the subject's placement in a monumental space—grand, overwhelming, and incommensurable in scope. Yet the reading of scale for earth works was often conflated with the notion of size, at best considering the *gigantism* of the art in comparison to the "puniness and mortality of humanity."[55] Some critics purported to think of "the scale of man" in its rapport with earth work, but the extent to which the art related to its site was largely ignored.

Where does Matta-Clark's work figure? Once again, Joel Shapiro's observations offer a partial clue, as they inadvertantly concatenate issues of scale, violence, and the sublime. Recalling his visit to *Day's End,* he remarks that it "was dangerous to the viewer. It was large; it had scale." He then adds, somewhat elliptically, "It wasn't like the earthworks of the same time."

While such claims are unspecific, the offhand distinction Shapiro draws between Matta-Clark's art and earth works points to the question of scale within the urban sphere. For Matta-Clark's work implicitly triangulates minimalism, land art, and urban space. Avoiding the trap of seeing scale as an immutable property of the work, as singular, absolute, and reducible, he remarked that "one of the things that intrigues me is the scale changes that come from the problems of doing a piece."[56] And when the notion of escalation entered into Matta-Clark's anarchitectural considerations, it was the change in scale of the urban surround that struck him. His peculiar fascination with the World Trade Center—two minimalist slabs—revolved partially around the buildings' "new scale and complexity": the way the buildings reshaped Lower Manhattan as an excessive verticality.[57] If Matta-Clark had been concerned with "nothing more complex than the limits of human scale," as he once acknowledged on a notecard, the terms of scale in the city had effectively transgressed those limits.

By extension, the artist's concerns with scale might be linked to the operations of the sublime. Holly Solomon's recollections of *Day's End* tacitly point to this. "I was afraid to cross the cut he made in the floor," she recalls; "I'm afraid of heights." Solomon's acrophobia confronts the question of scale and phenomenal space, in this instance, architectural space. For what is acrophobia if not a fearful reaction to a perceived *excess* of scale that occurs where the subject is least likely to consider scale's terms—at the ground upon which he or she stands? And doesn't acrophobia suggest a spatial contradiction of sorts: that the ground plan, a horizontal register, becomes subject to a terrifying escalation along its vertical axis?

When Matta-Clark cut a channel into the floor of *Day's End* (and other sites in which he cut into the ground) he effectively toyed with the scale of the work at the very place from which one makes determinations of scale. In opening up the floor to the sight of the water below (or to other floors of buildings, as he did in works such as *Circus, Conical Intersect, Office Baroque,* and *Splitting*), he revealed too many elements of the building and deprived his audience of any fixed point to relativize that space. The acrophobia that Solomon and many others experienced in Matta-Clark's work results partially from the body's seeming groundlessness in space, its dislocation. And what such an experience of scale enacts is a checking of the viewer's critical judgment, the degree of the subject's capacity to take cognitive measure of the proportion of things and the environmental surround.

Here Kant's notion of the "mathematical" sublime takes on pronounced relevance. Translating well to the problems of scale, it "begins with a question of quantity"[58] and then shades into questions of *relations* of quantity. Two mental operations are involved in this, apprehension and comprehension, respectively. Apprehension is the subject's capacity to take in sensory information, which "can go on *ad infinitum*"; comprehension is the ability to rationalize and make order of this influx of data. Standing in an inverse relationship to apprehension, comprehension produces an economy of spectatorship that might be condensed into the maxim "the more you see, the less you know."[59] Significantly, this economy is articulated through the terms of architecture. Paraphrasing M. Savary's 1787 *Lettres sur l'Egypte* to exemplify the analytic, Kant writes:

. . . we must keep from going very near the Pyramids just as much as we keep from going too far from them, in order to get the full emotional effect from their size. For if we are too far away, the parts to be apprehended (the stones lying one over the other) are only obscurely represented, and the representation of them produces no effect upon the aesthetical judgment of the subject. But if we are very near, the eye requires some time to complete the apprehension of the tiers from the bottom up to the apex, and then the first tiers are always partly forgotten before the imagination has taken in the last, and so the comprehension of them is never complete.[60]

The seemingly infinite number of stones that compose the pyramid sets the processes of apprehension into motion, and the mind virtually balks at the sheer boundlessness of it all. "The feeling of inadequacy of the imagination" is linked precisely to that bewilderment, the failure to rationalize the components by which a reading of scale is assessed.

Relative distance or proximity to the object further contributes to this sensibility, as confirmed by the experience within Matta-Clark's cuttings. When the viewer enters the building to be apprehended, a sublime contradiction underwrites the conditions of spectatorship. The beholder stands in such a close relation to the object and becomes so intimate with the inner workings of its space and its constitutive components, that the capacity to scale the building cut is rendered extremely difficult. What appears immediate, given over to sight as a visual excess, amounts to a kind of spectral blindness.

If the mathematical sublime is implicated in works such as *Day's End* through the question of scale, consider now the second formulation of the sublime—the "dynamical"—through the kinesis or temporality of the work, and, finally, the cut or the edge. "I think of it in terms of *time* as well as scale,"[61] Matta-Clark once offered with regard to a building cut, a remark that appeals strongly to the dynamical sublime. Kant notes that "the feeling of the sublime brings with it as its characteristic feature a *movement* of the mind bound up with the judging of the object."[62] That movement, he subsequently observes, is connected explicitly to the quality of its might or force, "that which is superior to great hindrances," or that which "must be represented as exciting fear."[63] Yet the dynamical sublime threatens, but by no means destroys its viewer, skirting the line between actual danger and imagined danger to the viewer.[64]

Such a reading can be applied to *Circus,* the last project Matta-Clark completed before his death in 1978. Produced at a site formerly adjacent to the Museum of Contemporary Art in Chicago, *Circus* was destroyed in the museum's expansion of the following year. It was Matta-Clark's only site project made specifically for a museum,[65] made possible by an invitation of the curator Judith Russi Kirshner. Worked on from January 17 to 27, *Circus* was staged in a three-story brownstone on East Ontario Street, whose cramped architecture "imposed a strict set of limitations on the form"[66] and dimensions of the artist's gesture (figure 3.10). Apart from these structural constraints, Booth, Nagle and Hartray, the architectural firm responsible for the museum's expansion, required that the brownstone's facade remain unscarred by cuts, and that no single rent exceed a width of twenty feet.[67]

The installation of *Circus* at the museum also forced Matta-Clark to confront obstacles that never occupied him when he produced his work illegally, particularly the insurance concerns that arose out of the fear that visitors to the exhibition might fall through the cuts in his work. Proper insurance for *Circus* was ultimately secured, though, and any potential danger to the viewers was largely undercut by the guidance offered by museum guards throughout the piece, conducted from January 28 to February 13. The artist noted that the project "was conceived for a safe visit by the public along the principal stairs and hallways up to the third floor," although Lawrence Weiner actually fell—fortunately unharmed—through a cut.[68] In spite of these logistical concerns, the general conditions for making the work were largely the same as any of his other cuttings. "The building is another one of those 'throw-aways,'" Matta-Clark observed, "a throwaway environment."[69]

The spatial disposition of *Circus* was perhaps the most complex of all of Matta-Clark's projects, although belied by the legibility of a section and plan of the work (figure 3.11). Likening the cutting to throwing a ball into space, he wrote: "the idea of the project is to generate a series of circular cuts . . . that become more energetically liberated as they take spherical shape along a diagonally ascending axis. These cuts dictate a progression of less enclosed to more open spaces as they break through

3.10 Gordon Matta-Clark, exterior view of site of *Circus* or *The Caribbean Orange,* 1978, 237 East Ontario Street, Museum of Contemporary Art, Chicago, IL.

Museum of Contemporary Art
SOURCERISTS UNLIMITED
SOURCERISTS UNLIMITED
SOURCERISTS UNLIMITED

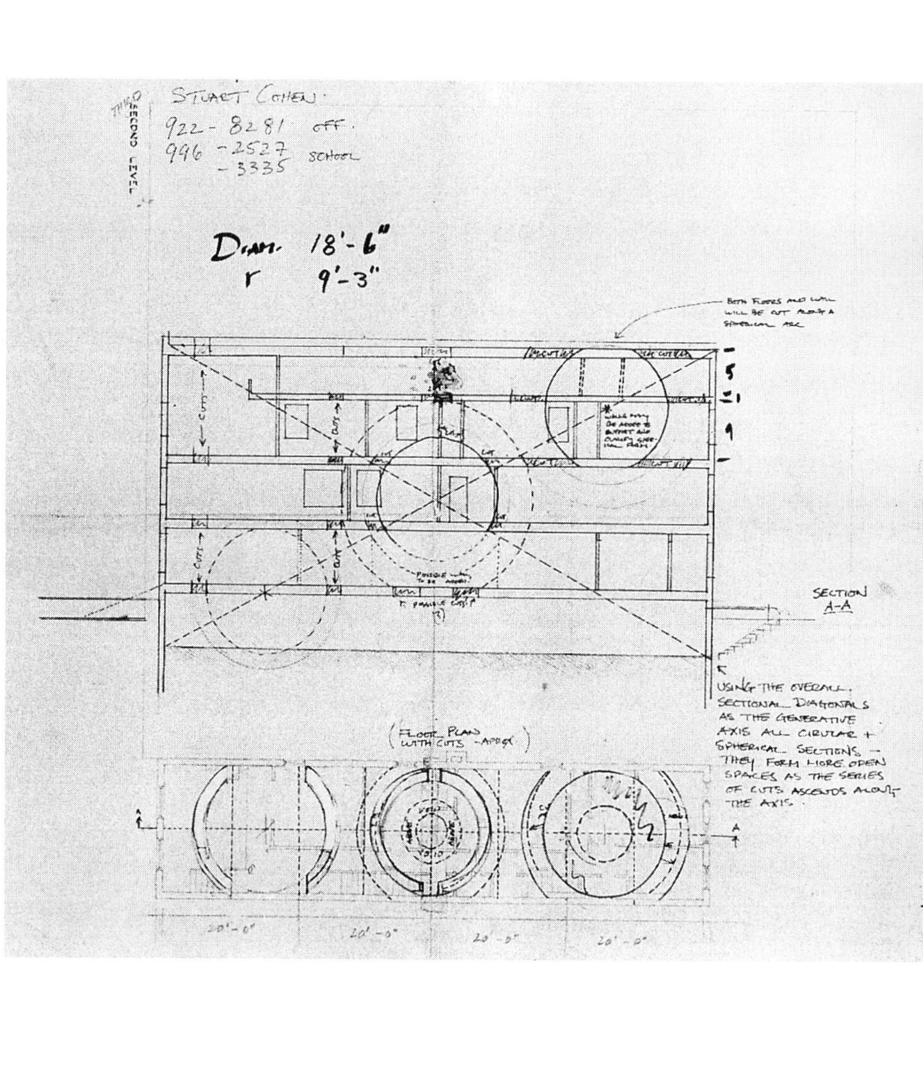
STUART COHEN.
922-8281 OFF.
996-2527
-3335 SCHOOL
THIRD
SECOND LEVEL
DIAM. 18'-6"
r 9'-3"
SECTION
A-A
USING THE OVERALL SECTIONAL DIAGONALS AS THE GENERATIVE AXIS ALL CIRCULAR + SPHERICAL SECTIONS - THEY FORM MORE OPEN SPACES AS THE SERIES OF CUTS ASCENDS ALONG THE AXIS.
(FLOOR PLAN WITH CUTS - APPROX)
20'-0"
20'-0"
20'-0"
20'-0"

the roof at the south end of the townhouse."[70] Upon entering, the first cuts one saw were large circular arcs removed from the first, second, and third floors of the building, which grew progressively incommensurable as one traversed the space and directed one's gaze upward (figures 3.12 and 3.13). The second floor contained a bowl-shaped room that mimicked the "Caribbean orange" of the work's alternate title—an orange cut along horizontal rather than vertical sections (figure 3.14). Then, as one approached the south end of the townhouse, one saw the base of a circle exposed to the famously bitter Chicago elements (figure 3.14), a fitting denouement to an increasingly destabilized treatment of place. Opening onto the frigid air, it positioned a horizontal ring against a skyline famous for its high-rises (figure 3.15).

The description offers some insight into the structure of the interior, but it remains disappointing as an ekphrastic exercise. Plan, section, elevation: these terms affirm a thinking toward place that is fixed, measurable, grounded in the ways that buildings are solid, massive, and volumetric. Doubtlessly, foregrounding such architectural vocabulary in describing Matta-Clark's work seems ironic, a point Judith Russi Kirshner takes up in her essay on the artist. Indebted to Yve-Alain Bois's reading of Richard Serra's site specificity (which theorizes his work through the picturesque and the sublime), Kirshner draws a parallel between Serra's sculpture and Matta-Clark's building cuts. She argues that both artists' works "are not reducible to plans, and depend on dislocation and the experience of the moving spectator."[71]

Kirshner's reference to Bois suggests a recurrent historiographic phenomenon. Bois's treatment of Serra considers the mathematical sublime at some length, underscoring the structural appropriateness of such models for the sculptural output of the period. Yet if both Serra and Matta-Clark reject the universalizing impulses of earlier minimalist readings, Matta-Clark's work proffers a destabilizing experience of place bound figuratively (and thematically) to the built environment.[72] I have suggested

3.11 Gordon Matta-Clark, section and plan of *Circus* or *The Caribbean Orange,* 1978, 237 East Ontario Street, Museum of Contemporary Art, Chicago, IL. Courtesy Gilbert Silverman.
3.12, 3.13, 3.14 (pages 146, 148, 150) Gordon Matta-Clark, *Circus* or *The Caribbean Orange,* 1978, 237 East Ontario Street, Museum of Contemporary Art, Chicago, IL.

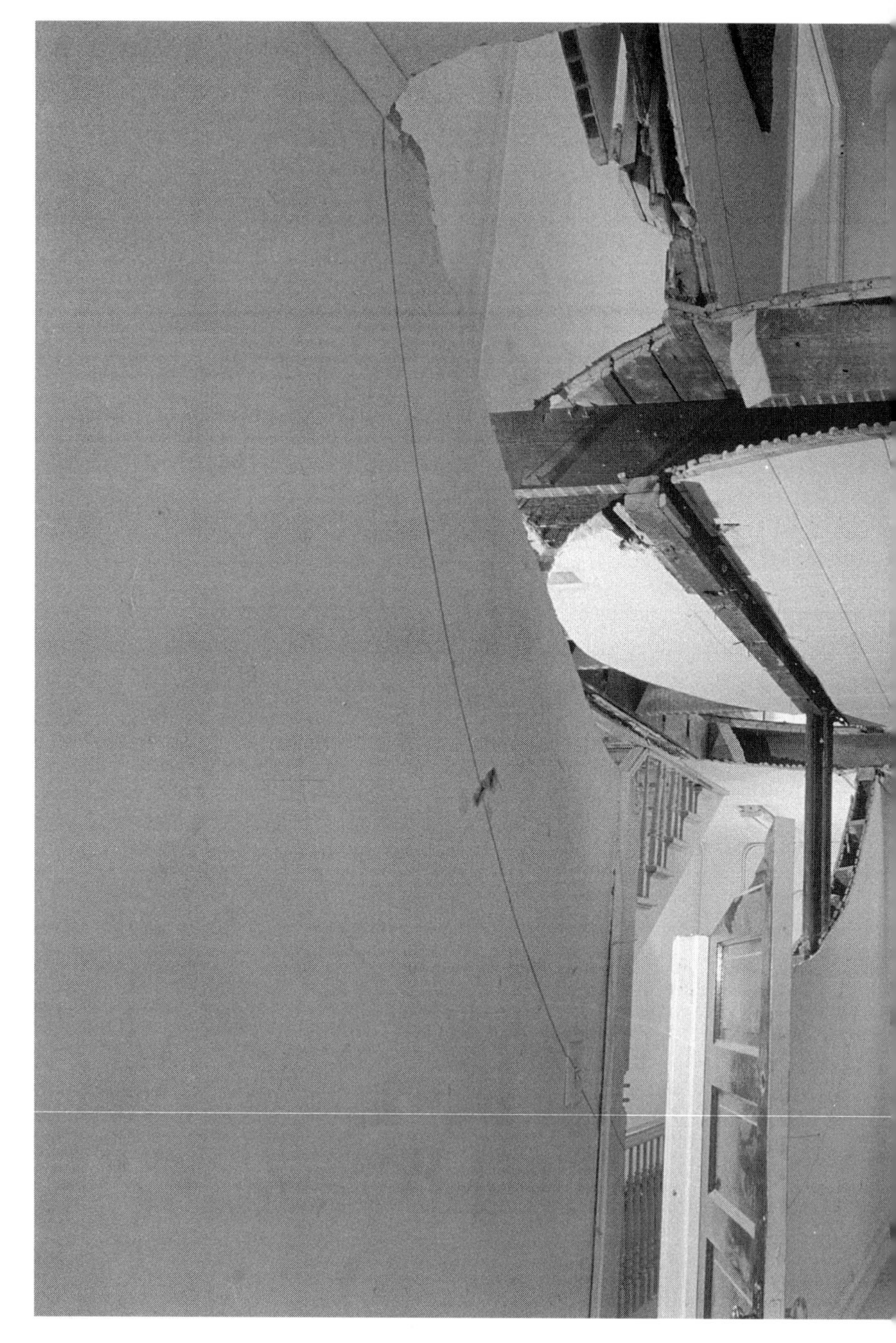

this experience appeals partially to the tenets of the "dynamical" sublime. Consider Matta-Clark's frankly inarticulate explanation of the title *Circus,* in which he reiterated the importance of moving through the piece:

> Everybody knows that circuses go south in the winter, right? So it's a winter circus. It's a circus because it sets a stage for people, sets a kind of stage from the ground up. Circus—basically the reason for "circus" in my own dyslexic manner means "circle" through which you operate. It means a circle in which you circle—a place of activity, a circle for action. And that's the way I understood this piece, that people were given a kind of circular stage to look at and circulate through.[73]

Circus, to follow Matta-Clark's puns and odd locutions, was not only a place where people looked through and at things, or a place where people were themselves viewed. It staged no less than the *circulation* of its audience in one of Matta-Clark's most ambulatory spaces.[74] As Matta-Clark observed:

> I think that they [the projects] are all different versions of some kind of preoccupation with a dynamic. The thing I would really like to express is the idea of transforming the static, enclosed condition of architecture on a very mundane level into this kind of architecture which incorporates . . . this sort of animated geometry or this animated, tenuous relationship between void and surface . . . [It] implies a kind of kinetic, internal dynamism of some sort.[75]

The peculiar disposition of architecture has long been described through the rhetoric of dynamism. The tumbling carriages of staircases, the ascension of ceilings and arches, the march of halls and corridors all contribute to the sense of a building's movement and recession in space. But Matta-Clark was speaking about two extremely different classes of dynamism in his building cuts, the first of which

3.15 Gordon Matta-Clark, *Circus* or *The Caribbean Orange,* 1978, 237 East Ontario Street, Museum of Contemporary Art, Chicago, IL.

offers a dramatic take on what happens to the spectator as he or she enters into the work:

When confronted with real time, with the real mysteries of time, there's a kind of central nervous spasm that takes place . . . which just amounts to a sort of all-consuming gag, an all-consuming quake . . . which you . . . can't understand.[76]

This kind of dynamism, experienced through the "confrontation with real time," is not that of the subject strolling casually, easily, through phenomenological space. We are far away from the free plan here; if anything, we have now given way to a free fall. For the artist characterized the movement through his work as the most embodied of dynamics, so much so that the viewer "can't understand" the experience. The litany of reactions invoked by Matta-Clark—quake, gag, spasm—are bodily impulses that arise from the subject's mental negotiation with real time and space, corresponding to the subject's literal passage within the building. Alternately halting and kinetic, it suggests a virtual seizure of the subject consumed by a violent force. The almost schizophrenic character of this encounter can be related generally to Kant's formulation of the dynamical sublime. The *time* of the object, at once "all consuming" and yet "gagging," begs the temporal integration or coherence of the viewer's experience.

But it is ultimately the cuts themselves that animate a broader notion of a dynamical sensibility. Described as one of the most terrifying elements of the work (aside from the building's scale), they engender the strange contradiction of the work's translucency on the one hand (the result of being able to look through the inner structure of the building) and the utter illegibility of the building on the other (figures 3.16 and 3.17). If, to revisit Merleau-Ponty's formulation, "the completed object is translucent, being shot through from all sides by an infinite number of present scrutinies . . . leaving nothing hidden," Matta-Clark overturns this principle by fulfilling it.

3.16 Gordon Matta-Clark, *Circus* or *The Caribbean Orange*, 1978, 237 East Ontario Street, Museum of Contemporary Art, Chicago, IL.

A closer analysis of the bowl-shaped chamber on the second floor of *Circus* supports this. Here, in literally cutting out a semi-circular shape from the room's former rectilinear configuration, the artist deprives one not only of the perpendicular axes by which architectural space is commonly regularized, but also the conventional disposition of one's body within it. Taking its place, a white ovoid form like a hollowed out egg shell offers a vivid contrast to the sharply cut circular rupture that swirls around its base. Yet Matta-Clark has all but confused the values of positive and negative space in this instance, of figure and ground; for here, the cut, traditionally read as a void, overwhelms the structure placed before us; whereas what is ontically present and visible (the room) is imparted with a recessional character, emphasized further by being steeped in shadow. Limned on all sides by a virtual blankness, and punctuated by twin doors at its only right angle, the room appears to be an island marooned in a sea of absence. The result is that the cuts that define the centrality of that space—which gives it is peculiar form—are the very elements that threaten to swallow it up.

Matta-Clark's exposure of the joists and the floor complex further reveals how the cut performs a two-fold operation, consolidating and defining form at the same time as it undoes it. The appearance of structural elements logically reassures the spectator of the security of the floor upon which he or she stands, but it also contributes to a protracted vertigo, another bodily experience conditioned by a halting and spasmodic movement—a sense of the body falling-in-place. Still, the vertiginous experience of the building is contradicted by the multiple purposes that the cut serves. If the cut produced a terrifying rift in the second-story floor, it also opened up the space of the room below, producing a desire to look up through it as an ascending feature of the architecture. A cut that once functioned at the level of its plan simultaneously impacted upon its section, perceptually disturbing the fixed axiality of the building's construction. One paradox unleashed by the placement of the cuts is that negative space appears to collide with negative space.

Attempting to articulate this phenomenon in his work, Matta-Clark offered: "I don't know if you read the negative space . . ."[77] The artist's declaration that one *does*

3.17 Gordon Matta-Clark, *Circus* or *The Caribbean Orange*, 1978, 237 East Ontario Street, Museum of Contemporary Art, Chicago, IL.

not read the negative space as its own property, that is, the space produced by the motion of the cut, confirms the most sublime characteristic of the gesture: that it denies the complete legibility of the thing into which it cuts as it denies its own capacity to be read (figure 3.18). He noted this peculiar aspect as he watched people ambulate throughout *Circus:* "Someone said something the other night that I thought was really interesting, he said 'you're using people as figure-figure instead of figure-ground.'"[78]

Figure-figure versus figure-ground. Matta-Clark's interlocuter tacitly underscores the importance of the audience in his work, whose members serve as elements within its "composition." Described as figure-figure instead of figure-ground, the "composition" is rhetorically vested with an allover character as if background, middleground, and foreground resist parting ways. Likewise, the clarity or legibility of spatial relationships is refused, the result of an apparent surfeit of movement and people within the space. And insofar as the people within the building provide an excess of figuration, so, too, might the claim be universalized for the experience of the work as a whole. It is not simply the presence of viewers that endows *Circus* with the quality of figure-figure but the proliferation of all of its figuring elements, which the gesture of the cut unleashes.

The relationship figure-figure versus figure-ground might be understood to recode earlier treatments of minimalism and architectural contextualism, particularly the gestaltist foundations informing those models. In sum, if the figure-ground paradigm was respectively analogized to the minimalist object's placement on a site, or a building type to its context within discourses on urbanism, the figure-figure relation spoke to the fundamental dislocation of both. And it is the cut that performs this dislocation as such an undecidable thing, neither figure nor ground nor one thing nor the other, but both, and at the same time. The cut recalls for us what Jean-Luc Nancy wrote of the sublime in a wholly different context: "In the sublime, it is a question of the figure of the ground, of the figure that the ground cuts, but precisely insofar as

3.18 Gordon Matta-Clark, *Circus* or *The Caribbean Orange,* interior details, 1978, 237 East Ontario Street, Museum of Contemporary Art, Chicago, IL.

the ground cannot constitute a figure . . . It does not constitute an infinite figure or image but the movement of cutting, delineation and seizure."[79]

The sublime, then, excessively figures the operations of Matta-Clark's cutting as groundless. Where this leads us in relation to its phenomenological dimension suggests much about Matta-Clark's critique of spatial experience.

CONTINGENCY AS EXCESS

An odd chiasma rests at the heart of Matta-Clark's "phenomenology of the sublime." On the one hand, treating his art through phenomenological terms renders these most destabilizing spaces into phenomenal objects. At the same time, however, the reading of the sublime offered here might be understood as the most radical attenuation of phenomenology—a virtual subversion of its principles that, paradoxically, occurs through their very fulfillment. For what else is Matta-Clark's art if not an engagement with space that indefinitely exposes its alloverness; that foregrounds its dimensionality; that throws into relief the perspectivism of the building as it sees, and is seen, by the viewer coursing throughout it; and that implicates the communicative and sensorial function of the body in that body's destabilization, vertigo, and even ascension? Are these not the same considerations by which Merleau-Ponty made claims for the *everywhereness* of architectural space?

The point at which the phenomenological shades into the sublime is, indeed, a matter of dimensionality, or, to put it in another vein, a degree of contingency. The acknowledgment of contingency within minimalism (or contextualism for that matter,) allowed one to relativize the relationship between subject and work, a relationship that was always subject to factors external to the art object or architecture, site-specific and irreducible to a singular spatial experience. But if Fried saw minimalism as itself theatrical, Matta-Clark's projects "theatricalize" minimalist contingency. They push the terms of theatricality to their logical extreme. They foreground the sense that contingency is *a priori* about a certain mode of cognitive excess, which cannot be totalized because it is endlessly conditional. They reveal that our experience as contingent beings guarantees that we are always already subjected to a state of perpetual vertigo.

Matta-Clark's building cuts thus unleash what is deeply repressed within the minimalist formulation of contingency: the cognitive failure to grasp fully an object in phenomenal space, and, by turns, the failure of a universalized phenomenological subject who would attempt to grasp it. In all of these respects, Hal Foster's discussion of the "crux" of minimalism is especially helpful in assessing Matta-Clark's art. In an essay that reads Michael Fried's "Art and Objecthood" with an acute sensitivity to its rhetorical shifts, Foster's argument rests on the ambivalence implicit to the reception of minimalist art as both the apotheosis of the modernist project in its formal reductiveness, and the inception of a viewing subject engendered as postmodern because no longer held as autonomous.[80] "Minimalism appears as a historical crux in which the formalist autonomy of art is at once achieved and broken up," Foster writes.[81] The tension that he identifies in Fried's condemnation of minimalism suggests that the minimalist work oscillates between a reading that is at once secure in its objecthood and perpetually dislocated along with its viewing subject.

The perceptual turning of Foster's argument bears marked implications for Matta-Clark's work. In the excess of contingent factors his art lays bare, it gives the lie to the phenomenological body, suggesting that the subject's intertwining with space is an actual shattering. But shattered along with it is the category of experience, structurally and thematically linked to architecture. For the building cuts broach the contingency of alienated space as always illegible, temporally riven. What Matta-Clark's critics mistook as his violence, then, is no less than a critique of the transparency of spatial experience. The political stakes of that lost space—as well as the communities left in its wake—are taken up with some urgency in Matta-Clark's projects in France.

4 ON THE HOLES OF HISTORY

If the person encountering the building cuts is phenomenologically "disintegrated"—traversed by contingency, overwhelmed by a surfeit of perceptual cues, and unmoored from the apparent givenness of architectural space—what might the work suggest about its production of spectatorship in general, its attitude toward the *community* of viewers that is often its local audience? What is one to make about the condition of the viewer's agency—the faith placed in a subject who acts conscientiously and autonomously? Do Matta-Clark's works sustain any political logic, embrace a political program? Or does his art engage a nihilism elevated to the ranks of art?

In work Matta-Clark produced in Paris in 1975 and 1977, a partial response is granted to these questions, tempered by a reading of nihilism described as "revolutionary"—Walter Benjamin's acutely politicized formulation of the term. Indeed, this chapter accepts as a given that community was fundamental to Matta-Clark's larger project: his commitment to the reclamation of social space, held against its alienation as property, has been discussed. But there is more than one model of community at play in Matta-Clark's work. The major site project *Conical Intersect* (1975) and a group of works that engaged with subterranean Paris undo the received knowledge about much site-specific art of the seventies, namely, its insistence upon the coherence of local communities in its reception, linked to the commonality of the work's place. On the contrary: the very dissipation of communities and the demolition of site served as the generating principles of much of Matta-Clark's work, and were its objects of critique. And to such ends, the form of the hole played a significant part.

"THE COMMUNITY OF THOSE WHO DO NOT HAVE A COMMUNITY"

How to define a community with nothing in common, with no shared experience or place? A community, to borrow Georges Bataille's words, "of those who do not have a community?" The history of *Conical Intersect* might tell us a great deal about the instability of the communal place and the ontological insecurity of its "audience." Opening up to an acutely local history, *Conical Intersect* presents a paradox for site-specific art. It recalls the history of that place, as it thematizes the limited communicability of *all* sites within the space of the city. Parallel to this, it dramatizes situations where ostensible communities are recognized as dispersed, powerless, outmoded—the terms of what might be called a "workless" community, a community whose commonality rests on its virtual loss rather than essential, shared identities.[1] It is a notion of community that seems acutely modern in its formulation.[2]

Such thinking, however, would seem fundamentally at odds with much criticism on public art and site-specific sculpture generated in the seventies, not to mention with some of Matta-Clark's projects themselves. For pervasive throughout these readings was a generalized notion of art's relationship to the public sphere, in which the work of art was to satisfy or express social consensus, rather than loss or lived differences. "What is needed," Lucy Lippard noted,

> is . . . an art that has to some extent originated in response to a broad audience or to a section, a community, of that audience—an art that rises up from the experience of the people . . . If public art is indeed to be public, if it is to fulfill the social needs of a specific environment . . . it must be able to engage at least a portion of its audience at the core of its own experience. The art must relate to the space in which it is located . . . in terms of the ambience, the spirit, the significance of that space for its residents.[3]

Typical of many accounts of the period, this rhetoric is informed by two basic premises about the *experience* of the work. At the level of individual reception, it assumes a subject who has an unmediated relationship to the object/site: a coherent site that might engage its audience "at the core of its own experience." In terms of the object, the language maintains a faith in quantifiable social interactions between public art and its community of viewers—the notion of the social "work" site-specific art might perform.

Clearly, Matta-Clark's own stance on community was fundamentally less arcane than what will be proposed in this discussion, although it does not disqualify its premises. In the most quotidian sense, the artist's notion of community translated into his much vaunted sociability, his love of entertaining and group dancing (personal accounts point repeatedly to a rather Dionysian character), and the gleeful sense of play he brought to projects staged at 112 Greene Street and Food, his Anarchitectural projects, and his early work with buildings. In short, if the destruction of the city was a principal concern for the artist, its non-productive use as art was also *la fête,* to borrow Lefebvre's phrase. His work, however serious, could also be seriously funny, absurd in its deep affection for trash and urban dejecta, things moldering, homely, and entropic. The critical motivations of his work did not mitigate their humorous qualities.

Even more important, the artist posed a larger sense of community against the alienation of modern housing his work assailed. For Matta-Clark, the participatory, social, and inclusive ritual of art making was understood as a democratic solution to the "state of isolationism" engendered by urban and suburban space. Graffiti represented an important means to address such concerns. Deeply utopian in spirit, such was the partial motivation for the work *Graffiti Truck* (figure 4.1) displayed in 1973 at an exhibition Matta-Clark organized titled *Alternatives to the Washington Square Art Fair.*[4] With this work, the artist invited residents from the South Bronx to spray-paint his truck, curiously named "Herman Meydag," with brilliant colors and baroque tag lines. (Subsequently, he would cut discrete "paintings" out of the truck with an acetelyne torch.) A related series of pictures from the same year, *Photoglyphs,* appealed also to the belief that the practice of art should be inclusive. Image after image of graffitied subway carriage (figure 4.2) suggested that the trains were not so much vandalized as they were artistically reclaimed, a challenge to city property alleged to be public. What some regarded as a gesture of defacement was for Matta-Clark an act of deeply social consequences, a protest against contemporary models of urbanism and notions of public and private space.

It was with two unrealized projects in particular that Matta-Clark demonstrated a communal ethos in keeping with a more conventional strain of social ac-

4.1 Gordon Matta-Clark, *Graffiti Truck,* 1973.

4.2 Gordon Matta-Clark, *Photoglyph,* 1973.

NATURAL
HIG

BRIGHTON BEACH
D 6th AVE
EXPRESS
KOOL

tivism. The most pressing example of this was the planned *Resource Center and Environmental Youth Program for Loisaida* (1977) (figure 4.3). Awarded a Guggenheim grant in 1977, Matta-Clark, Jene Highstein, Suzanne Harris, Fraser Sinclair, and others hoped to organize a community based project in a Lower East Side neighborhood of Manhattan.[5] "Throughout the Lower East Side," Matta-Clark wrote in a draft of the proposal,

> large amounts of reusable materials have become available because of the increasing rate of abandonment and demolition of buildings. This is a trend that will only continue as housing programs continue to be neglected and funding denied. On the Lower East Side there is a network of community groups and individuals engaged in open space and rehab projects, sweat equity, community gardens, playlots, cultural events, alternative living structures, etc. Loisaida has brought these groups together to share aims, problems and resources.[6]

The idea for the center, based loosely on other Sweat Equity programs in Manhattan, was to secure a building in which "donated and salvaged materials . . . could be stored for future use or resale."[7] A complimentary job training program would have local youths learn to run the organization as well as rehabilitate abandoned buildings in their own neighborhood for occupancy.[8]

This utopia of a place never came to fruition: Matta-Clark's death the following year effectively arrested the enthusiasm of its other participants. However, another proposed work, *Arc de Triomphe for Workers,* failed to be realized for reasons that suggest the frailty of projects based around traditional notions of community identity, particularly when they are conjoined with the terms of a unique site. In November 1975, Matta-Clark traveled to Milan at the invitation of the art dealer Salvatore Ala, where he produced an untitled wall cutting in the space of Ala's gallery. During the trip, he also sought an abandoned building to produce a larger cut, and came across an outmoded factory at Sesto San Giovanni, an industrial neighborhood in the

4.3 Gordon Matta-Clark, site for *Resource Center and Environmental Youth Program for Loisaida,* 1977, Lower East Side, Manhattan, NY.

city. The factory had been occupied by young members of the local Communist Party, and Matta-Clark proposed to cut an arch in the building to monumentalize their plight. "They had been taking turns holding down a section of the plant for over a month," Matta-Clark wrote. "[T]heir program was to resist the intervention of 'laissez-faire' real estate developers from exploiting the property. Their proposal was that the area be used for a much needed community services center."[9] Gerry Hovagimyan, who assisted Matta-Clark in a number of major building cuts, recalls the aborted outcome of the project. "Somehow," he remembers, "the authorities got wind of what he was going to do, and a day before the cutting, they went in on a trumped-up drug bust and chased everybody out."[10]

Well-intentioned as his gesture may have been, Matta-Clark's political aspirations for the group inadvertantly contributed to the dispersal of the squatters. Using art to champion a political cause in this instance could only lead to its failure, precisely because Matta-Clark would have made visible, that is to say, objectified, a community that had otherwise functioned without such dramatic exhortation. The attempt to establish a site for the communists did not simply have the effect of exposing their activities to the local authorities: it would also have secured the group's identity through a conservative reading of the monument, an idea of place that could perpetuate the values of a singular community in visual form. Instead, the notion of giving permanent expression to a political community worked against the conceptual foundation of Matta-Clark's other building cuts, to say little of his anarchitectural attitudes in general. For at the heart of his critique was the very insecurity of the built environment, a condition wrought by modernist notions of planning.

My comments on the proposed *Arc de Triomphe for Workers* do not seek to invalidate Matta-Clark's communitarian aspirations by any means. But there is a powerful, dialectical alternative to the treatment of community in Matta-Clark's work. Graver and more melancholic in its tone, it is considered through the notion of its "worklessness," attesting to the struggle in defining the terms of community through the historical conditions of urban space and its disappearance.

TELESCOPING PROGRESS

Perhaps no project articulates this idea as forcefully as *Conical Intersect* (figure 4.4), also known as *Etant d'art pour locataire.* Its history begins simply enough. In February 1975, Matta-Clark was invited to participate in the ninth Paris Biennale by Georges Boudaille, General Delegate of the Paris Biennale, and Jean Hubert-Martin, curator for the Musée national d'art moderne.[11] In September of that year, only a month after the opening of *Day's End,* Matta-Clark traveled to Paris to produce *Conical Intersect* on site at the Plateau Beaubourg. Connecting two seventeenth-century buildings with a spiraling, cone-like cut visible from the street, the work was described by the artist as "a wonder of good luck and timing," conceived when he "first heard of plans to build the Centre Pompidou as a hub of contemporary culture."[12]

In the earliest stage of its conception, Matta-Clark envisioned a somewhat different contribution to the Biennale: the on-site cutting of the Centre Georges Pompidou itself, still under construction at that time.[13] His original plan was to "inscribe through the walls and floors and ceiling of the exhibition space a series of one inch wide lines leaving long slivers of liberated space."[14] It soon became clear that this was not feasible, however, as letters to the organizers in the following month simply called for the conversion of "an abandoned structure slated for demolition into a work."[15] Matta-Clark was granted the use of two houses adjacent to the museum, close to Les Halles, the historic market district in the First Arrondisement. The location was fortuitous. "The site at 27–29 rue Beaubourg," Matta-Clark recalled, "was two modest town houses built in 1699 for Mr. and Mrs. Leisevilles as what appeared to be 'his or her' domiciles. These buildings were among the last left standing in the plan of modernizing the Les Halles-Plateau Beaubourg district."[16]

The area, a seven-and-a-half-acre expanse which had been cleared of old housing in the 1930s, was used as a crude parking lot for the delivery trucks that serviced the marketplace a few hundred yards to the west. But by 1975, the Plateau Beaubourg and the entirety of the Les Halles section of Paris had been subject to a massive reconstruction project inaugurated some twenty-two years earlier—a "Gaullist clearing," in Matta-Clark's words. The old parking lot was now sited as the future home of the Centre Georges Pompidou, the multiple use "cultural center" whose construc-

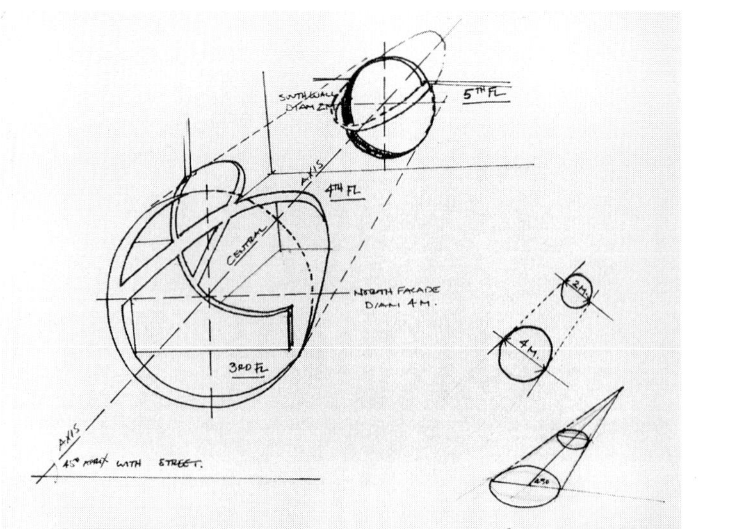
SOUTH WALL
DIAM 2M
5TH FL
AXIS
4TH FL
CENTRAL
NORTH FACADE
DIAM 4M.
3RD FL
AXIS
45° MAX WITH STREET.
2M.
4M.
SCHEMATIC FOR CONICLE INTERSECT

tion was as controversial as the vast demolition of the area that came before it. Thus, while Matta-Clark's work on the two houses in particular was largely incidental—made possible under the auspices of the Société d'économie mixte d'aménagement, de rénovation et de restauration du secteur des Halles (SEMAH)—he was certainly aware of how charged a site it was, perhaps *the* most appropriate backdrop for his building cuts. More than any of his other works, the Parisian site neatly illustrated the tension between narratives of historical progress—embodied in the construction of the Centre Pompidou—and the destruction of historical site that is a prerequisite for progress.[17]

A schematic drawing attests to this logic (figure 4.5). Within the two buildings themselves, a virtual knot of cut circles appeared to torque around an invisible thread, traveling up and through the twin houses as it grew smaller in diameter. Measuring twelve feet in wide, the center of the major cut on the building's north facade coincided roughly with the mid-point between the third and fourth floors. The hole was intersected at several points by other semi-circular incisions (figure 4.6), forming a more frenetic series of arcs that could be seen by looking up into the space of the building. Generated largely with hammers, chisels, and bow saws (apparently, very few electrical tools were used), the cuts were positioned from wall to floor to ceiling, not unlike the structure of honeycomb (figure 4.7). The normal coordinates of architectural orientation were interrupted to such a degree that a sense of vertigo was produced for the observer inside the building.

While the confusion of architectural orientation was pronounced enough at a phenomenal level, Gerry Hovagimyan remembers that this implied cone-like was in-

4.4 Gordon Matta-Clark, *Conical Intersect,* 1975, 27–29 rue Beaubourg, Paris, with Centre Georges Pompidou (under construction) in background.

4.5 Gordon Matta-Clark, schematic drawing for *Conical Intersect,* 1975. Private collection, Antwerp.

4.6 (page 172) Gordon Matta-Clark, *Conical Intersect,* 1975, 27–29 rue Beaubourg, Paris.

4.7 (page 174) Gordon Matta-Clark, *Conical Intersect,* 1975, 27–29 rue Beaubourg, Paris, in process.

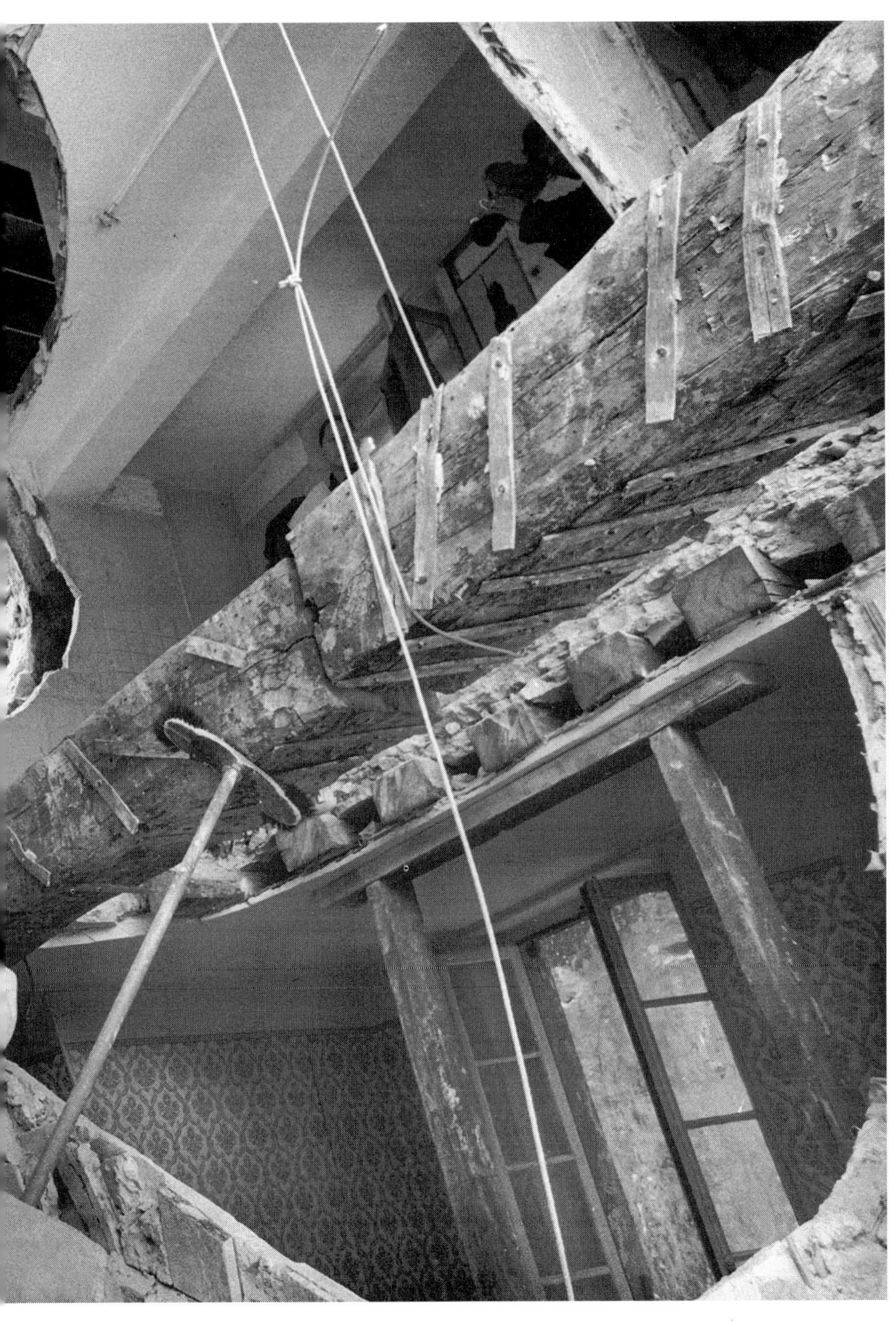

debted to Anthony McCall's film *Line Describing a Cone.*[18] "The film began with a dot of light," he notes, "the throw of the projector gradually made a cone of light in the room."[19] This cone of light, a non-material form, apparently generated the idea for the spiraling cut in *Conical Intersect.* In both McCall's film and Matta-Clark's building, a reference to optics—a cone of vision—is shaped by a literalized absence.[20] Like earlier projects in which visual tropes metaphorized the limitations of sight itself (as in the *Threshole* series, in which a perspectival "window" careens into a certain illegibility), Matta-Clark's opening up of this space did little to grant its viewers any stable sense of the object.

Along similar lines, one of the opening sequences of the documentary film of *Conical Intersect* is a view of the north wall of 29 rue Beaubourg (figure 4.8). With the camera tightly focused on its darkened facade, a small hole, seemingly no bigger than a pin prick at first, appears to bore its way spontaneously through the surface from the other side of the wall. The hole is of a deeper color than the wall itself, and as it expands in circumference, its blackness, rimmed by the white of the inner walls at which it progressively eats away, threatens to subsume the wall against which it is set. Several frames later, the hole begins to disgorge plaster and architectural rubble with only passing evidence of the hand responsible for the process. Seen in this light, the hole is not simply a central motif of the film, but precisely what structures and organizes its narrative.

What might this hole, this growing blackness, imply beyond a formal reading of the documentary sequence? Consider the place of the hole in the building. However complex the cutting may have been inside the apartments, it is unquestionable that most people observed the holes of *Conical Intersect* at street level. Matta-Clark and Hovagimyan were permitted to work at the site from September 24 to October 10, but French officers directed by SEMAH quickly escorted them out of the building the day it was completed. The building's entrance was boarded up shortly afterward, so that access to the site became extremely difficult. This did not deter a quasi-opening from happening, however, as the artist later broke through the barrier

4.8 Gordon Matta-Clark, still from film of *Conical Intersect,* 1975, 18 minutes, 16mm, color film.

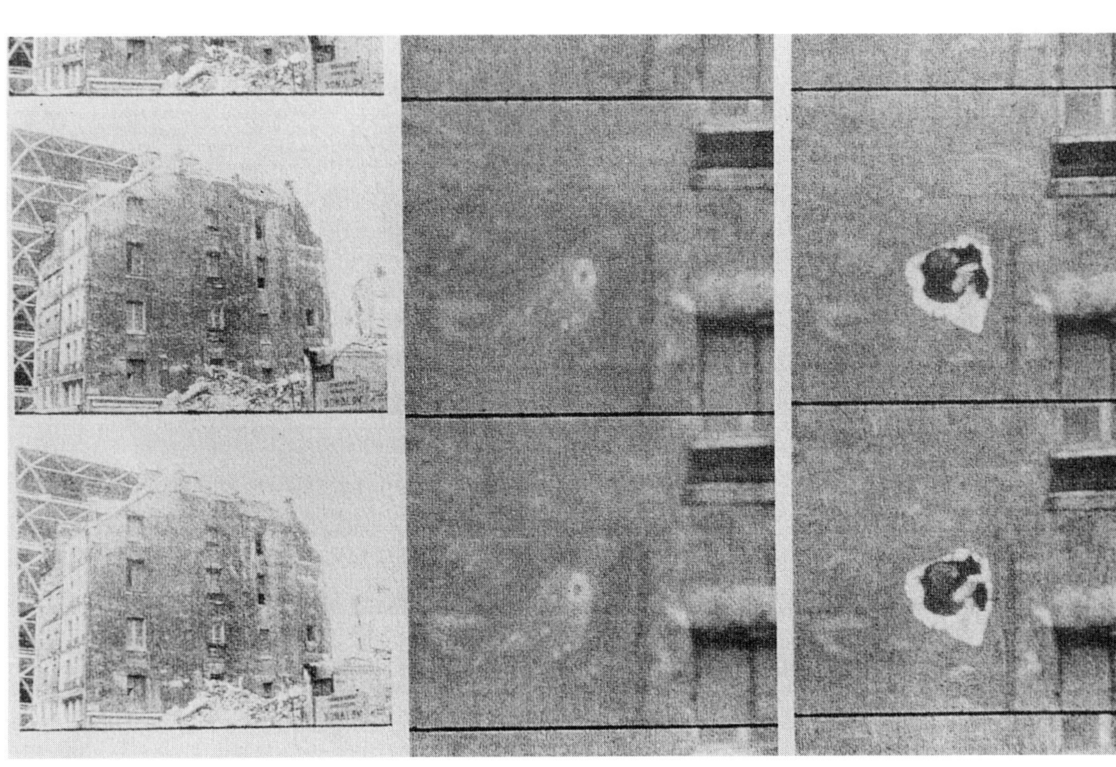

allowing limited access to the site. Finally, a performance of a type was staged at the future site of the museum's fountain, a performance most likely not construed as such by its audience. Titled *Cuisse de Boeuf,* it saw the artist roasting nearly 750 pounds of beef, which he made into sandwiches and distributed freely to the public. The gesture may have been inspired by the famous *abbatoirs* of the historic Les Halles, but it also clearly related to earlier performances in which food was served as a kind of primitive communion ritual.

As Thomas Crow has forcefully argued, the literal accessibility of Matta-Clark's cuttings is by no means incidental to the work, but tantamount to its first principle. Clearly, there were precedents for this concern. In projects such as *Fake Estates,* Anarchitecture, and the artist's interest in voyeurism and suburban "isolationism," Matta-Clark focused on alienated space—space rendered inaccessible—through the dictates of real estate and property lines. Following this trajectory, *Conical Intersect* obliquely questioned the pretensions of site-specific art to engage a local audience.[21] For what does it mean to stage an art work in the midst of the city, a work to which few have bodily access, or of which they may have little understanding? No doubt the work was highly "public" in a banal sense: the placement of the cone-like form on a wall exposed to the street, together with its siting in Les Halles, guaranteed its high visibility. Situated at the rue Beaubourg, "a very important north-south axis"[22] of Paris, it was seen from the outside by thousands of Parisians during its relatively short existence.

But *Conical Intersect* was not necessarily understandable for being so visible. In spite of its optical references and its seeming legibility to a broader public, its reception amounted to a type of blindness nonetheless. Doubtlessly a function of this was its enormous hole. "As you walked or drove down the street," Jean-Hubert Martin said, "the first thing you saw was this enormous circle of a hole in a building. People noticed it and talked about it on the street. It was a hole; people didn't know that it was an art work."[23] The film *Conical Intersect* documents this phenomenon, opening with a shot taken from a moving car. The camera lingers briefly over the deep black-

4.9 Gordon Matta-Clark, still from film of *Conical Intersect,* 1975, 18 minutes, 16mm, color film.

ness of the hole before panning over the Beaubourg's wiry facade directly behind it (figure 4.9), a looming, net-like structure that appears to ensnare the far smaller building adjacent to it. The effect is literally arresting. Groups of pedestrians are seen scratching their heads while staring up at the buildings. Shielding their eyes from the sun, they point to the mysterious form, seemingly uncertain as to its purpose or its source. And when Matta-Clark's work was demolished, it attracted a similarly perplexed audience (figure 4.10).

The hole of *Conical Intersect* did generate considerable confusion. Some of the speculation on the work was vaguely anti-American, or, at the very least, regarded the artist as psychologically unbalanced. "There were two main schools of thought at first," Matta-Clark reported to the *International Herald Tribune.* "One was that I'm just another American *fou*—or, say, a CIA man, looking over a potential site . . . and masquerading as an American *fou.* Another was that I was looking for treasure hidden in the walls."[24] By contrast, a seventy-year-old concierge was enthusiastically paraphrased by the artist. "Oh, I see the purpose of that hole," she observed, "it is an experiment into bringing light and air into spaces that never had enough of either."[25] In this freeing up of a typical bourgeois interior, the hole was granted a liberating function, described by the artist as a "son et lumière" experiment. But as many others commented, the hole was oriented as much toward the building's environs as it was to its interior, directing one's gaze toward the massive structure encroaching from behind: the hi-tech behemoth that was soon to become the Centre Georges Pompidou.

The hole recalled the structure of a telescope from outside the building, a periscope from within (figure 4.11). Oriented at a forty-five-degree angle from the street, it enabled pedestrians to peer up and through its telescopic form, radically juxtaposing the ascension of one era's architecture at the expense of another's disintegration. As Dan Graham noted, "With the aid of this 'periscope,' viewers could look not only into the interior of the Matta-Clark sculpture/building, but through the conical borings to these other buildings that embody past and present eras of Paris."[26] The

4.10 Gordon Matta-Clark, still from film of *Conical Intersect,* 1975, 18 minutes, 16mm, color film.

language of confrontation accordingly permeated the artist's own descriptions of the project. "Scruffy survivors," Matta-Clark called the old buildings, "facing off" with modernity itself.[27]

But how might one condense this operation rhetorically, give it a theoretical resonance specific to the project's environs? The artist's oblique interest in Walter Benjamin is instructive here. "I have enjoyed a term used in reference to Walter Benjamin, 'Marxist Hermeneutics,'" he once observed, "this phrase helps me think about my activities, which combine the inward . . . sphere of hermeneutics with the material dialectics of a real environment."[28] "Marxist hermeneutics" notwithstanding, Benjamin's notion of the dialectical image assumes profound relevance for discussions of *Conical Intersect.* For if Matta-Clark was concerned with "the material dialectics of a real environment," Benjamin's formulations on the temporality of the modern offer an acute critique of the ideology of progress.

In the "Konvulut N" section of the *Passagen-Werk* ("Re The Theory of Knowledge, Theory of Progress"), Benjamin describes a method of philosophical inquiry in which the juxtaposed images of past and present instantiate what he deems a "revolutionary recognition of the Now," an image necessarily opposed to illusions of immediacy and historical self-presence.[29] "It isn't that the past casts light on the present or the present casts light on the past," Benjamin notes:

> rather, an image is that in which the Then (*das Gewesene*) and the Now (*das Jetzt*) come into a constellation like a flash of lightning. In other words: image is dialectics at a standstill.[30]

The Now-time is such an image. For Benjamin, the raw material from which these images emerge is the "trash of history";[31] and the method, in its turn, is structured like montage. "I won't filch anything of value or appropriate any ingenious turns of phrase," he wrote, ". . . only the trivia, the trash—which I don't want to inventory, but simply allow it to come into its own way in the only way possible: by putting it to use."[32]

4.11 Gordon Matta-Clark, *Conical Intersect,* 1975, 27–29 rue Beaubourg, Paris.

To make use of things that have long outlived their usefulness: Benjamin is describing the logic of the outmoded in this passage, most famously articulated in his 1928 essay, "Surrealism: The Last Snapshot of the Revolution." Treating the pastness of things as a means to interrogate the very foundations of progress, Benjamin wrote about Andre Breton that

> He was the first to perceive the revolutionary energies that appear in the "outmoded," in the first iron constructions, the first factory buildings . . . the objects that have begun to be extinct . . . No one before these visionaries and augurs perceived how destitution—not only social but architectonic, the poverty of interiors, enslaved and enslaving objects—can be suddenly transformed into revolutionary nihilism.[33]

Benjamin describes a kind of local history of the basest, most quotidian order—a history of dirt and years-old fashions, of iron constructions and factory buildings. The revolutionary potential attributed to these things, things not long ago stripped of their novelty, is understood in terms of a particular conceptual disposition. "The trick by which this world of things is mastered" Benjamin states, "consists in the substitution of a political for a historical view of the past."[34] In such a displacement of history by politics, modernity's relentless pursuit of the new is now seen as an ever repeating process of construction and destruction. Yet Benjamin's notion of "revolutionary nihilism" intercedes in this cycle, for the outmoded bears witness to a process that has long assumed the status of myth.

To apply these concepts to *Conical Intersect* risks literalism, as if one could slavishly illustrate Benjamin's thesis with Matta-Clark's art. For what was the artist doing in Paris, after all, if not juxtaposing the "trash of history" with the new; considering the "banal obviousness of architecture"; or "telescoping the past with the present,"[35] to borrow Benjamin's own gnomic formulation, through the telescopic hole of *Conical Intersect?* Still, Matta-Clark's comment from 1977—"only our garbage heaps are growing as they fill up with history"[36]—resonates strongly with the larger considerations that consumed Benjamin throughout his Paris based investigations.[37] The patterns of progress and outmodedness Benjamin identifies in late nineteenth-century Paris, patterns organized specifically around building and technology, are revisited in their contemporary form at Les Halles by Matta-Clark.

Questions of temporality enable us to consider the problem of audience in Matta-Clark's work. The artist's use of obsolete buildings slated for demolition inherited a viewership linked to a long history of urban destruction in Paris. *Conical Intersect* literally telescoped the past through the present, and in doing so it opened onto two of the most important architectural and urban planning controversies in Paris in the postwar era. In the compacted narratives of Les Halles and the Centre Georges Pompidou that follow, the repetitive cycles of progress and destruction articulate a different reading of community for site-specific art.[38]

LE TROU DES HALLES AND "THE BUILDING WITH ITS TRIPES OUTSIDE"

Consider the rather hostile reception that greeted *Conical Intersect.* According to Hovagimyan, the building cut generated enormous hostility from the French Right: "Since it was near Beaubourg," he recalled, "the French officials and the Rightists were getting upset—they thought it was an insult to the new Beaubourg and a comment on the modernization of Paris."[39] Political as these claims were, they could not easily have been shrugged off by the artist.

But more shocking to Matta-Clark were the charges leveled against *Conical Intersect* by a different viewership: the Leftist press. On November 29, the French communist newspaper *l'Humanité* published a large photograph of the work on its front page (figure 4.12), accompanied by the sneeringly ironic caption:

> QUE D'ART! Il paratrait que ce trou est artistique, ayant été fait par un artiste. L'art dans ce domaine du trou, n'a pas peur du vide dans l'ancien quartier des Halles de Paris.
>
> C'était la rue Brantome, une des plus anciennes de Paris, et derrière se trouve le centre d'arts Georges-Pompidou.[40]

Lambasting Matta-Clark's "artistic hole," the anonymous editorial is unequivocal in its response to the project. This was bourgeois art at its worst, pretentious enough to render absence artistic, and brazen enough to stage itself in the ancient quarter of Les Halles. *L'Humanité* implied that the work only assumed the appelation of art because it was made by someone who claimed to be an artist.

LIVERPOOL JOHN MOORES UNIVERSITY
Aldham Roberts L.R.C.
TEL. 0151 231 3701/3634

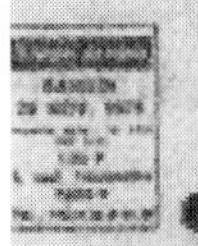

l'Humanité

ORGANE CENTRAL DU PARTI COMMUNISTE FRANÇAIS

Inflation, chômage, réduction du pouvoir d'achat...

2 décembre

JOURNÉE D'ACTIONS C.G.T.-C.F.D.T.

- GRÈVE DES CHEMINOTS
- Nombreux débrayages et manifestations

La C.G.T.

Répondre par une vaste lutte des travailleurs à l'intransigeance du pouvoir et du patronat

PRIX + 0,8 % (officiels) en octobre

mais le panier de la ménagère accuse des hausses que l'indice gouvernemental dissimule

Les troupes marocaines pénètrent au Sahara occidental

ESPAGNE

ENSEIGNANTS

Georges MARCHAIS

MAGISTRATS

SPORTS

Le vernis craque

QUE D'ART !

Préparation du XXIIe Congrès

Chacun compte pour un

Que veulent les communistes pour la France ?

Matta-Clark had never equated his cuttings with the wanton destruction of buildings, and he continued to be frustrated by the charges that his work amounted to a decadent gesture. "In Europe," he recalled, "I have had such heavy, absolutely devastating criticism of my work . . . based on European notions of social responsibility."[41] This criticism, he remarked, came from "people who think that what I'm doing is exploiting the sanctity of a certain kind of domestic space."[42] Even so, a heuristic function might be attributed to the attack in *l'Humanité* in spite of—or perhaps because of—its tone. No matter how trenchant, it is an elliptical caption, begging a closer reading. It positions Matta-Clark's project as a symptom of a social space already filled with emptiness or voids. Representing the very condition of its environment, this "holey" art is a function of the empty expanse that surrounds it.

Holes, voids, emptiness: a reader unversed in the urban history of Paris would find the passage in *l'Humanité* obscure; yet those familiar with the vicissitudes of planning in that city would detect pronounced implications. For this is an unofficial language, a journalistic and critical tradition in which the hole serves as a cipher of the area's destruction and modernization. As one historian lamented after the migrations of the marketplace in 1969, "[U]n 'trou' nous a été donné, plaie ouverte au coeur de la ville, comme si on avait voulu en vider toute trace ancienne, toute mémoire."[43]

In employing these turns of phrase, many contemporary writers suggested that the destruction of Les Halles in the seventies found precedent in the leveling of Paris by Baron Georges Eugène Haussmann during the Second Empire, a history Benjamin treated extensively in the *Passagen-Werk*.[44] But the destruction was also significant for specifically topographical reasons, as Les Halles was considered to be the very heart of Paris. Among the oldest neighborhoods in the city, its foundations are traceable to the era of Louis VI, when an open-air market was created around 1137.[45] Many centuries later, the site was eclipsed by the construction of the iron and glass pavilions built in the late nineteenth century, constructions that fixed the image of

4.12 *Conical Intersect* on the cover of *l'Humanité,* 29 November 1975, p. 1. Courtesy l'Humanité, Paris.

Les Halles in the minds of modern Parisians.[46] "Since the beginning of the century," wrote Emile Zola, "only one original monument has been built. . . . It is Les Halles."[47]

Ironically enough, this "monument" of the nineteenth century found its catalysts in the figures of Louis Napoleon and Haussmann, largely responsible for the demise of the old city. At the invitation of Haussmann in 1851, Victor Baltard inaugurated a building program that sought to give the markets more permanent form through the use of iron.[48] Construction of a building in stone was begun and later destroyed in the 1860s—an episode Benjamin recounts in his Konvolut on iron construction—but Baltard's subsequent plans were strongly supported by the Emperor.[49] The first building of the market opened in 1858 and the last of the complex was completed well after Napoleon III's demise in the 1930s.

Baltard's pavilions drew enormous attention to Les Halles, their modish materials signifying the most progressive building agenda to the crowds that flocked there—a strange fusion of the industrial and the seemingly organic. Yet not long after the pavilions were built, a tension between the new and the primordial or obsolete would animate the history of the site.[50] Like the cast-iron lofts in New York's SoHo with which they were roughly contemporary, the markets of Les Halles embodied the productivity and technological fortunes of the late nineteenth century; but they became as outmoded almost as rapidly as they had arisen. As early as 1913, the Commission d'Extension recommended that the marketplace be moved, stating a desperate need for modernization. By 1944, the Economic Council reiterated this proposal, citing problems of public hygiene on top of it. By 1961, a litany of complaints by government officials had been amassed against the marketplace, many of which contrasted its present decrepitude with the technological gains of the late nineteenth century. If once Les Halles was the very heart of Paris, now it was little more than an enormous traffic hazard that could not accommodate the growing number of automobiles that swept postwar France.[51] If the market was formerly described in terms of organic metaphors of fluorescence and growth, now it was considered a stinking, filthy place, rotten with both rats and prostitution. Perhaps most ironically, Les Halles was assailed as a potential fire trap, in spite of the fact that iron was championed in the nineteenth century for its high resistance to flame. Whatever the rationale for its removal, the controlling political body for Les Halles, SEMAH, decided that the markets would be moved south to the suburbs of Rungis.

The migration of the markets began in 1969, and the demolition of the pavilions took place two years later. Controversy erupted with populist force when the pavilions were destroyed in August 1971. Increasingly strident headlines attested to the shared investment in its loss. Architectural professionals, historians, and preservationists mourned the demolition of the architecture; while labor interests, socialists, and lower income families living near Les Halles protested the acts of land speculation that would necessarily displace them.[52] Although preservation of at least one of the pavilions had been guaranteed for another location, the future of the site itself had not been determined, even though competitions for its use were held some four years prior to the demolition. It wasn't until 1976 that a generalized plan for the area was formulated, and an unpopular one at best. The site was to be a complex containing a Metro station, a central power plant, and what was later to become an underground shopping mall, the "Forum des Halles."

Prior to the construction of the mall, the former location of the pavilions remained a hideous gash on the Parisian horizon for close to seven years (figure 4.13). Photographs of the site picture an enormous gaping hole amidst a Haussmannian cityscape otherwise organized by strong diagonals, straight boulevards, and the most monumental forms of architecture. With the ancient church of St. Eustache teetering at its perimeter the hole seemed even more violently implosive, the open wound of the old Paris a blight on the modern city.

"Le trou des Halles," as it simply came to be known, thus served as an image of modernization, a modernity ironically shaped by the very lack of an image. A feature of the built environment without purpose or end, a figure without apparent gestalt, it seemed an almost permanent condition of the urbanscape. Threatening to monumentalize the accelerated pace of the modern, it also served notice to the impossibility of the monument within modernity, to its alleged capacity to stabilize and communicate historical events and values in perpetuity. The insistence of the hole in the area was the "emptiness of the ancient quarter of Les Halles" so angrily denounced on the front page of *l'Humanité.*

Matta-Clark was obviously aware of the Les Halles controversy, but his shocked reaction at the hostility his project inspired suggests he did not consciously employ the hole as an icon of the situation. This was not a metaphor for the condition of the site, insofar as this would imply a sense of certainty about the area's longer history. For

in many respects, the history of Les Halles was as inaccessible to Matta-Clark as his work was to some viewers. *Conical Intersect* may have dramatized the destruction and development of the area from the artist's informed perspective, but its peculiar form (or lack of it) appeared to touch some collective psychic nerve, of which the artist had limited understanding. Its audience—by turns confused, bitter, or mildly amused—reacted to Matta-Clark's work in a manner that can be considered both site-specific and community-less, as if gathered around the passing of its own communal horizon.

The reception of *Conical Intersect* must be localized to an even greater degree, for compounding the already vexed history of Les Halles was the construction of the Centre Georges Pompidou. Sited in the former parking lot of the marketplace, its erection was inseparable from the demolition of the old neighborhood. And while the controversy surrounding it was largely organized around this destruction, it turned equally around the rhetoric of publicity its supporters espoused—namely, its pretensions to the democratizing of French culture in the wake of the mass strikes of May 1968.

Indeed, a little over a year after the events of May '68 and some two years before the destruction of the iron pavilions, an official announcement was made concerning the function of the former Plateau Beaubourg: "The French President decided to have a Centre erected in the Heart of Paris, not far from Les Halles, devoted to the contemporary arts, "it read.[53] Superseding the French Ministry of Culture, Georges Pompidou inaugurated a plan for a mixed-use cultural center, forming an ad hoc committee exclusively devoted to the organization of the complex. Two concerns came to preoccupy the President: first, the center was to contain several levels completely accessible to the public, including a public library and the Musée national d'art moderne; second, Pompidou was firm that the design competition be opened internationally, a curious gesture given the nationalistic purpose of the center itself. Calls for the competition were advertised in 1971, and 681 entries were submitted. When the jury finally arrived at a decision, the firm of Renzo Piano and Richard Rogers emerged victorious, together with the engineering company of Ove

4.13 "Le trou des Halles," photograph, Paris. Courtesy Centre Georges Pompidou.

Arup and Partners—a shock to followers of contemporary architecture. From the moment that the winners were made public until the official opening of the center on January 31, 1977, the Italian and British team became the focus of a heated debate about the nature of its proposed design, the design's place within French culture generally and its place within the old Les Halles neighborhood in particular.

Described as the "building with its tripes outside,"[54] the Centre Georges Pompidou was initially a shocking sight. With its color-coded assemblage of conduits, pipes, heating ducts, and escalators placed on the building's facade, it arose in the neighborhood like an irrepressible, scandalous machine, the monstrous child of a machine-age aesthetic of which it was the logical, if extreme, heir (figure 4.14). But if the sci-fi quality of the center bore a reference to the sixties designs of the British architectural collective Archigram, its street elevations were actually the outcome of an almost hypertrophied notion of functionalism on Piano and Rogers' part. Central to the conception of the building was the conviction that its spaces should be modular, that all its features share the capacity to be conveniently reversed, and that in line with the theories of social progress to which the firm subscribed, the entire structure was to accommodate change and growth easily. Flexibility in the service of evolution was the leitmotif of the design. "In a living and complex organism such as the Centre," the architects noted, "the evolution of needs is to especially be taken into account."[55] The desire to accommodate an almost biological expansion led to the idea that the building's structural system be pushed outside, a gesture that would maximize the possibilities of the empty interior (figure 4.15).

For all its superficial novelty and futuristic posturing, the "flexible envelope" of the Beaubourg was in many respects the ultimate reification of a functionalist platform. Its reception by the press was surprisingly positive, however, celebrating the seductiveness of its building agenda. Initially suspicious of the project, many factions of the leftist press grudgingly came to accept the center for its perceived populism, perhaps swayed by its supporters' appeals to the language of the public sphere.[56] More

4.14 Aerial view, Centre Georges Pompidou, Paris. Courtesy Centre Georges Pompidou.

4.15 Centre Georges Pompidou, Paris. Courtesy Centre Georges Pompidou.

vociferous supporters of the center were hyperbolic in ways that shed light on their own futuristic inclinations. Reyner Banham declared the center to be the ultimate example of his notion of the "Megastructure"—a structure that could be replicated, "spread about, and finally take over."[57] Intended as compliments, such pronouncements invariably planted the seeds for the criticism of the building. For the image of a structure "taking over" its environs is consonant with Matta-Clark's remarks on the building as an architectural trap, which he elliptically characterized as "a brave-new cobweb of culture."[58]

Apart from the general conception of the design, its interior and exterior modishness was also claimed by some to mask conservative ideologies. Attacking the building in his essay "Beaubourg-Effect: Implosion and Deterrence," Jean Baudrillard observed that the relationship between exterior and interior was an analogue to the ostensibly new and the fundamentally reactionary, conventionally organized social relations obscured by the spectacular character of the building's facades and its alleged populism. The unstructured interior of the center was assailed as "a model of absolute security, subject to generalization on all social levels, one that is most profoundly a model of deterrence," in sum, "an interior uptight with old values."[59] For Baudrillard, this uninterrupted space was "linked to the ideology of visibility, transparency, polyvalence, consensus, contact."[60] If the building was intended to be accessible and public, its interior would follow suit: transparency would be regarded as rational and unambiguous, the openness of the space adequated to the myth of an open society (figure 4.16).[61]

Baudrillard was equally acrimonious about the center's exterior. "This *thing,*" he called it, as if refusing even to acknowledge its classification as architecture, "openly declares that our age will no longer be one of duration, that our only temporal mode is that of accelerated cycle and of recycling: the time of transistors and fluid flow."[62] This thing, in other words, was a structure in which the historical was processed in the most breakneck of fashions: its mechanomorphic exterior, valorizing change and flow, seemingly churned up and spat out any sense of temporal *durée.*

4.16 Exterior, detail, Centre Georges Pompidou, Paris. Courtesy Centre Georges Pompidou.

And what was the ultimate effect of this, to follow Baudrillard's unforgiving rhetoric? The center was an "in-depth, irreversible implosion," "a vacumn-making machine."[63] It generated a violence fulfilling "the actual labor of the death of culture."[64] However coincidental the terminology, it is suggestive that Baudrillard characterized its implosiveness as "the deterrent efficacy of this huge black *hole,* this Beaubourg."[65]

It is tempting to read in this attack a broader critique of the entire Les Halles episode, with the black hole of the Centre Pompidou its inevitable outcome; a history that would progress to the point of its own self-effacement. True to its name, *Conical Intersect* literally intersected this history. With its own destruction as secure as that of the neighborhood upon which it trained its gaze so briefly, it internalized the mechanics of a process that ensured its disappearance. However momentarily, it arose to cast an unblinking eye on the thing responsible for its impending subsumption.

Aside from the externalizing features of its "gaze," the hole of *Conical Intersect* can be considered in relation to other aspects of the Beaubourg, specifically, the interior of the center, its aesthetics of transparency and the ideologies of public space attached to both. To follow Henri Lefebvre on "the illusion of transparency" in urban space,

> . . . space appears as luminous, as intelligible, as giving action free reign . . . The illusion of transparency goes hand in hand with a view of space as innocent, as free of traps or secret places.[66]

Yet it is precisely because space is *not* an innocent category that

> Sight and seeing, which in the Western tradition once epitomized intelligibility, have turned into a trap; the means whereby, in social space, diversity may be simulated and a travesty of enlightenment and intelligibility ensconced under the sign of transparency.[67]

If the open space of the Beaubourg stood metaphorically for publicness and communicability—as Enlightenment models of the public commons and greens were wont to convey—the open hole of *Conical Intersect* implicitly criticized such conceits as travesty. Not that the building cut intentionally commented on the interior of the museum, as the Centre Pompidou was far from completion when Matta-Clark staged his work at Les Halles. Rather, as the general reception of the cutting demonstrated, its literal openness belied the audience's inability to make sense of the site, to essentialize its purpose or function. At once excessively transparent and conceptually opaque, it challenged the equivalence between spatial and architectural transparency and consensus.

This oblique commentary on transparency and architecture might also be extended to the peculiar conditions of art and spectatorship at the Beaubourg. Indeed, the viewing of objects was to be regarded as public and democratic as its interior was open, the visual accessibility of its art reiterated by its pellucid architectural space. But just as *Conical Intersect* tacitly criticized the building's architecture, it also commented on the intertwining of art and architecture as comprehensible through these terms. It did this though literalizing that relationship. Using a building as its principal medium, it collapsed the mythical publicness of the architectural site onto the more obscure art object itself, the hole of Matta-Clark's project.

The holes of history best represented by this work were not fully plumbed by the artist, though. *Conical Intersect* engaged the controversy surrounding "le trou des Halles," but it was just one of Matta-Clark's works in Paris that addressed questions of community founded upon absence and loss.

"OUT OF THE GALLERIES AND INTO THE SEWER"

Manholes Expose Edges
of the Working Urban
Substrate—
A Cloud of Steam, A Burnout
Back Ups, Overflow, Explosion
—Gordon Matta-Clark[68]

When Matta-Clark returned to Paris two years later, he continued his explorations into other cavernous spaces. But now it was less the holes left in the wake of urban destruction that occupied him than the spaces into which trash and detritus were literally consigned: the catacombs and sewers of Paris.

A curious metaphor expressed Matta-Clark's interest in subterranean spaces. "I work similarly to the way gourmets hunt for truffles," he offered in an interview:

I mean, a truffle is a fantastic thing buried somewhere in the ground . . . Sometimes I find it. Sometimes I don't. In fact, the next area that interests me is an expedition into the underground: a search for the forgotten spaces left buried under the city as historical reserve or as surviving reminders of lost projects and fantasies . . . This activity should bring art out of the gallery and into the sewers.[69]

Matta-Clark's art prior to the Parisian works foreshadowed the gesture of displacing the gallery to the sewer, adequating art and architecture to garbage itself.[70] Detritus, as we know, played no small part in his work. Along with the *Winter Garden* installation, the early work *Garbage Wall* (1970) (figure 4.17) literalized the equivalence between trash and building. Here, the artist compressed trash into a makeshift architectural structure around which a three-day-long performance of hopelessly mundane activities was organized. And in *Open House* (figure 4.18), another piece from 112 Greene Street days, a dumpster served as a site for performance activities by Tina Girouard, Suzanne Harris, Ted Greenwald, and others, including a taped "soundtrack" by Greenwald driving his delivery truck for the *Village Voice.* A strangely contemporary dwelling, its "openness"—that is to say, its public dimension—underscored the ways that conditions of urban living were founded upon the site of their own waste.

These early pieces could be seen as particularly American in their critical inflection, referring to specifically American patterns of consumption and waste (*Winter Garden,* for instance, addressed the "throwaway" character of postwar American consumer culture). That these works from the 1970s were roughly contemporaneous with Manhattan's growing "garbage crisis" of the decade is also suggestive. Surely, the

4.17 Gordon Matta-Clark, *Garbage Wall,* 1970.

WOOSTER

site-specific concerns of Matta-Clark's art allow for an oblique, if not reflective, relationship to the sanitation problems that reached crisis proportions in New York in the late sixties and seventies.[71] Garbage was everywhere. In the most unavoidable sense, trash *was* the built environment. The combined result of a mounting fiscal crisis and longstanding labor struggles between sanitation workers and city hall, the problem was so pervasive in New York (and the rest of the country to a considerable extent) that one journalist was inspired to declare "garbage is politics."[72]

Garbage is politics. If garbage took on decidedly local implications for Matta-Clark's New York projects, the "political" character of detritus signified differently for him in France, appealing to environments, histories, and communities that were already lost. His French works of 1977 were more focused in exploring the *spaces* of historical waste, perhaps because their histories were themselves longer and more resonant. The photographic series *Underground Paris* (1977), for instance, documents four sites (Les Halles, Notre Dame, the Paris Opera, and St. Michel) in long scroll-like format (figure 4.19), each revealing "cross-sections of their foundation" at the bottom of the photograph.[73] The series offers an image of Paris that functions analagously to the critical model that structures *Conical Intersect.* Positioning lost or buried histories of the city against the immediately visible conditions of the built environment, the photographs dramatize the encounter between the pastness of things and the present.

This oscillatation between such temporal registers of experience is effectively conveyed in Matta-Clark's film *Sous-sol de Paris,* which found its precedent in his subterranean exploration of New York, *Substrait* (figure 4.20), made a year earlier. A nonlinear, black-and-white film, *Sous-sol de Paris* shows the artist negotiating the famous sewers of Paris. Among the technological accomplishments of the Second Empire, the sewers occupy a strangely overdetermined place within modern Parisian history,

4.18 Gordon Matta-Clark, *Open House,* 1972.

4.19 (page 202) Gordon Matta-Clark, *Underground Paris,* 1977.

4.20 (page 203) Gordon Matta-Clark, still from *Substrait (Underground Dailies),* 1976, 30 minutes, black and white and color with sound.

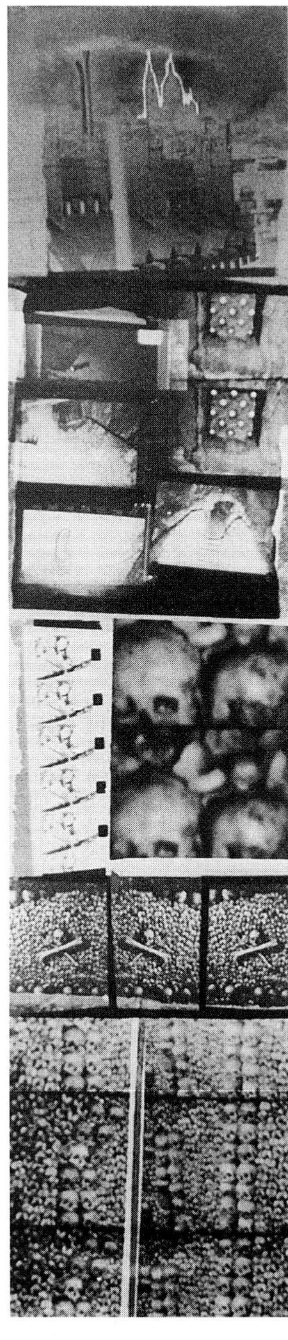

in part because they were thought to allegorize the processes of history itself. It is a notion most famously affirmed in Victor Hugo's exploration of the subject in *Les Miserables:*

The history of mankind is reflected in the history of cloaca. The sewer . . . is the resting place of all failure and all effort. To political economy it is a detritus, and to social philosophy, a residue . . . Every foulness of civilization, fallen into disuse, sinks into that ditch of truth wherein ends the huge social downslide, to be swallowed, but to spread . . . No false appearance, no white-washing, is possible . . . It is more than fraternity, it is close intimacy . . . A sewer is a cynic. It tells all.[74]

The sewer is the truth of history. The "sincerity of filth," as Hugo called it, carried political implications not unlike Benjamin's notion of the outmoded. When Daniel Cohn-Benedit, the student leader of May '68, declared, "we are the sewers of history," he called up the debased social status of the participants in the workers and student movement and imparted an almost revolutionary character to those nether regions.[75] Extending the seditionary character of the sewers back in time, the participants in the Commune, and later fighters of the Occupation, holed up in parts of the sewer. Rol-Tanguy, the leader of the Forces Françaises de l'Interieur (F.F.I.), worked closely with the head of the Parisian sewer system in establishing a stronghold of the Resistance, before moving his operations to the catacombs.[76]

Resistance in the sewers, in the catacombs: embedded within these specific historical events is a broader formulation regarding community—one that offers the possibility of thinking its terms through the fallen or debased. To speak of the sewer as being "a close intimacy," in Hugo's words, is to address tangentially the community engendered by things at the moment of their passing, defined through ruin or their acute marginalization. This seems to be the case especially for Matta-Clark's most deeply melancholic take on such issues, his pictures of catacombs and a site piece of 1977, *Descending Steps for Batan.*

In an image from the series *Underground Paris*, the profile of the church of St. Michel is strongly highlighted at the top of the work, crowning the photographic scroll with its crisply articulated spires. Moving downward, the sharp verticality of the architecture shifts to far more ambiguous images of the spaces beneath the building, tunnel-like forms whose spatial orientation is less than clearly given. That shift progresses as one follows the implied descent of the camera; for over half the lower part of the scroll is occupied by various horizontal registers of bones—masses of skulls and tibias and femurs arranged in precious, if disturbingly neat, patterns. So closely pressed are some of these bones to the picture plane that they assume a vaguely abstract quality as a result: eye sockets imply little more than blackened recesses, the curve of a cranial dome evaporates into shadowy line. Moving from the specific articulation of religious architecture to the graphic anonymity of bones, Matta-Clark offers an image progressively stripped of visual detail and life.

A similar operation occurs in the sequence shot in the famous catacombs at Denfert-Rocherau in *Sous-sol de Paris* (figure 4.21). Matta-Clark's camera lingers over an enormous pile of skulls organized with the same chilly precision as those represented in the still photographs. Again, the distance between the camera and the skulls is so short that their forms seem to waiver and blur, with the occular cavities remaining the only gestalt of the image. When the camera begins to retreat from the sockets, the pattern of black circles is intercut with another pattern of black circles, formed by rows and rows of wine bottles stored in an underground cellar (figure 4.22). The stillness of bones is positioned against an image suggesting the din of toasting and drinking, a jarring collision of images of the past and the present.

The clash between things mortified and the exuberant sociality associated with wine recalls the various legends that circulate around the catacombs themselves.[77] Established in 1785, the Parisian catacombs were old quarries in which the bones of six million individuals had been transferred from the ancient Cimetière des Innocents. One incident from the prehistory of the catacombs is telling in relation to Matta-Clark's project. In 1780, a restaurateur living near the Cimetière des Innocents went to retrieve some bottles of wine from his cellar, whereupon the smell of putrescence overwhelmed him. He was to discover its horrifying source shortly: the walls of a mass grave adjacent to his house had burst open, sending forth a heap of neighboring corpses into his basement.

While it's unlikely that Matta-Clark's splicing of skulls with wine in *Sous-sol de Paris* refers to this episode, as a coincidence it is instructive for treating the entirety of

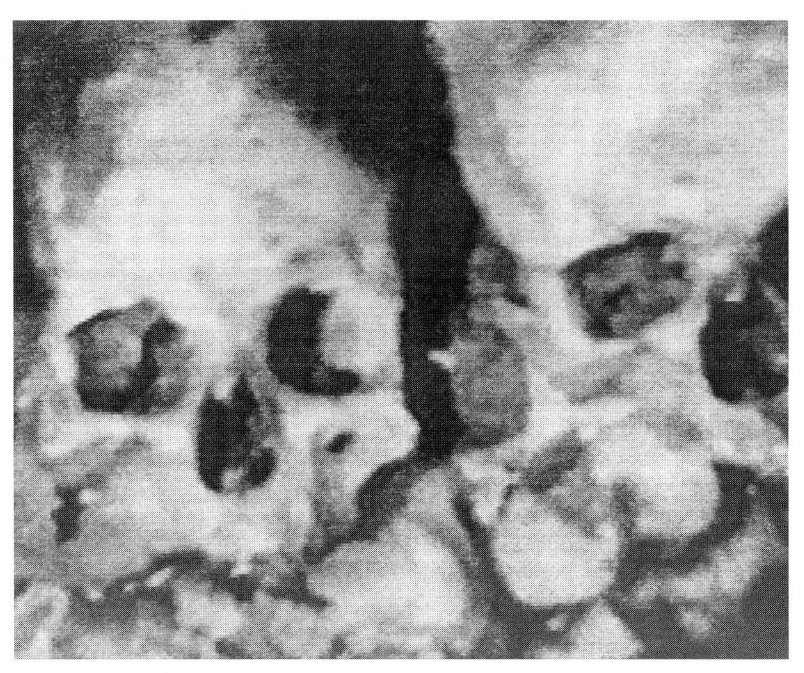

his Paris based work. In a grotesque and literal way, it illustrates an important debate within the urban planning of the Second Empire: the proximity of the dead to the living as a concern for the politics of modern Parisian urban history.[78] A situation in which familial and theological concerns clashed with the demand for public hygiene and the ever growing need for space in the city opened onto a question of more pressing theoretical and representational weight. For how does one acknowledge the presence of the past, its dead, in the urban present? How to defer to the *untimeliness* of the past in the space of the modern city?

This matter bridges the mechanics of *Conical Intersect* with Matta-Clark's Paris projects from two years later. When the past and its vestiges are set within the social fabric of contemporaneity, one is compelled to reflect upon the opacity of the present in relation to the past, "the illusion of permanence" as Lawrence Weiner described it, sustained by modern architecture.[79]

No work challenges this illusion as poignantly as the site piece Matta-Clark produced for Galerie Yvon Lambert, *Descending Steps for Batan* (figure 4.23). A deeply mournful piece, *Descending Steps for Batan* attenuates the issue of lost community through the example of the artist's own personal grief: it was dedicated to Gordon's twin brother Batan (Sebastian), who had allegedly committed suicide by jumping from the window of Gordon's studio the summer before.[80] Devastated, Matta-Clark produced a memorial to his brother in France, a cavernous hole dug directly into the foundations of the gallery. Every day of the exhibition, which began April 21, 1977, and lasted through the first week of May, he continued to dig deeper into the ground, creating a progressively larger and dirtier hole within a space traditionally pristine and white. Through the simple ritual of digging, he collapsed the work of art in the present with a figure who was now part of the past. In a place conventionally reserved for the new, a memorial to his brother was staged and was subsequently absorbed into the space of the gallery.

From *Conical Intersect* to *Descending Steps for Batan,* Matta-Clark's Parisian work bears no stable foundation in an equally unstabilized community. It assumes no

4.21, **4.22** Gordon Matta-Clark, still from *Sous-sol de Paris,* 1977.

productive relationship to changes in a site, engages no ideal of progress for its own sake, and thus does little of the "work" that site-specific art is often alleged to perform. Nihilistic, perhaps, but "revolutionary" in their nihilism, these "workless" projects offer a cogent political critique framed repeatedly through the form of the hole. Because the works' condition of possibility is the very impermanence of the built environment, Matta-Clark overturns the conventional relationship between art and its viewing public. Challenging any claims to an essentialized community of spectators, his work produces a viewership founded on loss, not the fullness of productive or performative experience. And it is the commonality of this loss, endlessly played out in the space of the city, that is the heart of the modern itself.

4.23 Gordon Matta-Clark, *Descending Steps for Batan,* Galerie Yvon Lambert, Paris, 1977.

5 CONCLUSION: TO BE CONTEMPORARY

When Matta-Clark died in August 1978 at the age of 35, a victim of liver failure and pancreatic cancer, he left behind a history rich in personal memory, if relatively few sculptural objects. To read the testimonials of his life given by his peers is to encounter the most exuberant of temperaments, a character whose boundless sense of engagement with people, things, community, threatened to outstrip any singular persona. All at once, Matta-Clark was the most Dionysiac of dancers; the sternest architectural critic; a punster; the most inventive (or, alternately, horrible) of cooks; a speculator; a child of surrealism; a Buddhist; a wastrel; a Marxist; a rich kid; a savior of builders; an infinite charmer; a student of garbage; a physical, life-affirming force; a man whose life was marked by illness, guilt, and loss. All descriptions possess some degree of truth value, but they do not so much consolidate a seamless gestalt of the artist as they amount to a historiographic incoherence.

Perhaps this incoherence is the founding principle of examining an artist who both is and is not contemporary, an artist who is a part of our recent historical horizon, but who is nevertheless historical because he is "past." For Matta-Clark's peers, the tragedy of his early death represents the passing of a different era for art making, one in which the can-do ethos of early SoHo suggested an endless horizon of possibility. For the historian, Matta-Clark's untimely passing inspires thoughts about the artist's potential, the work he might have produced had his career exceeded its short seven or eight years.

One needn't speculate too much, though. The notes and writings Matta-Clark left behind point clearly to the direction in which his work was heading. Of course, a number of building projects remained unrealized at the time of his death. Some were in their nascent stages, others were envisioned for museums, a few were little more than notes jotted down on index cards.[1] Yet, although Matta-Clark is best remembered for these cuttings, he was anxious to expand the range of his oeuvre.[2] If an interrogation into modern architecture and space was at the heart of his work, surely there were other means of conducting it, beyond the cuttings.

One way was to consider another register of space—namely, aerial space—and the artist's exploration of this area was to have taken pneumatic form.[3] While Matta-Clark had rejected the "verticalization" of the city as represented by the World Trade Center, he would also seek alternative uses of the space it ostensibly colonized. In *Documenta 6* in 1977, for example, Matta-Clark constructed a work titled *Jacob's Ladder* (figure 5.1), a looming netlike structure attached to the chimney of a factory that ascended into the sky. In *Tree Dance* (figure 5.2), a performance staged at Vassar College in 1971, a cluster of rope ladders enabled participants to dangle far above the ground in pod-like formations. And well before that, back in his undergraduate days at Cornell, Matta-Clark organized a memorial performance to Marcel Duchamp, in which the inflation of a pneumatic tunnel forced the audience out of the room.[4]

It was a couple of years before his death, however, that Matta-Clark threw himself into pneumatic technology. He researched extensively a project that attempted "to combine 'network enclosures' with the structural life of a series of a tethered balloons."[5] He wrote to a number of specialists in the field of ballooning, some of whom responded to the artist with puzzlement. Yet amid all the ballooning magazines and odd requests made of structural engineers, the end goal of Matta-Clark's research was an "alternative housing." However much a utopian solution to the question of livable space, it was doubtless in keeping with his anarchitectural motivations.

Aside from Matta-Clark's engagement with pneumatics, letters also reveal a nascent interest in "computer animation" and "computer graphics." He considered the use of computers "a part of my search to chart and reoccupy space," as if intuiting the discourses on cyberspace that were to proliferate shortly.[6] On at least two occasions, he wrote to the Center for Advanced Visual Studies at the Massachusetts Institute of Technology in an attempt to gain access to its computers—once, to the director Otto Piene, another time to a friend, video artist Peter Campus, who was in

5.1 (page 212) Gordon Matta-Clark, *Jacob's Ladder,* at Documenta 6, Kassel, Germany, 1977.

5.2 (page 213) Gordon Matta-Clark, *Tree Dance,* Vassar College, Poughkeepsie, NY, 1971.

LIVERPOOL JOHN MOORES UNIVERSITY
LEARNING SERVICES

residence at the program.[7] And a reference to working at UCLA, during a period Matta-Clark spent in Los Angeles with Chris Burden, communicates an interest in their computer facilities and advanced architecture programs.

These pneumatic as well as computer-based projects should not be viewed independently of his other work, although they may seem at odds with the relatively direct practices of his cuttings. If anything, they provide a dialectical corollary to the building cuts and his explorations underground. But apart from speculations about these unrealized works, Matta-Clark's death solicits a range of questions about the nature of contemporaneity and contemporary history. It calls up the seeming paradox of writing a history, an account of *pastness,* of things that are of the relative *present.*

The example of Matta-Clark's too-brief life is indeed suggestive for those who would attempt to historicize their subjects in a secure fashion. When friends and colleagues speak today about the "truth" of Matta-Clark and the seventies—his intentions, his psychological profile, and the acutely historical reasons motivating his art—they inadvertantly if poignantly illustrate two methodological truisms: that history is clearly determined in the present; and that the present, as the moment in which such historicizing takes place, is itself inaccessible to its participants. Their accounts are not to be held as suspect, however, for they are not. What they articulate is how personal memory and sometimes melancholy are at work in the most basic writings of history. Pastness and presentness collide so that nostalgic longing and historical distance refuse any easy distinctions.

Such, then, is the conundrum for the historian of recent art, the pronounced sense that to write a history of the contemporary is to dramatize a contradiction endemic to *all* productions of history. It is to make arguments about the transparency of contemporary events while continuously deferring to one's own embeddedness in the present—the impossibility of making claims of historical distance from the subject of one's study. Surely, Matta-Clark's projects contend with the *timeliness* and *untimeliness* of things—the past and the present of buildings, garbage, cities, people, and the question of futurity they open onto—and so the historiographic problems attached to the narratives of his biography are played out with equal intensity in his art.

In conclusion, two points regarding the legacy of Matta-Clark's work must be considered. The first regards the problematic terrain of the artist's influence for recent practice. The second considers how Matta-Clark's art thematizes questions of its own historiographic mediation.

Matta-Clark's reception within contemporary art and architecture is easy enough to track. Artists of both sculptural and neo-conceptualist stripes have made claims for his importance, critics and historians vouch for his influence.[8] And frequently, Matta-Clark's practice seems to have been unconsciously appropriated within recent art, yet his example is not explicitly credited.[9]

Some brief remarks need to be made about the seeming internalization of Matta-Clark's art by architecture in general, and his heroicization by young architects specifically. There is a supreme irony in thinking about recent architecture in terms of Matta-Clark's practice—one need only recall Matta-Clark's behavior at the Institute for Architecture and Urban Studies in 1976 to gauge his attitude toward the field. Nonetheless, names ranging from Frank Gehry to SITE are routinely invoked in the same breath as Matta-Clark. Likewise, the word "deconstruction" is erroneously linked to his work, as if to appeal to the literal disassembling of buildings as well as the theoretically acute notion of "deconstructivist" architecture. No doubt many architects genuinely respect the artist's work on its own terms (and some of them knew him personally), but a gross pseudomorphism takes place when Matta-Clark and these figures are leveled to the same visual field. The affinities suggested by writers on the subject represent a failure to acknowledge the critical and historical motivations of the artist's project.[10] Just why Matta-Clark's art exerts such fascination within the architectural community is open to debate,[11] although he himself offered some telling remarks. "I think that . . . architects would be fascinated," he declared, "because they spend so much time being so totally frustrated by having that kind of stuff . . . in their heads . . . and then not getting a chance to ever execute it."[12]

Questions of architecture notwithstanding, the place of Matta-Clark's art in the present represents the larger concern of concluding this book. This matter will be addressed through his use of the photographic document, followed by an account of the efforts to save the cutting *Office Baroque.*

THE SELF-EFFACING DOCUMENT

End at the beginning. At last we consider the image that inaugurated this discussion, a photograph of the site work *Splitting*. Horizontal in format, it is a slightly overexposed color picture, whose yellowish cast seems to thicken the focus of the image, blur the sharpness of its edges (see figure I.1). The house itself appears flat and without any distinguishing features: a charmless dwelling of the suburbs set against an appropriately dull blue sky. So characterless is the thing and so squarely placed on its photographic ground, that it appears to be a two-dimensional prop, an effect reinforced by the graphic swatch of shadow that cleanly organizes the lower register of the picture.

And what of the place of the cut, the wedge that bisects the house as though it were the thinnest cardboard? Pictured frontally, directly, the cut is represented with the same matter-of-factness as the rest of the image. The blankness of the house; the browning, weedy plot on which it stands; the shadeless trees; the violently-rent cleft: all are recorded with a prosaicness that dramatizes the uncanny situation depicted. Arguably it is this tension between the representation of the house and the cut, along with the gestalt of the building's exterior, that has secured the image of *Splitting* within art historical memory.

It seems a strange thing to say that we know of *Splitting* through this particular photograph—strange because the observation is at once so obvious as to verge on tautology, but imperative still for discussions of the historiographic concerns of the work. Perhaps it seems even more absurd to say that Matta-Clark's entire career is frequently assessed through the recollection of this one picture alone, but there is some truth to this as well. A conversation with an artist whose work deals with the historical imago of conceptual art confirmed this point when the discussion turned to the legacy of Matta-Clark.[13] He began to invoke Matta-Clark's image bank, and as he recalled pictures from the great art magazines of the seventies—*Avalanche, Arts, Artforum, Studio International*—he immediately cited the photograph of *Splitting*, which he alluded to by squaring his hands, as if to convey the blunt frontality of the house pictured. His remarks attested to the contemporary relevance of this work. In no less than three recent books on art of the postwar era, Matta-Clark's contributions were invariably represented by the image of *Splitting*, doubtless his most famous work.[14]

Thomas Crow usefully acknowledges Trisha Brown's recollections of Matta-Clark's art, or her failure to recollect the means by which she encountered them, as the case would have it.[15] Had she heard about them or actually visited them? Seen them in pictures? Was barred from even entering them? Brown's confusion, Crow argues, stems from the relative inaccessibility of Matta-Clark's work and its implied critique of the "imperious" beholder of more conventional readings of site-specific art. In chapter 3 I described the viewer's inability to make the experience of the building cuts cohesive and legible, and certainly this condition has been reinforced by the sheer impossibility of visiting Matta-Clark's site works in the present. The mechanics of Matta-Clark's photography must be touched upon as such, for in the absence of extant works, their function in mediating his art now is equivalent to studying the art itself. I will not speak about the artist's photographic montages, criticized by even his strongest supporters, but the photographs out of which my larger interpretations grow.[16]

How, then, are we to contend with the status of Matta-Clark's photographs? Are they documents in the literal sense of the word, little more than the dumb recordings of gestures past, or are they art objects in their own respect? When Matta-Clark once wrote of the "need to avoid purely photographic documentation," what were the implications of the word "purely"?[17] The artist gave a partial response regarding his attitudes toward photography. "I like the idea that the sacred photo framing process is equally 'violatable,'" he said. "And I think that's partly a carry over from the way I deal with structures to the way that I deal with photography."[18]

Matta-Clark was speaking of his photographic collages in this instance, but he could just as well have been describing his more conventional photography. For, surely, posing questions about the classification of his photography leads to an enormous debate about the nature of the document in art of the late sixties and seventies, of which the traditional formulation of documentary photography was especially taken to task by conceptual art. The question of this history could occupy the space of an entire book, but only the main threads of this debate need to be acknowledged in a treatment of Matta-Clark's work. Indeed, it is a basic assumption of conceptual art that its proliferation of new exhibition strategies—its performative dimensions (Vito Acconci and Chris Burden), its apparent allegiance to a dematerialization model (as in the *Inert Gas* series of Robert Barry), its inaccessibility to a broad public by virtue of its site-specificity (Robert Smithson, Michael Heizer)—required artists' statements, or the document that recorded an event. Thus these documents took on pronounced valence during the period. The photograph necessarily played a formative role in this shift, inaugurating what the artist Jeff Wall has identified as a "re-thinking and 'refunctioning' of reportage."[19]

Matters of the saleability of the photographic work notwithstanding, the photographic document was to be taken seriously on its own terms. In her popular account on conceptual art, Ursula Meyer notes:

> An essential aspect of Conceptual Art is its self-reference; often the artists define the intentions of their work as their art. Thus many Conceptual artists advance propositions or investigations. It is in keeping, then, with Conceptual Art that it is best explained through itself . . . In this sense, this book is not a "critical anthology," but a documentation of Conceptual Art and statements.[20]

That the book was regarded less as an anthology than as an actual presentation of conceptual art emphasizes the degree of transparency attributed to the conceptual document by Meyer. The documentation of the event, or the proposition, functioned as the art object alone, requiring no further mediation or interpretation by the critic or historian.

In stark opposition to these claims, much conceptual art called into question the notion of photographic or video documentation as so much neutral reportage, even as the document was elevated from its secondary role as artistic supplement to the material accident of conceptual performance itself. As Wall writes:

> The gesture of reportage is withdrawn from the social field and attached to a putative social event.

This introversion, or subjectivization, of reportage was manifested in two important directions:

> First, it brought photography into a new relationship with the problematics of the staged, or posed, picture, through new concepts of performance. Second, the inscription of pho-

tography into a nexus of experimental practices led to a direct but distantiated and parodic relationship with the art-concept of photojournalism.[21]

The documentary photographs of the conceptual event played with the historical nostrums of the photographic or video document itself. On the one hand, they were parodic, because the events they recorded were often staged privately, almost solipsistically; and the nature of the performances—a dog lapping up milk, say, or a figure plodding aimlessly with the stiff-legged gait of a Beckett character—seemed far too trivial to merit being recorded for all posterity, calling further into question the "reality" of performing bodies themselves.[22] On the other hand, the pictures were flagrantly amateurish. Lacking the slick finish and dramatic composition of contemporary photojournalism, the crudeness of the works reiterated their lack of a grand narrative.

The work of photo-conceptualism thus made ample reference to the strategies of documentary photography, just as it debased the conventions upon which documentary was founded. For even though the document became the central means by which to access conceptual work, it also presented itself for its own critical self-effacement.

The documentary photographs of Matta-Clark's site-projects operate by a parallel logic. While lacking the wry humor of much photo-conceptualism, they function as documents to the extent that they record specific and ephemeral places for posterity. At the same time, they reject the first principles of the genre: the aspiration to communicate historical events or things via the alleged transparency of the photographic medium. This is largely because many of Matta-Clark's pictures challenge the presumptions of visual accessibility when considered as individual objects. Mapping figure onto ground, plan with elevation, cuts with solid and void, they are pictures that must be studied intensively, and in series, if one is to extract any information from them. In spite of their formal conservatism, their "straight" documentary approach, they ultimately describe the limits of their own format just as they question the transparency of the space they represent.

It hardly seems an accident that the photograph of *Splitting* is reproduced *ad infinitum* in the art historical texts. It is by far the easiest image of Matta-Clark's site-works to read, the picture with the least amount of information presented, in the most lucid of compositional formats. Treated in these terms, a singular point about Matta-Clark's reception through his photography becomes clear: the mediation of the artist's work through that image speaks as much to the resistance of his work to be clearly re-presented, as it does to the formal merits of the photograph.

The refusal of the object to be translated in such a ready fashion was, of course, at play in the experience of the art when it actually existed. But the afterlife of the object, whether registered in photographic form or sculptural fragment, strongly underscores its historiographic mediation. The efforts to salvage Matta-Clark's last European site work, *Office Baroque,* represents at once a fulfillment of the building processes the work critiqued, and confirms much about the longevity of the work of art and its institutional relationship to property and bureaucracy.

TO SAVE *OFFICE BAROQUE*

From June 1977 to the time of its destruction some three years later, the site project *Office Baroque* (figure 5.3) found its home in the city of Antwerp, famous as the birthsite of Rubens and for a long history of maritime mercantilism. There, Matta-Clark worked in a waterfront environment, as he had with *Day's End* two years earlier. Set directly across the street from the historical site of the Steen, a tenth-century castle that presently houses a military museum, *Office Baroque* was within striking distance of a major tourist attraction in the city. At the time of Matta-Clark's cutting, the neighborhood bore the mildly seedy character common to a once heavily-trafficked industrial zone. An area whose former productivity had waned after the Second World War, most of its shipping activity had migrated north to Holland. However, the neighborhood was beginning to undergo the processes of gentrification organized around the city's growing tourist industry.

The building itself was a bland modernist affair erected in 1932 (figure 5.4). Five stories high, it was the former headquarters of the Seo shipping company; it had fallen into the possession of Marcel Peters and his company MP-Omega NV, who

5.3 Gordon Matta-Clark, *Office Baroque* with Steen in the background, 1977, Ernest van Dijckkaai 1, Antwerp.

planned to tear the building down and eventually rebuild on its site. For the purposes of Matta-Clark's project, use of the building was secured by Florent Bex, then director of the Internationaal Cultureel Centrum (ICC) in Antwerp. Bex, who had invited Matta-Clark to visit Antwerp in about 1976, finally met the artist at *Documenta* the following year. Discussions and letters were exchanged regarding the viability and nature of the Belgian project, with Matta-Clark insisting that the building be left standing "no less than a month."[23] He also intended the work to be very public, with its exterior cut open to the street. "The corner," he wrote Bex, "will be transformed into a segment of a spherical solid by separating it with an 'oxygen lance,' a tool that cuts reinforced concrete."[24]

Matta-Clark's first design was never realized, however. Bex presented the plan to the city authorities, who rejected it on the grounds that it would have been far too exposed to the street—too *public,* in a manner of speaking. Another proposal was submitted and then accepted in its stead, this time focusing on the building's interior. Inspired by two interlocking rings left by the wet imprints of a tea cup, Matta-Clark designed a plan in which "two semi-circular areas, of slightly different diameters," overlapped (figures 5.5 and 5.6).

These began on the first floor providing the constant motif as they were cut up through the floors and roof. Where these circles crossed, a peculiar, almost row-boat shaped hole resulted and was mutated from floor to floor as structural beams and available floor space dictated.

In this project . . . the disposition of spaces (large open offices near the ground, small interconnecting rooms toward the top) determined how the formal elements transformed from uninterrupted circular slices to shrapnel-like bits and pieces of the original form as they "collided" with partitions and walls.[25]

5.4 Site of *Office Baroque,* 1977, Ernest van Dijckkaai 1, Antwerp.

5.5, 5.6 (pages 224, 225) Gordon Matta-Clark, *Office Baroque,* 1977, Ernest van Dijckkaai 1, Antwerp.

"The most beautiful fugue of light, air, weather and sculpture,"[26] as Jane Crawford described it; or a "panoramic arabesque," to follow the artist's pronouncements. *Office Baroque* was in keeping with Matta-Clark's other works in its ambulatory quality (figures 5.7–5.9). Its internalization of wind, weather, and light, and the dynamic shifts in scale and movement were also enacted by the cuts and the exposed features of the building.

As graceful a passage as the site work offered to its viewers, its passage into being—and then demolition—was anything but seamless. From its origins in 1977, *Office Baroque* was subjected to a range of logistical difficulties that surpassed even the most trying dilemmas the artist had faced before. The rejection of the original, exterior plan was only the first in a series of problems, for others soon arose between the artist, the local authorities, and the owner of the property, Marcel Peters. When Peters gave Matta-Clark a key to the building, he abruptly commented, "I know nothing," as if to absolve himself in advance of any liability.[27] Liabilities would indeed develop. One evening, Matta-Clark and Crawford were marking the place of the cuts with grease sticks, when a group of policemen, who had stealthily tracked the activities of the couple, surrounded the two, hauled them off, and then threw them in jail. Bex was soon called in the middle of the night to bail them out; whereupon it was explained that the long-abandoned building had a secret history as a drug den for hippies and vagrants.

Other less melodramatic events were to take place around *Office Baroque,* foreshadowing the bureaucratic confusion that would descend upon the site in time. The work opened without incident to the public on October 7, with Matta-Clark acting as a tour guide throughout the building; an exhibition of photographs and building fragments was simultaneously staged at the ICC. On Saturday, October 16, however, a small advertisement appeared in the real estate section of the *Gazette van Antwerpen* (figure 5.10), a rough translation of which reads as follows:

5.7, 5.8, 5.9 (pages 227, 228, 229) Gordon Matta-Clark, *Office Baroque,* 1977, Ernest van Dijckkaai 1, Antwerp.

T. 40.32.36 of 27.90.43.

Tel. 30.78.30 - 35.00.24.

ZOERSELBOS te huur villa. Tel. 12.37.28. Weekd. na 18 u.

Luxe studio - EPI gem. of ongem., gr. nekant, zicht op keuk. en badk., gr. v.c., ingem. kasten, tel. - T. 031/30.22.69

d. ongemeub. studio uin, slechts 4.500 fr. Martin Belgiëlei 118

aglandweg, nieuw ap- 2 slaapk., badk., hof., onmidd. beschikb.

achtegalenpark) Gou- aan 11, gelijkvloers, geinst. keuken en arage.

e appart., gr. liv., hall, ng. keuk. en badk., gar. keld. Bist 30 Wil- 2.64

M: Draaiboomstraat utoweg) 2e verd. 2 slk. ver groen zone. 6.500 .80.

HT: Studio op gelijk- uff., tapis-plain. Pr. 36.43.17.

PEN: 2 slaapka- ern komfort - Kruis- 3, 15de verdieping. ar 1 december 1977. er maand + kosten. de inlichtingen tel.

gem. huis te huur. st. N.V. Tel. 30.79.77.

AT: pracht. landh.

TE HUUR

Buiten klassement 1802

ANTWERPEN

River - View Studio's

Burelen, op een verrassende artistieke manier verbouwd, tegenover het «Steen». Zeer ruime, bewoonbare werkruimte's, 1200 m2, uniek ontwerp, prachtig zicht, volledige acclimatisatie, stromend water op alle verdiepingen, zeer zonnig, zeer lage huurprijzen (vanaf 5.000 - fr/md.).

Te bezichtigen: elke zaterdag van 12 - 17 u.
Ernest Van Dyckkaai 1

3.200 **Amerikalei:** mod. studio
5.000 **Centrum:** app. 2 slpk.
5.000 **Zuid:** winkel en 4 plaats.

APP

2 SLPK.
3 SLPK.
4 SLPK.

De gemeub twee jaar in rijke intern hun buiten dergebrach

De tarieven ten gelden

Voor prijze en voor all tel. op nr.

MP BEHE

WINKE

— nabij De
— nabij Hu
— Amerikal
— Bisschop
— Turnhout
— Astridple

BUREL

— Amerikal
— Frankrijk
— Bisschop
— Appelma
— Oudaan:
— Van Scho
— Turnhout

RIVER-VIEW STUDIO'S
A dramatically reworked office building in front of the Steen. Artistically carved into lofty live-in professional studios 1200 sq. M. each . . . raw but flexible. Fully climatized, running water, sun all day long. Can be had for a song. . . . 5000 BF and up. GUIDED TOURS this Saturday from Noon to Five. No. 1 Ernest Van Dyckkaai [sic].[28]

Replete with the hyperbolic rhetoric of real estate advertising, the notice was a satyric gesture by Matta-Clark. But the advertisement caused enough attention among the speculating public that Peters was significantly annoyed. "I extend my apologies for any alarm or embarrassment this may have caused to you, and for having placed it without your prior knowledge," a sheepish letter from Matta-Clark to Peters reads:

In retrospect all I can offer is this explanation of my motives which were totally non-commercial. My purpose was to present what I thought a mildly absurd add [sic] for an art work out of the art context, and thereby attract the attention of an unprepared "bargain-hunter" so that I could then interview him for a film I was shooting that day in the building.[29]

Apropos of all of Matta-Clark's work, the intertwining of property and art fueled this minor confrontation. Not until after the artist's death, however, did the magnitude of such a conflict become fully apparent, culminating with the destruction of *Office Baroque.*

Indeed, although the site was only open to the general public for a little more than a month, it survived its producer by almost two years. Its relative longevity was a function of intensive efforts to save the work. Shortly after Matta-Clark's death on August 27, 1978, Crawford and Bex began a valiant if ultimately unsuccessful drive to preserve the building from destruction, recognizing that it was the only fully ex-

5.10 Gordon Matta-Clark, "River-View Studio's," Gazette van Antwerpen, October 16, 1977.

tant building cut by the artist. Bex has acknowledged that Matta-Clark's site-objects were never intended to be permanent works, but longer debates soon took place over the importance of saving it, and Bex was convinced of the effort.[30] "Gordon had always maintained that the buildings were the real work of art," Crawford also pointed out, "so I was desperate to preserve this last art piece."[31]

Bex and Crawford developed a plan to purchase the building through funds raised from an auction of art works donated by friends and colleagues. It soon became clear that the artist had more supporters than he could have ever imagined: some 230 artists from twenty countries donated works, "including Vito Acconci, Alice Aycock, Christo, the composer Robert Kushner, Sol LeWitt, Isamu Noguchi and Robert Rauschenberg."[32] This outpouring of support was so unexpected that Crawford and Bex expanded the focus of their plans. They decided to establish a contemporary museum that was principally organized around *Office Baroque,* what Crawford would call "the first artist's museum."[33] An adjacent property was to be purchased as part of the larger institution.

The second plan for saving *Office Baroque* and establishing the museum revolved around convincing the Belgian government of the viability of the institution, having the state "purchase" the works for the museum (through sponsors), and then using the money to buy *Office Baroque* and the nearby property. A long paper trail between Bex, Crawford, and the local authorities was shortly initiated, with the recently established Gordon Matta-Clark Foundation acting as the central organizing body of the effort. Several Belgian collectors agreed to sponsor the project, raising the necessary funds requested by Peters, who was more than willing to sell the property. But during the course of these negotiations, Peters experienced personal bankruptcy, which forced him to place the title to the building under his larger company, MP-Omega, NV, over which he did not have complete authority. With this gesture, yet another round of transactions began. The cost of the property continued to rise, in spite of the foundation's offers that met the previous asking price.

For all of these real estate maneuverings, exchanges between the city, the real estate group, and the foundation appeared to be proceeding smoothly enough. It thus came as a shock to Bex when he received a panic-stricken phone call one morning in the summer of 1980: the building was being torn down. By the time Bex arrived at the site, close to two floors had been demolished by a wrecking ball; by day's end,

Matta-Clark's cutting had been reduced to a pile of rubble. Revisiting this series of events today, Bex is convinced that the company thought it could secure more capital for the property alone. It is an observation made even more bitter by the company's total bankruptcy the following month.

MATTA-CLARK'S IMPOSSIBLE PLACE TODAY

But what does this sad episode tell us about the contemporary legacy of Matta-Clark's art? As laudable as the efforts were to save *Office Baroque,* its fate was in keeping with the theoretical tenor of all Matta-Clark's works: the terms of contemporary building programs ensure the destruction of the building's earlier incarnations; and property values play parasite to the burgeoning places of art and culture, a tired but necessary reminder of the processes of gentrification. The imbrication of *Office Baroque* in a tangle of governmental bureaucracy, money, real estate, and the international art world, demonstrates the implicit force of Matta-Clark's larger critique. It is a critique that goes to the heart of what it means to be contemporary—to be with the time.

Perhaps Matta-Clark's critical legacy is best understood attending to the actual outcome of his former sites. A parodic appropriation of an art historical trick—the juxtaposing of a work of art and the actual site from which it was drawn—becomes useful in thinking about the fate of his art and its relationship to the contemporary. Usually when an art historian engages in such gestures, placing a picture of a landscape next to a photograph of a mountain, for instance, it is as if to say, "This artist was here; he painted this work at this site; these are the similarities between the site now and its representation." The *then* and the *now* of the object and the site serve to confirm one another, stabilize the historical groundedness of the place in question. But employing such conventions for Matta-Clark's purposes bears witness to a radical ironizing of these premises; for to return to these sites is to encounter a fate prefigured by the longer histories of each place. To wit: property values and an influx of high-end boutiques have driven a great many galleries away from SoHo; the piers near *Day's End* now play host to an outpriced gymnasium and entertainment center; the Centre Pompidou is among the most heavily visited tourist attractions in Paris; and the former site of *Conical Intersect* is now known as "Le Quatier d'Horloge," a

Aldham Robarts L.R.C.
TEL. 0151 231 3701/3634

reference to time at once poignant and bathetic in light of this discussion. Only the actual site of *Office Baroque* demonstrates the tenuous, liminal status of the contemporary as it relates to building and construction. As of the Spring of 1994, a good fourteen years after *Office Baroque* was destroyed, the site remained an unused plot of land—in essence, a hole—an uncanny reminder of the losses upon which the terms of the present are partially shaped.

And what is to be salvaged from this failure of sorts, the incapacity of the art to survive today? Its worklessness, really? Perhaps the inability of the art to be integrated with our time offers a resistance to the material conditions of the present, even as these conditions succumb to art's techniques. But the building cuts by extension also refuse a future staked upon the gestures of the contemporary, offering the possibility of a space outside the proper and legislatable. For Matta-Clark, the object to be destroyed—its proleptic temporality—is always already an object projected for a later moment, as it is an opportunity for a new intervention.

The fate of Matta-Clark's dynamic and brilliant site works thus guarantees a strange place for the artist's legacy. His place for us is secure because, paradoxically, it is insecure. A restive place, it is at once sublime and impossible, its contemporaneity of no matter now.

NOTES

INTRODUCTION

1. On the classicist notion of work, described through the antinomy of form and matter, see Martin Heidegger, "The Origin of the Work of Art," in *Poetry, Language, Thought* (New York: Harper and Row, 1971), p. 27. Considerations of the work of art (as well as craft and applied science) are also bound to the notion of *techne,* which was not to be understood as practice or technique as such, but rather as the comprehension of the measurability of the art work, the possession of which guarantees its production. On *techne,* see Aristotle, *Nichomachean Ethics,* trans. M. Ostwald (Indianapolis: Bobbs-Merrill Co., 1962), pp. 151–52. It bears saying that theoretical discussions on the avant-garde have long turned around the status of the work of art. See Peter Bürger, *Theory of the Avant-Garde* (Minneapolis, MN: University of Minnesota Press, 1984), pp. 55–82.

2. On practice, particularly "spatial practice" in the city, see Michel De Certeau, *The Practice of Everyday Life* (Berkeley: University of California Press, 1984), p. 96.

3. See John Chandler and Lucy Lippard, "The Dematerialization of Art," *Art International,* February 20, 1968, pp. 31–36.

4. Ursula Meyer, "Introduction," in *Conceptual Art* (New York: Sutton, 1972), p. xi.

5. For an important account of conceptual art, see Alexander Alberro, "Deprivileging Art, Seth Siegelaub and the Politics of Conceptual Art" (Ph.D. diss., Northwestern University, 1997).

6. For artist's critiques of the notion of dematerialization or the disappearance of the art object, see Mel Bochner, "Excerpts from Speculation (1967–1970)," *Artforum* 8, no. 9. (May 1970), p. 70; and Daniel Buren, "Mise en Gard," in *Konzeption/Conception* (Leverkusen, Germany: Stüdtischen Museum, 1969), n.p. Many artists also took issue with the rather romantic notion that such work could resist the commodifying drives of the market. On this, see Alberro, pp. 3–5. Critics also detected a traditional model of artistic selfhood in these discussions, because they were dependent on the artist's autonomy as bearer of transparent meaning. See Benjamin Buchloh, "Conceptual Art 1962–1969, From the Critique of Institutions to the Aesthetics of Administration," in *October* 55 (Winter 1990) pp. 105–143 and Rosalind Krauss, "Sense and Sensibility: Reflections on Post 60's Art," in *Artforum* (November 1973), pp. 43–53.

7. Georges Bataille, *The Accursed Share,* vol. 1, trans. R. Hurley (New York: Zone Books, 1990), p. 21; also see Georges Bataille, *Inner Experience,* trans. Leslie-Anne Boldt (Albany: State University

of New York Press, 1988). My account is informed by Denis Hollier's crucial work on Bataille, *Against Architecture* (Cambridge, MA: MIT Press, 1989). Hollier's book bears relevance here in that it specifically treats the notion of architecture according to both Hegel and Bataille: for Hegel, architecture's place was, of course, primary or formative, and not only in the history of art; for Bataille, the destruction of architecture represented a resistance to the anthropocentric rationality of the Hegelian model and the logic of *Aufhebung* that underlay it.

As Hollier and others note, Bataille's theorization of the general economy contains an implicit critique of both the traditional notion of work and, by extension, the dialectics of Hegel. To think Hegel through Bataille's terms, the narrative of the dialectic suggests that all things are made useful—"put to work," in a manner of speaking—in the dialectic's totalizing drive toward Absolute Knowledge. The dialectic can therefore be regarded as the ultimate form of a restricted economy, as much as it assimilates, preserves, and sublimates everything in its idealist questing. The vicissitudes of alterity are overcome; negativity is enjoyed as a positive virtue; difference is obliterated; even death is made an object of understanding in Hegel's teleology. On Hegel's desire to internalize death itself for the progress of reason, see G. W. F. Hegel, *The Phenomenology of Spirit,* trans. A. V. Miller (Oxford: Oxford University Press, 1977), p. 20. For a critique of Hegel, see Bataille, "Hegel, Death and Sacrifice," reprinted in "On Bataille," *Yale French Studies,* no. 78 (1990), p. 9. On the difference between Hegel's reading of the dialectic and Bataille's, see Bataille, *The Accursed Share,* vol. 3, p. 369.

For an important reading of restricted and general economies, see Jacques Derrida, "From Restricted to General Economy, A Hegelianism without Reserve," *Writing and Difference,* trans. A. Bass (Chicago: University of Chicago Press), p. 259. Also resonant here is Maurice Blanchot's notion of "desoeuvrement" (literally, a revocation of work, or worklessness): Maurice Blanchot, *The Space of Literature,* trans. Leslie Smock (Lincoln: University of Nebraska, 1982), p. 46. Henri Lefebvre discusses Bataille's general economy as it relates to the production of space. See Henri Lefebvre, *The Production of Space,* trans. Donald Nicholson-Smith (Oxford: Blackwell Publishers, 1991), pp. 19–20, 176–180.

It bears saying that this mine is not the first reading to propose a connection between Matta-Clark and Bataille. Marianne Brouwer's essay "Laying Bare" also addresses the relation between the two, although she is less concerned with principles of economy than a certain thematization of architecture. See Marianne Brouwer, "Laying Bare," in *Gordon Matta-Clark,* exh. cat. (Valencia, Spain: IVAM Centre Julio Gonzalez, 1992), pp. 363–365. Far more incisive is Yve-Alain Bois and Rosalind Krauss's consideration of Matta-Clark's work as "formless." See Yve-Alain Bois and Rosalind Krauss, *Formless, A User's Guide* (New York: Zone Books, 1997).

8. Thierry de Duve, "Ex Situ" *Les Cahiers du Musée national d'art moderne,* no. 27 (Spring 1978), pp. 37–59. De Duve describes the sacrificial logic of much installation based work (including Matta-Clark's) in an essay that considers its virtual sitelessness.

9. Bataille, *The Accursed Share,* vol 1, p. 21.

10. Ibid., p. 23.

11. Henri Lefebvre, "Right to the City," reprinted in *Writings on Cities,* ed. and trans. Eleonore Kofman and Elizabeth Lebas (Oxford: Blackwell Publishers, 1996), pp. 66–70.

12. Matta-Clark quoted in Corinne Diserens, "The Greene Street Years," in *Gordon Matta-Clark,* p. 360.

13. Gordon Matta-Clark, proposal (c. 1974), The Estate of Gordon Matta-Clark, Weston, CT.

14. Lefebvre, *The Production of Space,* p. 85.

CHAPTER 1

1. See Joan Simon, "Gordon Matta-Clark: 1943–1978," *Art in America* (December 1978), p. 13. Also see Judith Russi Kirshner, "Non-uments," *Artforum* (October 1985), pp. 104–105.

2. Martica Sawin, *Surrealism in Exile* (Cambridge, MA: MIT Press, 1995), p. 290.

3. Anne Alpert, in conversation with the author, April 1, 1994, New York.

4. Roberto Matta, interviewed in *Gordon Matta-Clark,* exh. cat. (Valencia, Spain: IVAM Centre Julio Gonzalez, 1992), p. 396.

5. Caroline Goodden, interviewed by Joan Simon in *Gordon Matta-Clark, A Retrospective,* p. 40.

6. Harold Bloom, *The Anxiety of Influence* (Oxford: Oxford University Press, 1973).

7. Le Corbusier, *The Radiant City,* (New York: Orion Press, 1967), title page.

8. Nancy Miller, "Interview with Matta," *Matta: The First Decade,* exh. cat. (Waltham, MA: Rose Art Museum, Brandeis University, 1982), p. 18.

9. Ibid., p. 19.

10. The notion that Le Corbusier's architecture is categorically rationalist and unambiguous represents something of a surrealistic caricature of the architect. A growing body of work attests to the architect's surrealistic leanings, in spite of his avowed hatred of the movement. See Rem Koolhaas, "Europeans: Bieur! Dali and Le Corbusier Reconquer New York," in *Delirious New York,* (New York: The Monacelli Press, 1994), pp. 235–281.

11. Le Corbusier, *L'Urbanisme* (Paris: Vincent, Fréal et Cie, 1966), p. 166.

12. Roberto Matta, "Mathématique Sensible—Architecture du Temps," *Minotaure,* no. 11 (Spring 1938), p. 43. Reprinted in translation as "Sensitive Mathematics—Architecture of Time," in *The Surrealists on Art,* ed. Lucy R. Lippard (Englewood Cliffs, N.J.: Prentice Hall, 1970), pp. 167–169.

13. Anthony Vidler, *The Architectural Uncanny: Essays in the Modern Unhomely* (Cambridge, MA: MIT Press, 1992), pp. 150–156.

14. Sigmund Freud, "The Uncanny," in *The Collected Papers of Sigmund Freud,* vol. 4 (London: The Hogarth Press, 1923), p. 370.

15. Ibid., p. 375.

16. The uncanny's repetition of motifs both familiar and strange parallels the compulsion to repeat that is at the heart of the repressed moment that constitutes the Oedipal threat. The desire to occupy the womb thus suggests the homeostatic tendency of all organic life, famously known as the death drive. Sigmund Freud, *Beyond the Pleasure Principle,* trans. James Strachey (New York: W. W. Norton, 1975).

17. Kirshner, "Non-uments," pp. 104–106. Also see Brouwer, "Laying Bare," pp. 363–365.

18. "The very nature of my work with buildings takes issues with the functionalist attitude to the extent that this kind of self-conscious vocational responsibility has failed to question or reexamine the quality of life being served." Gordon Matta-Clark interviewed by Donald Wall,"Gordon Matta-Clark's Building Dissections," *Arts Magazine* (March 1976), p. 76.

19. Gordon Matta-Clark, letter to "The Mob" (The Anarchitecture Group), c/o Caroline Goodden, New York, December 10, 1973, The Estate of Gordon Matta-Clark, Weston, CT (hereafter referred to as E G M-C.). Also note Matta-Clark's garbled Le Corbusier reference in the same letter. "A living place to (carry-all) responses to the perfect man or modulor as he would serve as a bearer for housing building—not building."

20. The term "defunctionalizing" is Matta-Clark's, and is understood in opposition to the "engineering" purpose of the building. Gordon Matta-Clark, typed notes, c. late 1974–1975, p. 3, E G M-C.

21. Wall, "Gordon Matta-Clark's Building Dissections," p. 40.

22. Gordon Matta-Clark, typed notes, c. late 1974–1975, p. 3.

23. Gordon Matta-Clark interviewed by Liza Bear, "*Splitting:* The Humphrey Street Building," *Avalanche* (December 1974), p. 37.

24. Ibid.

25. *Gordon Matta-Clark: A Retrospective,* op. cit., p. 68.

26. Bear, "Splitting: The Humphrey Street Building," p. 36.

27. Christopher Knight, "How the Art World Gained Through Division," *Los Angeles Times,* October 17, 1995, F1 and F4.

28. Maud Lavin, "Gordon Matta-Clark and Individualism," *Arts Magazine* 48 (January 1984), pp. 138–141.

29. Interview with Gordon Matta-Clark (interviewer unnamed), in *Gordon Matta-Clark,* exh. cat. (Antwerp: Internationaal Cultureel Centrum, 1977), p. 10.

30. Kenneth Jackson, *Crabgrass Frontier* (New York and Oxford: Oxford University Press, 1986), p. 6.

31. On philosophical models of privacy (in relation to the terms of the public sphere) see Seyla Benhabib, "Models of Public Space: Hannah Arendt and the Liberal Tradition and Jürgen Habermas," in *Habermas and the Public Sphere,* ed. Craig Calhoun (Cambridge, MA: MIT Press, 1992), pp. 90–93.

32. Jürgen Habermas, *The Structural Transformation of the Public Sphere* (Cambridge, MA: MIT Press, 1989).

33. A central text on this topic is Oskar Negt and Alexander Kluge, *Public Sphere and Experience* (Minneapolis: University of Minnesota Press, 1993). Also see Jürgen Habermas, "Modernity, An Incomplete Project," in *The Anti-Aesthetic,* ed. Hal Foster (Port Townsend, WA: Bay Press, 1983), pp. 3–16; and Jean-François Lyotard, *The Postmodern Condition: A Report on Knowledge* (Minneapolis: University of Minnesota Press, 1985).

34. The inscription of private, suburban space as feminine belied woman's inaccessibility to the public sphere, coded as masculine. For an urban studies analysis of women's inaccessibility to the public sphere, see Dolores Hayden, *Redesigning the American Dream: The Future of Housing, Work and Family Life* (New York: W. W. Norton, 1984), p. 50. For historical and sociological analyses of womens' access to the public sphere, see Joan Landes, *Women and the Public Sphere in the Age of the French Revolution* (Ithaca, NY: Cornell University Press, 1988); Mary P. Ryan, "Gender and Public

Access: Women's Politics in Nineteenth Century America," in *Habermas and the Public Sphere,* pp. 259–289; and Mary P. Ryan, *Women in Public* (Baltimore, MD: Johns Hopkins University Press, 1990).

35. Gordon Matta-Clark, undated notecard, E G M-C.

36. Gordon Matta-Clark, proposal for Guggenheim Fellowship, (draft, August 18, 1976), E G M-C.

37. Matta-Clark, proposal for Guggenheim Fellowship.

38. For instance, compare Matta-Clark's treatment of the "private" space of the suburban home with the public space of the city. In his work *Open House* (1972), a dumpster that served as the site of performance-based activities, the urban and, by extension, public sphere is literalized as an "open house," which is then equated to urban detritus.

39. Matta-Clark, proposal for Guggenheim Fellowship.

40. On Englewood, see John K. Lattimer, *This is Early Englewood* (Englewood, NJ: Englewood Historical Society, 1990); and Daniel Bennett Mazur, "People, Politics and Planning: The Comparative History of Three Suburban Communities" (Ph.D. diss., Rutgers University Department of Urban Planning, 1981), pp. 94–160; 485–660.

41. See Jackson, *Crabgrass Frontier,* p. 241; and Wall, "Gordon Matta-Clark's Building Dissections," op. cit., p. 76.

42. One of the last censuses taken in Englewood before Matta-Clark's work was executed suggests that Humphrey Street was already quite depressed in the early sixties. In the census of city blocks recorded in 1960, Humphrey Street (Tract #69, Block #49) was listed as having seventy-nine housing units of which twenty-eight were considered "deteriorating" and eleven completely "dilapidated"—nearly half of the housing units on the street. Of the total population of 317 individuals, seventy-six were listed as non-white. *U.S. Census of Housing, 1960, City Blocks, Englewood, N.J.*, prepared under the supervision of Wayne F. Daugherty, Chief Housing Division, U.S. Department of Commerce, Bureau of the Census, p. 3.

43. On this field trip, see A. R., "Anarchitecture in Englewood: Clean Cut," and Laurie Anderson, "Take Two," both in *Art-Rite,* no. 6 (Summer, 1974).

44. On Matta-Clark's notion of voyeurism, see Bear, "*Splitting:* the Humphrey Street Building," p. 37, as well as chapter 2 of this book. Also consider the title of one of his videos, *Chinatown Voyeur* (1971).

45. Kirshner, "Non-uments," p. 389.

46. See Bear "*Splitting,* The Humphrey Street Building," p. 36.

47. Alice Aycock interviewed by Joan Simon, in *Gordon Matta-Clark: A Retrospective,* p. 33.

48. On this urban renewal scheme in Binghamton, see "New superblock will turn downtown into a plaza," *The American City,* vol. 83, no. 7, July 1968, p. 131.

49. Gordon Matta-Clark, academic transcript, Registrar of Cornell University, 1968.

50. Quoted in Bear, "*Splitting:* The Humphrey Street Building," p. 36.

51. On the internal politics of the department and its history, see Kenneth Frampton and Alessandra Latour, "Notes on American Architectural Education"; and on the particularities of its design program, see David Blakeslee Middleton, "The Combining of the Traditional City and the Modern City: The Work of the Cornell Graduate School of Urban Design," both in *Lotus International,* no. 27 (1981), pp. 5–39; and pp. 47–65.

52. *Announcement of Cornell University,* School of Architecture, Ithaca, NY, vols. 53, 54, 55, 56, 57, 1961–1966. Also see Alexander Caragonne, *The Texas Rangers: Notes from the Architectural Underground* (Cambridge, MA: MIT Press, 1994); and Colin Rowe, *As I was Saying: Recollections and Miscellaneous Essays, Cornelliana,* ed. Alexander Caragone (Cambridge, MA: MIT Press, 1995).

53. On the "New York Five," see *Five Architects,* exh. cat., (New York: The Museum of Modern Art, 1969).

54. Frampton, "Notes on American Architectural Education," p. 29.

55. Caragonne, *The Texas Rangers,* p. 345.

56. Frampton, "Notes on American Architectural Education," p. 29.

57. The term was not coined by Rowe but by two graduate students, Stuart Cohen and Stephen Hurtt, who wrote a master's thesis on Le Corbusier. See Thomas L. Schumacher, "Contextualism: Urban Ideals and Deformations," in *Casabella,* nos. 359–360 (1971), pp. 79–86.

58. See William Ellis, "Type and Context in Urbanism: Colin Rowe's Contextualism." In *Oppositions* 22 (Fall 1979), p. 4; and Frampton, "Notes on American Architectural Education," p. 29.

59. Ellis, "Type and Context in Urbanism," p. 4.

60. Fred Koetter and Colin Rowe, *Collage City* (Cambridge, MA: MIT Press, 1978), p. 149.

61. Rowe and Koetter themselves discuss the importance of ambiguous space in *Collage City,* p. 168.

62. An architectural statement that crystallizes this attitude is Arthur Drexler's preface to *Five Architects,* p. 1.

63. The title of an exhibition held at Cornell, *Cornell Then: Sculpture Now,* presents a neat homology between former students of the university and the state of contemporary sculpture in the seventies. See the exhibition catalogue, *Cornell Then: Sculpture Now* (Ithaca, NY: 1977).

Of course, Cornell was also known for explicitly political events in the late sixties: from December 1968 to June 1969, the student union was occupied by some 80–100 black students who were protesting against (and protecting themselves from) white extremists on campus. Matta-Clark had graduated from Cornell by that time, but he still lived in Ithaca (the *Earth Art* show was staged in February 1969).

64. *Earthworks* opened at the Dwan Gallery, New York, on October 5, 1968, four months before the Cornell show in 1969.

65. Willoughby Sharp, *Earth Art,* exh. cat. (Ithaca, NY: A. D. White Museum, 1970), n.p.

66. Among the most sophisticated accounts written by artists are Robert Smithson, *The Writings of Robert Smithson,* ed. Nancy Holt (New York, New York University Press, 1979); and Robert Morris, *Continuous Project Altered Daily* (Cambridge, MA: MIT Press, 1994). For critical and historical writing, see Rosalind Krauss, "Sculpture in the Expanded Field," in *The Originality of the Avant-Garde and other Modernist Myths* (Cambridge, MA: MIT Press, 1985), pp. 276–290; and Rosalind Krauss "The Double Negative: A New Syntax for Sculpture," in *Passages in Modern Sculpture* (Cambridge, MA: MIT Press, 1981), pp. 243–287. Also see Yve-Alain Bois, "A Picturesque Stroll Around *Clara Clara,*" reprinted in *October: The First Decade* (Cambridge, MA: MIT Press, 1987), pp. 342–371. For an account on Serra, devoted largely to the *Tilted Arc* controversy, see Douglas Crimp, "Redefining Site-Specificity," in *On the Museum's Ruins* (Cambridge, MA: MIT Press, 1993). An excellent critical genealogy of the notion of site specificity is found in Miwon Kwon, "One Place after Another: Notes on Site Specificity," *October* 80 (Spring 1987), pp. 85–111; also see James Meyer, "The Function of Site," *Documents* 7 (Fall 1996), pp. 20–29.

67. Kwon, "One Place after Another," p. 109.

68. See John Beardsley's observation on earth art, in *Earth Art and Beyond* (New York: Harry N. Abrams, 1984), p. 7: "Most of these works are inextricably bound to their sites, and take as a large part of their content a relationship with the specific characteristics of their particular surround-

ings. . . . These are not isolated objects, intended for isolated appraisal, but fully engaged elements of their respective environments, intended to provide an inimitable experience of a certain place for both the artist and the viewer."

69. Just as the legitimacy of the public sphere has been questioned, so, too, have the terms of public art. On the problematics of public art and the public sphere, see Rosalyn Deutsche, *Evictions* (Cambridge, MA: MIT Press, 1996).

70. Smithson, *The Writings of Robert Smithson,* p. 105.

71. Nancy Holt recalls Smithson's visiting and working on site at the campus at least twice, first in December 1968, the second time in January of the following year (Nancy Holt in telephone conversation with the author, February 11, 1994, New York-Cambridge). A couple of artists did not personally install their work because of bad weather conditions in New York.

72. Louise Lawler in conversation with the author, January 9, 1995, New York.

73. Dan Graham in conversation with the author, February 7, 1995, New York; also see Dan Graham, "Gordon Matta-Clark," reprinted in *Rock My Religion,* ed. Brian Wallis (Cambridge, MA: MIT Press, 1993), p. 194. For statements by Keith Sonnier and Lawrence Weiner, see *Gordon Matta-Clark: A Retrospective,* pp. 141–142.

74. Nancy Holt, in phone conversation with the author, February 11, 1994, New York-Cambridge.

75. See James Lingwood and Maggie Gilchrist, "El Entropologo," in *El Paisaje Entropico* (Valencia, Spain: IVAM Centro Julio Gonzalez, 1993), pp. 17–25. Also see Gary Shapiro, *Earthwards: Robert Smithson and Art after Babel* (Berkeley: University of California Press, 1995).

76. A useful account of the physical bases of entropy is Martin Goldstein and Inge F. Goldstein, *The Refrigerator and the Universe: Understanding the Laws of Energy* (Cambridge, MA: Harvard University Press, 1993); also see Max Planck, *Eight Lectures on Theoretical Physics* (New York: Columbia University Press, 1915).

77. Robert Smithson, "Entropy and the New Monuments," reprinted in *The Writings of Robert Smithson,* pp. 9–18.

78. See Rudolf Arnheim, *Entropy and Art: An Essay on Disorder and Order* (Berkeley: University of California Press, 1971), pp. 7–9.

79. Claude Levi-Strauss, "Clocks and Steam-engines," in Georges Charbonnier, *Conversations with Claude Levi-Strauss,* (New York: Grossman, 1969), pp. 33–42; Thomas Pynchon, "Entropy," *The Kenyon Review,* vol. 22, no. 2 (Spring 1960), pp. 277–293.

80. Smithson, "Entropy and the New Monuments," p. 9. In the sense that entropy refuses teleology, temporally regresses, or suggests an "energy drain," a theoretical continuum between the theorization of the entropic and the death drive (which has its origins in the uncanny) can be evinced. Rudolf Arnheim makes such a connection between entropy and the death drive. See Arnheim, *Entropy and Art,* pp. 42–43.

81. Ibid., p. 10.

82. Ibid., p. 11.

83. Anne Alpert in conversation with the author, April 1, 1994, New York.

84. Tina Girouard, in *Gordon Matta-Clark: A Retrospective,* p. 121.

85. John Gibson, in *Gordon Matta-Clark: A Retrospective,* p. 23.

86. See Cindy Nemser, "The Alchemist and the Phenomenologist," *Art in America,* no. 59 (March 1970), pp. 100–103.

87. Quoted by Mary Jane Jacob, in *Gordon Matta-Clark: A Retrospective,* p. 26.

88. A "recipe" for a number of works from this period was found in the pages of Matta-Clark's copy of Claude Levi-Strauss's *The Raw and the Cooked* in the artist's library in Weston, CT.

89. Robert Smithson interviewed by Allison Skye, "Entropy Made Visible," in *The Writings of Robert Smithson,* p. 191.

90. Quoted in Wall, "Gordon Matta-Clark's Building Dissections," op. cit., p. 77.

91. Robert Smithson, "A Tour of the Monuments of Passaic, New Jersey," in *The Writings of Robert Smithson,* p. 54.

92. Smithson, "Entropy Made Visible," p. 191.

93. Smithson, "Frederick Law Olmsted and the Dialectical Landscape," in *The Writings of Robert Smithson,* pp. 117–129.

94. Ibid., p. 119.

95. Frederick Law Olmsted, *The Papers of Frederick Law Olmsted: The Years of Olmsted, Vaux and Company, 1865–1874,* vol. 6, eds. D. Schuyler and J. Turner Censer (Baltimore, MD: Johns Hopkins University Press, 1992), p. 195.

96. Jacques Derrida, "The Principle of Reason: The University in the Eyes of its Pupils," *Diacritics,* vol. 13, no. 3 (December 1983), p. 5.

97. Ibid., p. 6.

98. Richard Bernstein, "Another fatal plunge has Cornell asking whether its gorges inspire student suicides," *New York Times,* November 5, 1994, Metro Section, pp. 25–26.

99. Derrida, "The Principle of Reason," p. 3.

100. For the full range of this argument, see Martin Heidegger, "Lecture Three," *The Principle of Reason,* trans. R. Lilly (Bloomington: University of Indiana Press, 1991), pp. 17–25.

101. Derrida, "The Principle of Reason," p. 9.

102. See Hobbs, *Robert Smithson: Sculpture* (Ithaca: Cornell University Press, 1981), pp. 131–132; Nancy Holt in conversation with the author, February 11, 1994, New York.

103. Louise Lawler (in conversation with the author, January 9, 1994, New York) suggests that the two met during the installation of the *Earth Art* show in February 1969, but cannot precisely confirm this. If this were in fact the case, then the idea for Matta-Clark's *Rope Bridge* effectively predates Smithson's *Mirror Wedge.*

104. Alois Riegl, "The Modern Cult of Monuments: Its Character and Its Origin," trans. Kurt Forster and Diane Ghirardo, *Oppositions* 25 (Fall 1982), p. 21.

105. Ibid., p. 22.

106. Ibid., p. 35.

CHAPTER 2

A version of this chapter was published as "Objets impropres de la modernité," in *Les Cahiers du Musée national d'art moderne,* no. 60 (Winter, 1997).

1. G. W. F. Hegel, *Elements of the Philosophy of Right,* ed. A. W. Wood (Cambridge, U.K.: Cambridge University Press, 1991), p. 76.

2. Les Levine interviewed by Joan Simon, in *Gordon Matta-Clark: A Retrospective,* ed. Mary Jane Jacob (Chicago: Museum of Contemporary Art, 1985), p. 96.

3. Gordon Matta-Clark interviewed by Liza Bear, "*Splitting:* The Humphrey Street House," *Avalanche* (December 1974), pp. 34–37.

4. For a survey on the development of alternative spaces in the late 1960s and early seventies, see Jacki Apple, *Alternatives in Retrospect,* exh. cat. (New York: The New Museum of Contemporary Art, 1981); *New York-Downtown Manhattan: SoHo,* exh. cat. (Berlin: Akademie der Kunst, 1976); and Stephanie Edens, "Alterative Spaces Soho-Style," *Art in America,* vol. 61, no. six (November–December 1973), pp. 38–39.

5. See *Soho—Cast Iron Historic Designation Report,* prepared for the City of New York Parks, Recreation, and Cultural Affairs Administration, Landmarks Preservation Commission, 1973, p. 104.

6. For an account of the founding of the space, published shortly after it opened, see Alan Saret and Jeffrey Lew "112 Greene Street, An Interview," *Avalanche* (Winter 1971), pp. 12–13. Also see Alan Saret quoted in *112 Workshop/112 Greene Street,* ed. Robin Brentano with M. Savitt (New York: New York University Press, 1981), p. xii.

7. Jene Highstein in conversation with the author, November 7, 1995, Cambridge, MA.

8. Suzanne Harris quoted in *112 Workshop/112 Greene Street,* p. vii.

9. Highstein in conversation with the author, November 7, 1995, Cambridge, MA.

10. Highstein, ibid. Also see Alan Saret's recollections on the founding of 112 Greene Street in *112 Workshop/112 Greene Street,* p. xii.

11. For the connection between the early and the later generation, see Lawrence Alloway, "SoHo as Bohemia," in *New York-Downtown Manhattan: SoHo,* pp. 142–150.

12. George Trakas's site-specific piece (the "demolition piece") from November 1971 involved removing sections of the floor of 112 Greene Street, and was installed without Lew's knowledge. See *112 Workshop/112 Greene Street,* p. 10.

13. Jeffrey Lew, quoted in *112 Workshop/112 Greene Street,* p. 2.

14. Mary Jane Jacob, *Gordon Matta-Clark: A Retrospective,* p. 31.

15. Gordon Matta-Clark quoted in *Gordon Matta-Clark,* exh. cat. (Valencia, Spain: IVAM, Centro Julio Gonzalez 1993), p. 369.

16. Caroline Goodden Ames in telephone conversation with the author, December 19, 1995, Cambridge, MA-Ruidoso Downs, New Mexico.

17. Jeffrey Lew quoted in Edens, "Alternative Spaces Soho-Style," p. 38.

18. Richard Nonas quoted in *Gordon Matta-Clark,* p. 398.

19. Matta-Clark's fascination with basements might also recall Gaston Bachelard's phenomenology of cellars popularized in *The Poetics of Space* (Boston: Beacon Press, 1994), pp. 22–23. The book was originally published in France in 1958 and translated into English in 1964. In Chapter 3, I address the phenomenology of the house through the terms of Merleau-Ponty (not Bachelard).

20. See Caroline Goodden quoted in *112 Workshop/112 Greene Street,* p. 7, and in conversation with the author, December 19, 1995.

21. Gordon Matta-Clark interviewed by Donald Wall, "Gordon Matta-Clark's Building Dissections," *Arts Magazine* (March 1976), pp. 74–79.

22. Interview with Gordon Matta-Clark (interviewer unnamed), in *Gordon Matta-Clark,* exh. cat. (Antwerp: Internationaal Cultureel Centrum, 1977), p. 10.

23. "Rumbles," *Avalanche* (Fall 1971).

24. Goodden, in conversation with the author, December 19, 1995.

25. Letter from Gordon Matta-Clark to Lee Jaffe, August 1, 1971, E G M-C.

26. Goodden, quoted in *Gordon Matta-Clark: A Retrospective,* pp. 39–40.

27. Henri Lefebvre, *The Production of Space,* trans. Donald Nicholson-Smith (Oxford: Blackwell, 1991), p. 87.

28. Rodolphe Gasché, "Ideality in Fragmentation," introduction to Friedrich Schlegel, *Philosophical Fragments* (Minneapolis: University of Minnesota Press, 1991), p. vii.

29. Gordon Matta-Clark, letter to Harold Stern, Department of Real Estate, New York, July 10, 1971, E G M-C.

30. Of *Bronx Floors,* Goodden recalls that it was less the illegality of his removals that was at issue than the safety of those who might occupy the buildings. Also see Manfred Hecht interviewed by Joan Simon in *Gordon Matta-Clark, A Retrospective,* p. 73.

31. In 1967 William Anastasi exhibited silkscreened images of the walls of the Dwan gallery on the walls of the Dwan Gallery, but the reputation of the gallery casts a different critical light on the relationship of art to its site.

32. Rosalind Krauss, "Notes on the Index, Part 2" *in The Originality of the Avant-Garde and Other Modernist Myths* (Cambridge, MA: MIT Press, 1985), p. 217.

33. Ibid., p. 211.

34. Ibid., p. 217.

35. See "Art and Industry in SoHo," *The Village Voice,* January 28, 1971, p. 1.

36. A notable exception to this tendency is Thomas Crow, "Site-Specific Art: The Strong and the Weak," in *Modern Art in the Common Culture* (New Haven, CT: Yale University Press, 1996), pp. 131–152. Some artists have consistently testified to this connection: see, for example, the statement by Lawrence Weiner in *Gordon Matta-Clark, A Retrospective,* p. 141. That Daniel Buren, a friend of Matta-Clark's, and Dan Graham, a social acquaintance, speak glowingly about his work in terms that are congruent with their own interests suggests a certain oversight on the part of earlier historians of Matta-Clark. See Dan Graham, "Gordon Matta-Clark," in *Rock My Religion* (Cambridge, MA: MIT Press, 1992), pp. 194–206. Further testimony was provided by Daniel Buren in conversation with the author, Paris, April 25, 1994; and Dan Graham in conversation with the author, New York, February 7, 1995. Finally, Matta-Clark referred to "Dan Graham's milestone work on the American home" (presumably, Graham's important *Homes for America*) on two occasions: Gordon Matta-Clark, letter to Caroline Goodden and "The Meeting" (the Anarchitecture group), December 6, 1973, from the Netherlands; and a notebook, c. 1973, E G M-C.

37. On the critique of institutions, see Benjamin Buchloh, "Conceptual Art 1962–69: From the Aesthetics of Administration to the Critique of Institutions," *October* 55 (Winter 1990), pp. 105–143; and Hal Foster, "Who's Afraid of the Neo-Avant-Garde" (along with other essays) in *The Return of the Real* (Cambridge, MA: MIT Press, 1996). The classic text on the avant-garde as "institution" to which the "neo-avant-garde" responds as critique is Peter Bürger, *Theory of the Avant-Garde* (Minneapolis: University of Minnesota Press, 1984). On the white cube, see Brian

O'Doherty, *Inside the White Cube: The Ideology of the Gallery Space* (San Francisco: Lapis Press, 1976).

38. Daniel Buren, "Notes on Work in Connection with the Place where it is Installed Taken between 1967 and 1975," *Studio International* 190, no. 977 (September 1975), pp. 124–129. This essay appears in an issue of *Studio International* entirely devoted to the theme of the relation between art and architecture.

39. Michael Asher, *Writings: 1973–1983 On Works 1969–1979,* ed. Benjamin Buchloh (Halifax: The Press of the Nova Scotia College of Art and Design, 1979), p. 76.

40. Ibid., p. 81.

41. Michel de Certeau, *The Practice of Everyday Life* (Berkeley: University of California Press, 1984), p. 91.

42. Gordon Matta-Clark, undated notecard (c. 1973), #1177, E G M-C.

43. For a comprehensive survey on SoHo's cast-iron buildings, see *SoHo—Cast Iron Historic Designation Report.* Cast-iron technology was deployed in New York as early as 1812, but it was in the 1840s that its merits were simultaneously recognized by the competing Manhattan-based companies of Daniel Badger and James Bogardus.

44. Henri Lefebvre, "Industrialization and Urbanization," *Right to the City,* reprinted in *Henri Lefebvre: Writings on Cities,* p. 69.

45. Ibid., p. 70.

46. Ibid., p. 70.

47. On the debate concerning the theorization of space through Marxian categories of production, see Manuel Castells, *The Urban Question: A Marxist Approach* (London: E. Arnold, 1977). A useful review of the Lefebvre/Castells debate is M. Gottdiener, *The Social Production of Urban Space* (Austin: University of Texas Press, 1985).

48. Lefebvre, *Rights to the City,* p. 66.

49. Ibid.

50. Lefebvre's account on the production of space owes something to Bataille's notion of the general economy; his emphasis on the city as *oeuvre*—a kind of use value irreducible to the logic of ex-

change—is informed by Bataille's *Accursed Share.* See Lefebvre, *The Production of Space,* pp. 177–180.

51. On historical accounts of urban space as festival or play, see Mona Ozouf, *Festivals and the French Revolution* (Cambridge, MA: Harvard University Press, 1988).

52. For a comprehensive discussion of this history see Robert Fitch, *The Assassination of New York* (London: Verso, 1993).

53. Lefebvre, *The Production of Space,* p. 73.

54. Lefebvre, "Space: Social Product and Use Value," in J. W. Freiberg, *Critical Sociology: European Perspectives* (New York: Wiley, 1979), p. 291.

55. The Department of Housing and Urban Development (HUD) was granted cabinet-level status by Lyndon Johnson in 1965. It bears saying that the term "deconcentration" is not neutral; to follow M. Gottdiener, deconcentration "refers to the absolute increase of population and density of social activities outside traditional city regions," although in the past it has referred to "a general demographic leveling of population density across metropolitan regions." On the use of "deconcentration" and the related term "decentralization," see Gottdiener, *The Social Production of Urban Space,* p. 9. On the ideology of "concentration" in cities, see Jane Jacobs, "The Need for Concentration," in *The Death and Life of Great American Cities* (New York: Vintage Books, 1961), pp. 200–205.

56. American urban renewal proper begins in the forties and not in New York but Chicago, when federal urban renewal legislation is enacted in 1949. My thanks to Sarah Whiting for her incisive criticisms of my reading.

57. Nathan Silver, *Lost New York* (New York: Random House/Wing Books, 1967).

58. On the Lindsay Plan, see Fitch, *The Assassination of New York,* pp. 119–121.

59. Sharon Zukin, *Loft Living: Culture and Capital in Urban Change* (New Brunswick, NJ: Rutgers University Press, 1989), p. 76.

60. Among the best known examples is Robert Venturi, *Complexity and Contradiction in Architecture* (New York: The Museum of Modern Art, 1966). For a reclamation of the streetscape from a non-architect's perspective (indeed, from a figure who made claims for a "non-pedigreed architecture"), see Bernard Rudofsky, *Streets for People* (New York: Doubleday and Company, 1969). Note that a copy of Rudofsky's exhibition catalogue *Architecture without Architects* (New York: The Museum of Modern Art, 1964) was found in Matta-Clark's library.

61. Gottdiener, *The Social Production of Urban Space,* p. xv. On contemporaneous debates, see Robert Goodman, *After the Planners* (New York: Simon and Schuster), 1971.

62. Jane Jacobs, *The Death and Life of American Cities,* pp. 4–5.

63. Ibid., p. 25.

64. Gordon Matta-Clark, undated (and unaddressed) proposal, c. 1974, E G M-C.

65. Charles R. Simpson, *SoHo: The Artist in the City* (Chicago: University of Chicago Press, 1981), p. 119. The average lofts consisted of roughly 2,500 feet of unpartitioned space, and were rented for $90.00 per month up until the mid–1960s.

66. An incisive account on the economic development of SoHo is found in Zukin, *Loft Living: Culture and Capital in Urban Change;* also extremely informative are Simpson, *SoHo: The Artist in the City,* and J. R. Hudson, *The Unanticipated City: Loft Conversion in Lower Manhattan* (Amherst: University of Massachusetts Press, 1987).

67. Simpson gives a useful brief on the word "slum" in the complex rhetoric of urban politics. The designation of an urban area as a slum guarantees the availability of state and federal funds for urban renewal under Title 1 Slum-Clearance Legislation. The "Slum-Clearance" Rationale was used in the demolition of many urban areas in the Northeast after World War II. But slums have traditionally been considered residential neighborhoods, and not manufacturing areas, as the South Houston Industrial Area was designated under current zoning laws then. As Simpson notes, "Advocates for redevelopment [of SoHo] attempted to extend the definition of slum to include areas without residents" (see *SoHo,* p. 133).

68. Chester Rapkin, *South Houston Industrial Area: Economic Significance and Condition of Structures in a Loft Section of Manhattan,* City of New York, Department of City Planning, 1973.

69. See, for example, R. Park, E. Burgess, and Robert Mckenzie, *The City* (Chicago: University of Chicago Press, 1925); and Amos Hawley, *Human Ecology* (New York: Ronald Press, 1950).

70. Quoted in Simpson, *SoHo,* p. 125.

71. Among its other problems, Article 7-B tacitly discouraged owners from renting to artists. First it prohibited manufacturers and artists from sharing the same lofts, effectively negating advances made for mixed-use occupancy of buildings. Beyond this, Article 7-B demanded that the building's owners meet expensive building codes (primarily fire codes) that were standard in residential housing.

72. See Simpson, *SoHo,* p. 155; and Zukin, *Loft Living,* pp. 52–55.

73. On the efforts to preserve the cast-iron architecture, see *SoHo—Cast-Iron Historic District,* pp. 24–30.

74. The first two art galleries in the area were Paula Cooper's on Wooster Street, and Richard Feigan's "warehouse" exhibition space. Both opened in 1968.

75. Gordon Matta-Clark, undated notes, E G M-C.

76. It is with George Maciunas's Fluxhouse Cooperatives (80–82 Wooster Street and then 16–18 Greene Street), founded in the South Houston Industrial Area in 1966, that the role of artist and real estate developer converged so dramatically that artistic practice could never again declare itself innocent of the business of speculation. On this history, see, Simpson, *SoHo: The Artist in the City,* pp. 156–157. It bears saying that Matta-Clark was also involved in a small-scale real estate operation called Table Top Realty, although the nature of his dealings was hardly of the scale (not to mention dubiousness) of Maciunas's.

77. Dan Carlinsky, "'Sliver' Buyers Have a Field Day at City Sales," *New York Times,* October 14, 1973, Real Estate Section, p. 1 and p. 12.

78. On the *Fake Estates,* Hubert Damisch has noted the interstitial relationship of Matta-Clark's property to the modernist grid, describing the artist's property as falling between the separate units of the grid as it simultaneously confirms the intractability of the model for modernist practice. Hubert Damisch in conversation with the author, Washington, D.C., September 19, 1996.

79. See Rosalind Krauss, "Grids," in *The Originality of the Avant-Garde and Other Modernist Myths,* pp. 8–22. Krauss has also written about the "exploded section" of the grid in works by Peter Eisenman and Rem Koolhaas: see Rosalind Krauss, "Some Notes on the Subject of the Grid," in *ANYone,* ed. Cynthia P. Davidson (New York: Rizzoli International Publications, 1991), pp. 214–226.

80. Carlinsky, "'Sliver' Buyers Have a Field Day at City Sales," p. 12.

81. Gordon Matta-Clark interviewed by Liza Bear, p. 34.

82. Karl Marx, *Economic and Philosophical Manuscripts,* in *Selected Writings,* ed. D. McClellan (Oxford: Oxford University Press, 1977), p. 91.

83. Gordon Matta-Clark, letter to Caroline Goodden and "The Meeting," (the Anarchitecture group), op. cit. Also see notes from the same year, #1283A, E G M-C.

84. On Anarchitecture's interest in cultural paradox and contradiction, see Richard Nonas, quoted in *Gordon Matta-Clark,* p. 374.

85. Gordon Matta-Clark, notecard #1153, c. 1973, E G M-C.

86. Gordon Matta-Clark, notecard #1146, c. 1973, E G M-C.

87. Gordon Matta-Clark, interviewed by Liza Bear, "*Splitting,* The Humphrey Street House," p. 34. The attention paid to spaces of "interruption" or "movement" spaces bears similarities to the rhetoric of the Situationist International, whose theories of psychogeography and drift provided a non-rationalized relationship to the space of the city. The parallels between Matta-Clark's concerns and the SI have been noted before. See Elizabeth Sussman, "Introduction," in *On the Passage of a Few People Through a Very Brief Moment in Time,* exh. cat. (Boston: ICA, 1998), p. 10.

88. For example, Matta-Clark writes about the only form of privacy "enjoyed" by homeless alcoholics (people who don't possess private space). Calling this "paper bag privacy," he writes: "all the empty bottles in paper bags to be found at the corner of Houston and Bowery—large photo of such a multiple container and explanation of how within the law it ensures a drunkard's privacy." The irony implicit in this note is the extent to which the privacy of the "paper bag" is guaranteed under the law, while the privacy of the "drunkard's" living situation is not. Gordon Matta-Clark, letter to "The Meeting," op. cit.

89. Gordon Matta-Clark, Anarchitecture notebook, c. 1973 (#1335), E G M-C.

90. Gordon Matta-Clark, letter to "The Meeting," op. cit.

91. Matta-Clark writes, "Scroll of Endless City World Trade Towers printed top to top, bottom to bottom on a long roll." The sketch that accompanies his description pictures a handscroll—a horizontal ground—that would implicitly serve to reorient the vertical thrust of the buildings." Letter to "The Meeting," op. cit.

92. De Certeau, *The Practice of Everyday Life,* p. 91.

93. Gordon Matta-Clark, letter to Robert Ledenfrost, January 16, 1975, E G M-C.

94. Crawford B. Macpherson, "The Meaning of Property," in *Property: Mainstream and Critical Positions,* ed. C. B. Macpherson (Toronto: University of Toronto Press, 1978), pp. 1–15.

95. Etymology further allows us to establish a longer genealogy of the notion of property as *what one is* and *what one owns.* Finding its root in the Latin *proprious*—one's own—the word "property" subsequently evolved into *pro privo*—private, personal, or proper—in thirteenth-century English. For a discussion of the etymology of private property, see V. G. Kiernan, "Private Property in His-

tory," in *Family and Inheritance: Rural Society in Western Europe 1200–1800,* ed. Goody, Thirsk, and Thompson (Cambridge, UK: Cambridge University Press, 1976), pp. 361–396.

96. For a critical/historical treatment of this theme, see Margaret J. Radin, "Property and Personhood," *Stanford Law Review* 34 (1982), p. 957.

97. Hegel, *Elements of the Philosophy of Right,* p. 76.

98. G. W. F. Hegel, *Phenomenology of Spirit,* trans. A. V. Miller (Oxford: Oxford University Press, 1977), pp. 258–259.

99. The use proviso is among the most important theories surrounding the justification of property. Its most famous formulation is John Locke's "On Property," in *Two Treatises of Government,* in which Locke claims that "Everyman has property in his own person," and that "mixing one's labor" with the environment in a state of nature guarantees one's right to that property. John Locke, *Two Treatises of Government* (London: Everyman Library, 1993), pp. 127–140.

CHAPTER 3

1. Maud Lavin, "Gordon Matta-Clark and Individualism," *Arts Magazine* (January 1984), pp. 138–141 (emphasis added).

2. Ibid., p. 141.

3. Gordon Matta-Clark, letter to Melvyn Kaufman, New York, January 31, 1975, E G M-C.

4. Melvyn Kaufman, memo to Gordon Matta-Clark, New York, February 9, 1975, E G M-C.

5. Judith Russi Kirshner, unpublished notes for interview with Gordon Matta-Clark, the archives of the Museum of Contemporary Art, Chicago, p. 6, (undated, c. winter 1977–1978).

6. Matta-Clark interviewed by Liza Bear, "*Splitting,* The Humphrey Street Building," *Avalanche* (December 1974), p. 36.

7. On Eisenman's "disinheritance" of Rowe's theories on contextualism, see *Cities of Artificial Excavation* (Montreal: CCA, 1994), pp. 118–119. On the IAUS, also see Alexander Caragonne, *The Texas Rangers: Notes from the Architectural Underground* (Cambridge, MA: MIT Press, 1994), p. 405.

8. Rosalyn Deutsche hypothesizes that at least one of the images from *Window Blowout* is Richard Meier's Twin Parks Project in the Bronx. Deutsche examines *Window Blowout* through the rhetoric of "urban decay" and the uses to which that rhetoric was put for urban politics in the Bronx (and present day urban policies in New York). See Rosalyn Deutsche, "The Threshole of Democracy,"

in *Urban Mythologies, The Bronx Represented Since the 1960's,* exh. cat. (Bronx, NY: The Bronx Museum of the Arts, 1999).

9. See, for example, the statement by Andrew MacNair in *Gordon Matta-Clark, A Retrospective,* ed. Mary Jane Jacob (Chicago: Museum of Contemporary Art, 1985), p. 96.

10. Ibid., p. 96; also see Thomas Crow, "Site-Specific Art: The Strong and the Weak," in *Modern Art in the Common Culture* (New Haven, CT: Yale University Press, 1996).

11. It has long been claimed that the pier was demolished two years after the cutting (see, for example, *Gordon Matta-Clark,* exh. cat. [Valencia, Spain: IVAM Centre Julio Gonzalez, 1992], p. 383), but no municipal records for the city of New York document its destruction. In fact, Bella Abzug secured "emergency" money for the rennovation of Pier 52 (as well as Piers 48 and 51) in 1976. See "U.S. Giving Pier-Renovation Aid," *New York Times,* May 26, 1976, p. 23. An on-site inspection by the author revealed that its structure is still intact. This was finally confirmed by the author in conversation with Dan Klein, Director of Real Estate for the Department of Sanitation, New York, August 1998.

12. See the "Rent Roll" section of the *Annual Report of the New York City Department of Docks and Ferries,* New York, 1879–1939, New York Municipal Reference Room, Surrogate Court. Although it is difficult to determine precisely when the Baltimore and Ohio Railroad Company first occupied Pier 52 (the annuals of the Department of Docks were not available during the war years), press releases suggest that this took place in the 1950s. During that time, the Baltimore and Ohio also rented Piers 20, 21, 22, 23, 39, 40, and 66. *Press Release on the Baltimore and Ohio Railroad,* Department of Marine and Aviation, City of New York, May 1, 1958, Vertical File "Piers," New York Municipal Reference Room, Surrogate Court. The occupation of the piers by the Baltimore and Ohio Railroad was firmly opposed by local labor, namely the ILA (International Longshoreman's Association) and the IBL (International Brotherhood of Longshoreman), because of the threat posed to longshoreman jobs. See *Press Release on the Baltimore and Ohio Railroad,* Department of Marine and Aviation, City of New York, June 9, 1958, Vertical File "Piers," New York Municipal Reference Room, Surrogate Court.

13. George Gent, "City Plans to Use Piers as Cultural Playground," *New York Times,* June 3, 1970, pp. 1 and 36; also see *Press Release, City Pier to be used as Sunbathing and Recreation Area,* New York City Economic Development Administration, June 3, 1970, Vertical File "Piers," New York Municipal Reference Room, Surrogate Court.

14. See John Turcott, "The Village Piers, A Mugger's Paradise?" *Our Town* (New York), November 14, 1975, p. 1; and John Turcott, "The Piers: Living Two Lives Amidst Spreading Crime and Broken Glass," *Our Town* (New York) November 21, 1975, p. 1. Turcott's articles are ostensibly about the crime surrounding the piers, but the tone of his argument is homophobic. For a nostalgic rec-

ollection of cruising around Pier 45, see Guy Trebay, "Tears for Piers," *The Village Voice,* September 14, 1993, p. 19.

15. Gordon Matta-Clark interviewed in *Gordon Matta-Clark,* exh. cat. (Antwerp: International Cultureel Centrum, 1977), p. 11.

16. Gordon Matta-Clark, letter to Wolfgang Becker, Aachen, Germany, September 8, 1975, E G M-C.

17. On *Day's End* as "public domain," see Matta-Clark, letter to Wolfgang Becker. Matta-Clark left New York shortly after the work was discovered but this was because he was scheduled to produce the site work *Conical Intersect* for the Paris Biennale in early September. A letter to Matta-Clark from Gerald Ordover, his attorney, warns that the artist "would be classified as a fugitive" if he didn't cooperate with New York's Economic Development Administration. The EDA later dropped the investigation against Matta-Clark. Gerald Ordover, letter to Gordon Matta-Clark, Paris, September 19, 1975, E G M-C.

18. Matta-Clark interviewed in *Gordon Matta-Clark* (Antwerp), p. 11.

19. Ibid.

20. Holly Solomon quoted in *Gordon Matta-Clark: A Retrospective,* p. 25.

21. Joel Shapiro quoted in *Gordon Matta-Clark: A Retrospective,* p. 142.

22. Gordon Matta-Clark, undated notecard, E G M-C.

23. Yve-Alain Bois, "Matisse and 'Arche-Drawing,'" in *Painting as Model* (Cambridge, MA: MIT Press, 1990), pp. 24–25.

24. On the question of scale and its relationship to site in modern sculpture, see Thierry de Duve, "Ex Situ," *Les Cahiers du Musée national d'art moderne* no. 27 (Spring 1978), p. 38.

25. See Robert Morris, "Notes on Sculpture, Part 2," reprinted in *Continuous Project Altered Daily* (Cambridge, MA: MIT Press, 1993), p. 15.

26. Michael Fried, "Art and Objecthood," reprinted in *Art and Objecthood and Other Essays* (Chicago: University of Chicago Press, 1998) p. 153.

27. Ibid., p. 155.

28. Judith Wechsler, "Why Scale?" *Art News* 66, no. 4 (Summer 1967), pp. 32–37.

29. Lucy Lippard, "Escalation in Washington," *Art International* 12, no. 1 (January 1968), pp. 42–46.

30. See Barbara Rose, "Blowup—The Problem of Scale in Sculpture," *Art in America,* 56, no. 4 (July–August 1968), pp. 83–91; Sidney Tillim, "Scale and the Future of Modernism," *Artforum* (October 1967), pp. 14–18; and Andrew Hudson, "Scale as Content: Bladen, Newman and Smith at the Corcoran," *Artforum* 6, no. 4 (December 1967), pp. 46–47. Also see the exhibition catalogue, E. Green, *Scale as Content* (Washington, D.C.: The Corcoran Gallery of Art, 1967).

31. See Richard Serra's discussion of the "cut as line" in sculpture and drawing. Richard Serra, "Notes on Drawing," in *Richard Serra: Writings, Interviews* (Chicago: University of Chicago Press, 1994), p. 179.

32. An extremely insightful analysis of this transition is found in James Meyer, "The Genealogy of Minimalism: Carl Andre, Dan Flavin, Donald Judd, Sol LeWitt and Robert Morris" (Ph.D. diss., Johns Hopkins University, 1995).

33. Robert Morris, "Notes on Sculpture, Part 1," reprinted in *Continuous Project,* pp. 7–8.

34. Robert Morris, "Notes on Sculpture, Part 2," reprinted in *Continuous Project,* p. 15.

35. Ibid., p. 16.

36. Rosalind Krauss has written the most important work to this end. See Rosalind Krauss, *Passages in Modern Sculpture* (Cambridge, MA: MIT Press, 1977), particularly the chapter "The Double Negative: A New Syntax for Sculpture," pp. 243–288. Also see her "Richard Serra: A Translation," in *The Originality of the Avant-Garde* (Cambridge, MA: MIT Press, 1985). See, too, Robert Morris, "Some Notes on the Phenomenology of Making," in *Continuous Project;* and Mel Bochner, "Serial Art, Systems, Solipsism," in *Minimal Art: A Critical Anthology* (New York: E. P. Dutton, 1968), pp. 92–103. Bochner describes "an acute awareness of the phenomenology of rooms" in works by Carl Andre and Dan Flavin.

37. Maurice Merleau-Ponty, *The Phenomenology of Perception* (London: Routledge, Kegan & Paul, 1989), p. 92.

38. Merleau-Ponty, *The Phenomenology of Perception,* pp. 66–69.

39. John Baldessari quoted in *Gordon Matta-Clark: A Retrospective,* p. 19.

40. Susan Rothenberg quoted in *Gordon Matta-Clark, A Retrospective,* p. 73.

41. Ibid., p. 366.

42. Maurice Merleau-Ponty, "Eye and Mind," in *The Primacy of Perception,* (Evanston, IL: Northwestern University Press, 1964), p. 166.

43. Jackie Winsor interviewed in *Gordon Matta-Clark: A Retrospective,* p. 72.

44. Gordon Matta-Clark interviewed by Judith Russi Kirshner in *Gordon Matta-Clark* (IVAM) p. 367.

45. My discussion evolves almost exclusively out of the Kantian reading and from more recent continental philosophers who return to discuss the Third Critique. See Immanuel Kant, *Critique of Judgment,* trans. J. H. Bernard (New York: Hafner, 1951).

46. Ibid., p. 108.

47. For critical treatments of the sublime and presentation, see the collected essays in *Of the Sublime: Presence in Question,* trans. Jeffrey Librett (Albany: State University of New York Press, 1993). For a brilliant psychoanalytic and semiotic account of the sublime in literary romanticism see Thomas Weiskel, *The Romantic Sublime* (Baltimore, MD: Johns Hopkins University Press, 1976).

48. Kant, *Critique of Judgment,* p. 121.

49. Ibid., p. 96.

50. Jean-François Lyotard, "Newman: The Instant," in *The Lyotard Reader,* ed. Andrew Benjamin (Oxford: Basil Blackwell, 1989). Lyotard also considers the Third Critique through the "Interest of the Sublime"—that is, as a kind of economy, at moments sacrificial. See Lyotard, "The Interest of the Sublime," in *Of the Sublime: Presence in Question,* trans. Jeffrey S. Librett (Albany, NY: State University of New York, 1993), pp. 109–132.

51. See Jean-François Lyotard, *Lessons of the Analytic of the Sublime* (Stanford, CA: Stanford University Press, 1994).

52. See Robert Rosenblum, "The Abstract Sublime," *Art News* 59 (February 1961). Also see Jean-François Lyotard, "Newman: The Instant," and "Sublime and the Avant-Garde," in *The Lyotard Reader;* on Lyotard's discussion on abstraction and photography viz. the sublime, see "Presenting the Unpresentable," *Artforum* 29 (April 1989). Also see the literature on Agnes Martin, e.g., Carter

Ratcliff, "Agnes Martin and the 'Artificial Infinite,'" *Art News* 72 (May 1973); Thomas McEvilley, "Grey Geese Descending: The Art of Agnes Martin," *Artforum* 25 (Summer 1987); and Rosalind Krauss, "Clouds," reprinted in *Inside the Visible* (Boston: The Institute of Contemporary Art; Cambridge, MA: MIT Press, 1996).

53. Kant, *Critique of Judgment,* p. 100. On earth works, see John Beardsley, "Traditional Aspects of New Land Art," *Art Journal* 42 (Fall 1982), pp. 226–232; and John Beardsley *Earthworks and Beyond* (New York: Abbeville Press, 1984); Henry Sayre, "Open Space: Landscape and the Postmodern Sublime," in *The Object of Performance: The American Avant-Garde since 1970* (Chicago: University of Chicago Press, 1989), pp. 211–246; Melinda Wortz, "Walter de Maria's 'The Lightning Field,'" *Arts Magazine* 54 (May 1980), pp. 170–173.

54. Walter de Maria's *Lightning Field* is often cited as one such work. A critique of the *Lightning Field* as sublime is found in John Beardsley, "Art and Authoritarianism, Walter de Maria's Lightning Field, *October* 16 (Spring 1981), pp. 35–38.

55. Beardsley, *Earthworks and Beyond,* p. 63. Also see Gregoire Muller, "The Scale of Man," *Arts Magazine* 44 (May 1970), pp. 42–43. The notable exception is Robert Smithson's essay on *The Spiral Jetty,* reprinted in *The Writings of Robert Smithson,* pp. 109–116. Smithson describes how "a crack in the wall if viewed in terms of scale, not size, could be called the Grand Canyon."

56. Matta-Clark interviewed by Bear, "*Splitting:* The Humphrey Street House," p. 37.

57. Gordon Matta-Clark, letter to Robert Ledenfrost, January 16, 1975, E G M-C.

58. Kant, *Critique of Judgment,* p. 85.

59. Ibid., p. 90.

60. Ibid.

61. Matta-Clark quoted by Bear, "*Splitting,* The Humphrey Street House," p. 37.

62. Kant, *Critique of Judgment,* p. 85.

63. Ibid., p. 99.

64. Ibid., p. 109.

65. Apart from Matta-Clark's original plans for *Conical Intersect* (discussed in chapter 4), he had also proposed work for the Museum of Modern Art, New York.

66. Judith Russi Kirshner, press release, "Circus or The Carribean Orange," the Museum of Contemporary Art, Chicago, 1978.

67. Ibid.

68. Letter from Gordon Matta-Clark to Alene Valkanas, December 26, 1977, Archives of the Museum of Contemporary Art, Chicago.

69. Gordon Matta-Clark quoted by Judith Russi Kirshner, unpublished notes for an interview with Matta-Clark, Archives of the Museum of Contemporary Art, Chicago, p. 1 (undated, c. winter 1977–1978).

70. Matta-Clark, Letter to Alene Valkanas, op. cit.

71. Judith Russi Kirshner, "Non-uments," *Artforum* (October 1985), p. 104 (reprinted in *Gordon Matta-Clark* [IVAM], p. 367).

72. Thomas Crow points out that Serra implicitly critiques Matta-Clark in saying that he "wouldn't go to a leftover, picturesque pier" to produce his art. See Crow, "Site-Specific Art: The Strong and the Weak," p. 146.

73. *Gordon Matta-Clark,* p. 392.

74. Tina Girouard staged a performance within the work titled *Spread* that involved some twenty-one performers who occupied all levels of the work.

75. Gordon Matta-Clark quoted in "Interview with Gordon Matta-Clark" by Judith Russi Kirshner. *Gordon Matta-Clark* (IVAM), p. 389.

76. Ibid., p. 367.

77. Ibid., p. 364.

78. Ibid., p. 368.

79. Nancy's statement resonates strongly here, although he makes clear that the sublime is not an aesthetic and has little to do with art. Nancy, "The Sublime Offering," in *The Sublime: Presence in Question,* p. 35.

80. Hal Foster, "The Crux of Minimalism," *Individuals,* exh. cat. (Los Angeles: Museum of Contemporary Art; New York: Abbeville Press, 1988), pp. 162–183.

81. Ibid., p. 162.

CHAPTER 4

A version of this chapter appeared in *October* 85 (Summer 1998).

1. The concept of a "workless community" is indebted in part to Georges Bataille, with reformulations in the generation of philosophers who were contemporary with or followed Bataille's writing. Much of this writing turns around the Heideggerean thematics of finitude, the acutely temporal sense in which a being is oriented toward death. The notion of a "workless community" alluded to generally in this discussion suggests that communities are organized around the commonality of each member's finitude or loss. Such communities are described as "workless" because their members are not brought together through a shared work, project, set of interests, or lived experiences. Rather, it is mutual recognition of the finitude or radical otherness of the community's members, witnessed in the other's passing, that is the foundation of the workless community. Jean-Luc Nancy effectively condenses this notion when he writes, "Nothing is more common than being, it is the self-evidence of existence. Nothing is more uncommon than being, it is the self-evidence of community." See Jean-Luc Nancy, "Of Being in Common," in *Community at Loose Ends,* ed. Miami Theory Collective (Minneapolis: University of Minnesota Press, 1991), p. 8; Georges Bataille, *Inner Experience,* trans. Leslie Anne Boldt, (New York: State University of New York Press, 1988); Maurice Blanchot, *The Unavowable Community*, trans. P. Jorris (New York: Stations Hill Press, 1988); and Jean-Luc Nancy, *The Inoperative Community* (Minneapolis: University of Minnesota Press, 1991).

2. This is not to suggest that there ever existed such essentialized communities, but that the modern condition radically underscores the "workless" character of all community.

3. Lucy Lippard, "Community and Outreach: Art Outdoors, in the Public Domain," reprinted in *Get the Message: A Decade of Art for Social Change* (New York: E. P. Dutton, 1984), p. 38; also see John Beardsley, *Art in Public Spaces* (Washington, D.C.: Partners for Livable Spaces, 1981).

4. Matta-Clark had been rejected from the Washington Square Art Fair, leading him to organize a kind of "anti-salon" exhibition on Mercer Street.

5. The project was to be funded by a $12,000 grant given by the Guggenheim Foundation. Gordon Ray, President of the John Simon Guggenheim Foundation, letter to Matta-Clark, New York, March 16, 1977, E G M-C. Jane Crawford recalls that the interest in starting a community center began around 1975, when Matta-Clark, Alanna Heiss, Robert Rauschenberg, Robert Morris, and others casually discussed the formation of such a center in the Bronx. Jane Crawford, in conversation with the author, August 2, 1998, Weston, CT.

6. Gordon Matta-Clark, draft of *A Resource Center and Environmental Youth Program for Loisaida: A Proposal,* August 18, 1976, E G M-C.

7. *Gordon Matta-Clark, A Retrospective,* ed. Mary Jane Jacob, op. cit., p. 97. Sweat Equity programs in the seventies were designed to acquire "tax defaulted properties from the city, closing them up against further deterioration and vandalism while a group of potential tenants apply to the city for rehabilitation funding." The goal was to exchange the tenant's labor for ownership. Gordon Matta-Clark, *A Resource Center and Environmental Youth Program for Loisaida* (proposal for a Guggenheim Fellowship), undated, fall 1976, E G M-C.

8. Matta-Clark was deeply inspired by the Lower East Side organization "Adopt a Building," with which he hoped to collaborate. Gordon Matta-Clark, letter to Ruth Garcia, Adopt a Building, New York, July 29, 1976, E G M-C.

9. Gordon Matta-Clark, *A Resource Center and Environmental Youth Program for Loisaida* (proposal for a Guggenheim Fellowship).

10. Gerry Hovagimyan interviewed by Joan Simon in *Gordon Matta-Clark, A Retrospective,* p. 88.

11. Georges Boudaille, letter to Matta-Clark, February 14, 1975, and April 16, 1975, E G M-C.

12. "Interview with Gordon Matta-Clark, Antwerp, September 1977," (interviewer unnamed), in *Gordon Matta-Clark* exh. cat. (Antwerp: Internationaal Cultureel Centrum, 1977), p. 12.

13. Gordon Matta-Clark, letter to Georges Boudaille, Paris, June 1975, E G M-C.

14. Gordon Matta-Clark, draft of a letter to Nina Felshin, Director of American entries to the Paris Biennale, Washington, D.C., June 1975, E G M-C.

15. Gordon Matta-Clark, letter to Georges Boudaille, Paris, July 30, 1975, E G M-C.

16. Ibid.

17. *Conical Intersect* required authorization not only from the museum, but also from the Société d'économie mixte d'aménagement, de rénovation et de restauration du secteur des Halles. SEMAH allowed Matta-Clark to work on site from September 24 to October 10, 1975; it also provided information about structural engineers in Paris. Dominique Saglio, letter from the office of the General Director, SEMAH, to Gordon Matta-Clark, September 24, 1975, E G M-C. SEMAH was widely regarded as responsible for the demise of the neighborhood. Gordon Matta-Clark, letter to Georges Boudaille, Paris, July 30, 1975, E G M-C.

18. Matta-Clark expressed his interest in McCall's work, particularly his "use of the total projection space for its experience." Gordon Matta-Clark, letter to Wolfgang Becker, Neue Galerie, Sammlung Ludwig, Aachen, June 10, 1976, E G M-C.

19. Hovagimyan interviewed by Simon in *Gordon Matta-Clark, A Retrospective*, p. 88.

20. According to Hovagimyan, it also bore a rather Duchampian reference in the form of a bad pun: Matta-Clark also called the cutting "Quel Con," which obliquely acknowledged Duchamp's word play in *L.H.O.O.Q*, i.e., "she's got a hot ass." Matta-Clark's pun turned on this reference as it did the twinned resonances of the word "Con" as both "cone" and "cunt." See Hovagimyan interviewed in *Gordon Matta-Clark, A Retrospective*, p. 88.

21. Thomas Crow, "Site Specifity: The Strong and the Weak," in *Modern Art in the Common Culture* (New Haven, CT: Yale University Press, 1996), p. 135.

22. Jean-Hubert Martin, quoted in *Gordon Matta-Clark, A Retrospective,* p. 89.

23. Ibid.

24. Irving Marder, "The Art of Putting Holes in Houses," *International Herald Tribune,* October 20, 1975, p. 9.

25. Matta-Clark, interviewed by Donald Wall in "Gordon Matta-Clark's Building Dissections," *Arts Magazine* (March 1976), p. 76.

26. Dan Graham, "Gordon Matta-Clark," reprinted in *Rock My Religion,* ed. Brian Wallis (Cambridge, MA: MIT Press, 1993), p. 202.

27. Gordon Matta-Clark, notes, Paris 1975, E G M-C.

28. Matta-Clark quoted in Wall, p. 76. For another reading that considers the relation between Matta-Clark's art and Benjamin, see Graham, "Gordon Matta-Clark," in *Rock My Religion.*

29. On the dialectical image, see Susan Buck-Morss, *The Dialectics of Seeing: Walter Benjamin and the Arcades Project* (Cambridge, MA: MIT Press, 1989).

30. Walter Benjamin, "Konvolut N (Re The Theory of Knowledge, Theory of Progress)," in *Benjamin: Philosophy, History, Aesthetics,* ed. Gary Smith (Chicago: University of Chicago Press, 1987), p. 49.

31. Ibid., p. 48.

32. Ibid., p. 47.

33. Benjamin, "Surrealism," in *Reflections,* ed. Peter Demetz (New York: Schocken Books, 1978), pp. 181–182.

34. Ibid., p. 182.

35. Benjamin, "Konvolut N," p. 60.

36. Matta-Clark quoted in Corinne Diserens, "The Greene Street Years," in *Gordon Matta-Clark,* exh. cat. (Valencia, Spain: IVAM Centre Julio Gonzalez, 1992), p. 360.

37. Walter Benjamin, "Theses on the Philosophy of History," in *Illuminations,* trans. Harry Zohn (New York: Schocken Books, 1978), p. 258.

38. On Les Halles, see Jean Herbert, *Sauver Les Halles: Coeur de Paris* (Paris: Denoel, 1971); Bertrand Lemoine, *Les Halles de Paris: L'histoire d'un lieu* (Paris: L'Equerre editeur, 1980). On the Beaubourg, see Jean Baudrillard, *L'effet Beaubourg: Implosion et Dissuasion* (Paris: Editions Galilée, 1977), reprinted as "The Beaubourg Effect: Implosion and Dissuasion," trans. Rosalind Krauss and Annette Michelson, *October* 20 (1982); Maurice Leroy, *Le Phenomene Beaubourg* (Paris: Editions Styros, 1977). For a trenchant critique of the building, see Louis Chevalier, *The Assassination of Paris* (Chicago: University of Chicago Press, 1994); for a celebratory account, see Nathan Silver, *The Making of Beaubourg* (Cambridge, MA: MIT Press, 1994).

39. Hovagimyan interviewed by Simon in *Gordon Matta-Clark, A Retrospective,* p. 89.

40. *l'Humanité,* November 25, 1975, p. 1.

41. Gordon Matta-Clark interviewed by Judith Russi Kirshner, in *Gordon Matta-Clark* (IVAM), p. 392.

42. Ibid.

43. Lemoine, *Les Halles de Paris: L'histoire d'un lieu,* p. 7.

44. Articles that appeared toward the end of the controversy employing this rhetoric include Jean-Francois Dhuys, "Paris, un Trou au Coeur," *Nouvelles Litteraires,* August 11, 1978, p. 3; M.-C. Husson, "L'enseigne architecturale du trou des Halles," *Liberation,* March 13, 1978, pp. 15–16; and "Halles, toujours le trou," *L'Express,* August 7–October 14, 1978, pp. 110–112. Note also an article on Matta-Clark linked to this rhetoric, J.-M. Poinsot, "Un Trou de Gordon Matta-Clark," *Data* 20 (March–April, 1975), p. 40.

45. A standard text on this history is David Pinkney, *Napoleon III and the Rebuilding of Paris* (Princeton, NJ: Princeton University Press, 1958), pp. 9–10. Also see Norma Evenson, *Paris: A Century of Change 1878–1978* (New Haven, CT: Yale University Press, 1979), p. 303.

46. See Siegfried Giedion, *Building in France, Building in Iron, Building in Ferroconcrete,* trans. J. Duncan Berry (Santa Monica, CA: Getty Center for the History of Art and the Humanities, 1995).

47. Emile Zola quoted in Evenson, *Paris: A Century of Change,* p. 303.

48. Walter Benjamin, "Construction en Fer" (Konvolut F, F1A, 5; F2a, 1; F5, 3), in *Paris, Capitale du XIXe siècle, le livre des passages,* (Paris: Cerf, 1989), pp. 174–176; p. 183.

49. Ibid, p. 183. Also see G. E. Haussmann, *Mémoires du baron Haussmann,* vol. 3 (Paris: Victor-Havard, 1890–1893), p. 478.

50. See Emile Zola's famous discussion of the pavilions in *The Belly of Paris,* trans. E. A. Vizatelly (Los Angeles: Sun and Moon Press, 1996), p. 30. On Benjamin's linking of nature and technology, see Buck-Morss, "Mythic Nature, Wish Image," in *The Dialectics of Seeing,* pp. 110–159.

51. See Chevalier, "The Bagnole and the Tree," in *The Assasination of Paris,* pp. 44–56.

52. Opposition to the removal of the marketplace was organized along two lines. First, many newspapers argued for the architectural importance of the pavilions to French culture. See Jacques Michel, "La Bataille des Halles: des Artistes Francais et Americains addressent des Messages a M. Pompidou," *Le Monde,* July 4–5, 1971, p. 7; A.C., "Une grand historien de l'architecture moderne juge les pavillions des Baltards," and J.M., "H.-R. Hitchcock, un monument-clé du XIXe siecle," *Le Monde,* July 14, 1971, p. 10. The second line of criticism came principally from the communist press and concerned itself with the people who would lose their homes as a result of increased real estate speculation in the area, about 1,300 families. See "Halles: Abandon de l'actuel plan d'amenagement," *l'Humanité,* July 10, 1971, p. 5.

53. Official announcement of plans to build the Centre Georges Pompidou, cited in Silver, *The Making of Beaubourg,* p. 3.

54. Silver, *The Making of Beaubourg,* p. x.

55. Renzo Piano and Richard Rogers quoted in Silver, *The Making of Beaubourg,* p. 24.

56. Silver, *The Making of Beaubourg,* p. 174. Also see "L'Amenagement du quartier des Halles a Paris: Les explications du directeur de la SEMAH," *Le Monde,* June 11, 1978, p. 22.

57. Reyner Banham quoted in Silver, *The Making of Beaubourg,* p. 185.

58. Matta-Clark, unpublished notes, undated (c. fall 1975), E G M-C.

59. Baudrillard, "The Beaubourg Effect: Implosion and Deterrence," pp. 3–4.

60. Ibid., p. 4.

61. On other notions of the aesthetic of transparency and modern architecture, see Colin Rowe and Robert Slutzky, "Transparency, Literal and Phenomenal," *The Mathematics of the Ideal Villa and Other Essays* (Cambridge, MA: MIT Press, 1976), pp. 159–185; and Anthony Vidler, "Transparency," in *The Architectural Uncanny* (Cambridge, MA: MIT Press, 1992), pp. 217–225.

62. Baudrillard, "The Beaubourg Effect," p. 5.

63. Ibid., p. 3.

64. Ibid., p. 6.

65. Ibid., p. 7 (my emphasis). Baudrillard's apparent interest in Matta-Clark's work is not coincidental. A letter from Sylvie Deswarte, assistant at Editions C.C.I. (Centre de création industrielle, Centre Beaubourg), suggests that Baudrillard was interested in using Matta-Clark's *Photoglyphs* series to illustrate an essay on graffiti in New York. Sylvie Deswarte, letter to Gordon Matta-Clark, Centre de création industrielle, Centre Beaubourg, Paris, January 9, 1974, E G M-C.

66. Henri Lefebvre, *The Production of Space,* trans. Donald Nicholson-Smith (London: Blackwell, 1991), pp. 27–28.

67. Ibid., p. 76.

68. Gordon Matta-Clark, undated note card #1186 (c. 1975?), E G M-C.

69. Matta-Clark interviewed by Wall, "Gordon Matta-Clark's Building Dissections," p. 79.

70. Yve-Alain Bois has made this observation about Matta-Clark's *Threshole* series, which he treats as a pun on Trashhole and its "cloacal" implications. Yve-Alain Bois and Rosalind Krauss, *Formless: A User's Guide* (Cambridge, MA: MIT Press, 1997), p. 190.

71. New York suffered a garbage crisis in the late sixties through the mid-seventies, the worst years being 1974–1976. John V. Lindsay once declared that his administration spent "more time on sanitation" than any other subject. "Lindsay Defends Administration on Sanitation Service," *Long Island Press,* July 22, 1970, n.p. (see Vertical File—NYC Sanitation, Dept. of., Municipal Reference Room, Surrogate Court, New York). Also see Craig R. Whitney, "Garbage Collection Poses Mounting Political Problem for Lindsay," *New York Times,* July 26, 1970, p. 48; Donald Singleton, "New

York: Slob Capital of the World, Part 1," "Lifting the Lid on a Litter Basket Fiasco, Part 2," and "To Get Clean, New Yorkers Must Start Thinking Clean, Part 3," *New York Daily News,* September 16, 17, and 19, 1974, pp. 38; 30; 60. In July 1975, 1,432 sanitation workers were laid off as a result of the recession, exacerbating what was already a crisis situation. See David Vidal, "Rapid Garbage Pileup is Laid to Layoffs, Confusion and Slowdowns," *New York Times,* July 26, 1975.

72. Whitney, "Garbage Collection Poses Mounting Political Problem for Lindsay," p. 48.

73. Matta-Clark interviewed by Wall, "Gordon Matta-Clark's Building Dissections," p. 100.

74. Victor Hugo, *Les Miserables,* trans. N. Denny (London: Penguin Books, 1976), p. 1065.

75. Daniel Cohn-Benedit, quoted in Donald Reid, *Paris Sewers and Sewerman: Realities and Representations* (Cambridge, MA: Harvard University Press, 1991), p. 18.

76. Reid, ibid., p. 52.

77. For histories of the catacombs, see M.-F. Arnold, *Paris: Catacombes* (Paris: Editions Romillat, 1993); and Pietro Saletta, *A la decouverte des Souterrains de Paris* (Paris: Sides, 1990).

78. See Shelley Rice, "Souvenirs," *Art in America* 76, no. 9 (September 1988), pp. 157–166.

79. Lawrence Weiner interviewed by Joan Simon in *Gordon Matta-Clark: A Retrospective,* p. 141.

80. Whether or not John Batan Matta committed suicide is open to debate; Jane Crawford remarks that some considered it an accident. Jane Crawford, in conversation with the author, August 2, 1998, Weston, CT.

CHAPTER 5

1. In 1978, only a few months before his death, Matta-Clark proposed a cutting for a program called "Twentieth-Century Ruins," organized by his longtime supporter, Alanna Heiss. He hoped to cut the corner of buildings located on 54th Street and Eighth Avenue, not unlike his original plan for the work *Office Baroque.*

2. Jane Crawford in conversation with the author, September 9, 1998, Weston, CT.

3. The possibility of using pneumatic technology in architecture and the arts had already been explored in the sixties, in among, others, the architectural proposals of the French group Utopie and the British collective Archigram, as well as in projects by Group Zero, Jeffrey Shaw and Christo.

4. Jane Crawford reports that an old college friend of Matta-Clark's, Serpic Angelini, described this performance as dedicated to the memory of Marcel Duchamp, who died in October 1968. (Teeny Duchamp was Matta-Clark's godmother.) Jane Crawford, in conversation with the author, August 2, 1998.

5. Gordon Matta-Clark, letter to Piccard Balloons, Newport Beach, CA, November 20, 1977, E G M-C. Matta-Clark also communicated with Dick Brown of the magazine *Ballooning,* as well as Gill Schjeldahl, "father of Peter" (the art critic), who had worked in the field. Matta-Clark, undated notes (late 1977?), E G M-C. For the most comprehensive account of Matta-Clark's interest in balloon housing, see Peter Fend, "New Architecture from Matta-Clark," in *Reorganizing Structure by Drawing Through It: Drawings by Gordon Matta-Clark,* exh. cat. (Vienna: E. A. Generali Foundation, 1997), pp. 46–55.

6. Gordon Matta-Clark, letter to Wolfgang Becker, Neue Galerie, Aachen, June 10, 1976, E G M-C.

7. Otto Piene's rejection of Matta-Clark's proposal is dated December 8, 1975. Peter Campus's reply is undated, as is the copy of the letter Matta-Clark wrote to him. One assumes the correspondance with Campus was roughly contemporary with Piene's. E G M-C. Matta-Clark's interest in cybernetics and computer technology more generally is confirmed by several books in his library, notably Norbert Wiener, *Cybernetics: or Control and Communication in the Animal and Machine.*

7. Gordon Matta-Clark, letter to Wolfgang Becker, Neue Galerie, Aachen, June 10, 1976, E G M-C., Weston, CT.

8. Among others, two well-known contemporary artists—Rachel Whiteread and Rirkrit Tiravanija—have acknowledged the links between their own work and Matta-Clark's art. See Jerry Saltz, "A Short History of Rirkrit Tiravanija," *Art in America* (February 1996), pp. 82–85, 107; and Lynn Zelevansky, *Sense and Sensibility: Women Artists and Minimalism in the Nineties,* exh. cat. (New York: The Museum of Modern Art, 1994), p. 5.

9. See Benjamin Forgey, "The House that Art Unbuilt," *Washington Post,* June 18, 1994, G1 and G8. Forgey's article reviews the collaborative group Art Attack, who "deconstructed" an old farmhouse in Arlington, VA, in 1994.

10. See, for example, Aaron Betsky, *Violated Perfection: Architecture and the Fragmentation of the Modern* (New York: Rizzoli, 1990), pp. 104–105; 49–53. For notable exceptions, see Rem Koolhaas, interviewed by John Rajchman, "Thinking Big," *Artforum* 33 (December 1994), p. 99; and Mark Wigley, "Deconstructivist Architecture," in *Deconstructivist Architecture* (New York: The Museum of Modern Art; Boston: Little, Brown and Company, 1988), p. 11.

11. This was the theme of a conference surrounding Matta-Clark's films, co-sponsored by the UCLA Department of Architecture, the Los Angeles Forum for Architecture and Urban Design, and SCI-ARC, October 9–10, 1997.

12. Gordon Matta-Clark interviewed by Judith Russi Kirshner in *Gordon Matta-Clark,* exh. cat. (Valencia, Spain: IVAM Centre Julio Gonzalez, 1992), p. 392.

13. The artist is Matthew Antezzo.

14. See Thomas Crow, *Modern Art in the Common Culture* (New Haven, CT: Yale University Press, 1996); Corinne Robbins, *The Pluralist Era: American Art,* 1968–81 (New York: Harper and Row, 1984), p. 107; and Brandon Taylor, *Avant-Garde and After: Rethinking Art Now* (New York: Harry N. Abrams, 1995).

15. Crow, "Site-Specific Art: The Strong and the Weak," in *Modern Art and the Common Culture,* p. 135.

16. See the statements of Joseph Kosuth and Lawrence Weiner, *Gordon Matta-Clark, A Retrospective,* ed. Mary Jane Jacob (Chicago: Museum of Contemporary Art, 1985), p. 111 and p. 141.

17. Gordon Matta-Clark, letter to Wolfgang Becker, Aachen, February 2, 1976, E G M-C.

18. Matta-Clark interviewed by Kirshner, p. 393.

19. Jeff Wall, "'Marks of Indifference,' Aspects of Photography in, or as, Conceptual Art," in *Reconsidering the Object of Art: 1965–75,* (Cambridge, MA: MIT Press, 1995), p. 248.

20. Ursula Meyer, *Conceptual Art,* (New York, NY: Dutton Press, 1972), p. viii.

21. Wall, "'Marks of Indifference,'" p. 253.

22. Frazer Ward, for example, considers performance art of the sixties and seventies in relation to notions of critical publicity, rather than conventional readings of performance through the body. Ward challenges the "reality" or immediacy of the lived performing body in the work of Acconci and Burden in particular through the terms of the public sphere. See Frazer Ward, forthcoming dissertation on Vito Acconci and Chris Burden (Ph.D. diss., Cornell University, 2000).

23. Letter from Gordon Matta-Clark, New York, to Florent Bex, Antwerp, March 30, 1977. Courtesy Florent Bex, Antwerp.

24. Ibid.

25. “Interview with Gordon Matta-Clark, Antwerp, September 1977” (interviewer unidentified), *Gordon Matta-Clark,* exh. cat. (Antwerp: Internationaal Cultureel Centrum, 1977), 13.

26. Jane Crawford interviewed by Joan Simon in *Gordon Matta-Clark: A Retrospective,* p. 111.

27. Florent Bex, in conversation with the author, June 4, 1994, Antwerp, and Jane Crawford, March 9–10, 1994, Weston, CT.

28. Gordon Matta-Clark, New York, translation of advertisement cited in letter to Marcel Peters, Antwerp. Letter undated. Courtesy Florent Bex, Antwerp.

29. Undated letter to Marcel Peters from Gordon Matta-Clark, ibid.

30. Florent Bex, in conversation with the author, June 1994, Antwerp. Also see Jean Desalle, “Pour Sauver l'Office Baroque de Gordon Matta-Clark, il faut creer un Musée d'Art Contemporain a Anvers,” *29,* April 1980, pp. 4–7.

31. Jane Crawford quoted in *Gordon Matta-Clark* (IVAM), p. 387.

32. Grace Glueck, “People: A Drive to Save Split Sculpture,” *New York Times,* March 14, 1980, C18. In another context, Crawford cites “350 artists from 17 countries” (*Gordon Matta-Clark* [IVAM], p. 387).

33. Jane Crawford quoted in Glueck, “People: A Drive to Save Split Sculpture,” C18.

INDEX

Note: Pages numbers for illustrations are in *italics.*

LIVERPOOL JOHN MOORES UNIVERSITY
Aldham Robarts L.R.C.
TEL. 0151 231 3701/3634

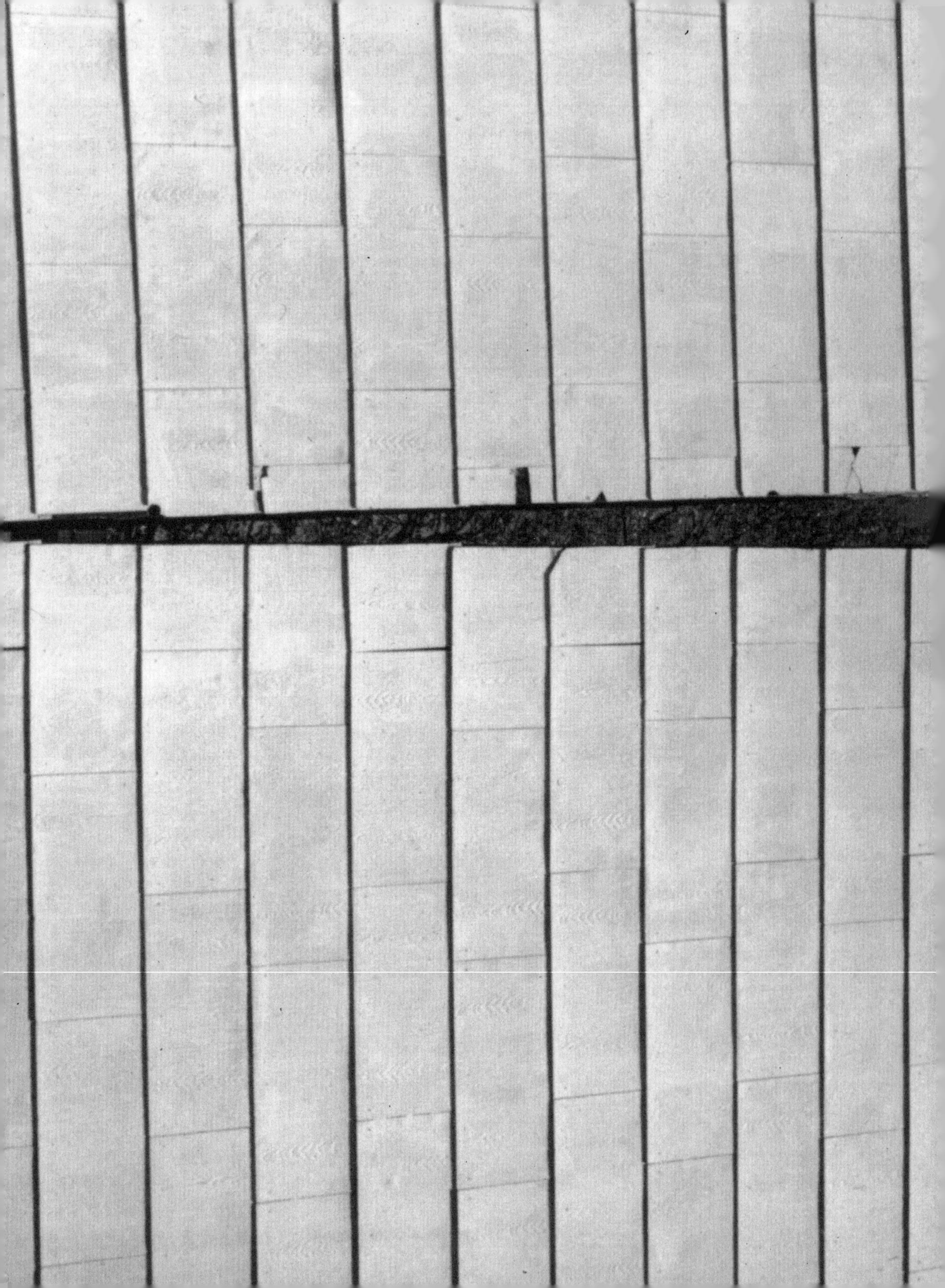